THE SCIENCE OF REVOLUTION

an introduction

by lenny wolff

RCP Publications, Chicago

Copyright © 1983 by RCP Publications

Cover Design by RCP Publications Art Group
Cover Photo by Morton Shapiro

Library of Congress Cataloging in Publication Data

Wolff, Lenny.
  The science of revolution.

  1. Revolutions and socialism. 2. Communism.
I. Title.
HX550.R48W64 1983   321.09   80-51229
ISBN 0-89851-035-X
ISBN 0-89851-036-8 (pbk.) 88-1659

First Printing: 1983
Printed in U.S.A.

Published by:
RCP Publications, P.O. Box 3486 Merchandise Mart
Chicago, IL U.S.A. 60654

This book was made possible by the aid and efforts of the leadership of the Revolutionary Communist Party, USA.

L. Wolff

Table of Contents

Below are abbreviations used for works commonly cited in the text.

Anti-Dühring — *Anti-Dühring,* by Frederick Engels, FLP, Peking, 1976.

Basic Principles — *Basic Principles for the Unity of Marxist-Leninists and for the Line of the International Communist Movement.* A Draft Position Paper for Discussion Prepared by Leaders of the Revolutionary Communist Party of Chile and of the Revolutionary Communist Party, USA. January 1, 1981.

Capital — *Capital,* 3 Volumes, by Karl Marx, edited by Frederick Engels, International Publishers, New York, 1967 (pagination is identical to the hardcover edition, Foreign Languages Publishing House, Moscow, 1961)

Conquer the World?. . . . — *Conquer the World? The International Proletariat Must and Will,* by Bob Avakian, *Revolution,* No. 50, Dec. 1981, RCP Publications, Chicago.

Feuerbach — *Ludwig Feuerbach and the End of Classical German Philosophy,* by Frederick Engels, FLP, Peking, 1976.

FLP — Foreign Languages Press, Peking.

Immortal — *Mao Tsetung's Immortal Contributions,* by Bob Avakian, RCP Publications, Chicago, 1979.

Imperialism — *Imperialism, The Highest Stage of Capitalism,* by V.I. Lenin, FLP, Peking, 1973.

LCW — *Collected Works,* 45 Volumes, by V.I. Lenin, Progress Publishers, Moscow, 1965.

Manifesto — *Manifesto of the Communist Party*, by Karl Marx and Frederick Engels, FLP, Peking, 1972.

Materialism — *Materialism and Empirio-Criticism*, by V.I. Lenin, FLP, Peking, 1972.

MEM — *Marx Engels Marxism*, by V.I. Lenin, FLP, Peking, 1978.

MESW — *Selected Works*, 3 Volumes, by Karl Marx and Frederick Engels, Progress Publishers, Moscow, 1970.

MSR — *Selected Readings from the Works of Mao Tsetung*, FLP, Peking, 1971.

MSW — *Selected Works*, 4 Volumes, by Mao Tsetung, FLP, Peking, 1965.

New Programme and New Constitution — *New Programme and New Constitution of the Revolutionary Communist Party, USA*, RCP Publications, Chicago, 1981.

Origin — *The Origin of the Family, Private Property and the State*, by Frederick Engels, FLP, Peking, 1978.

Renegade — *The Proletarian Revolution and the Renegade Kautsky*, by V.I. Lenin, FLP, Peking, 1975.

RW — *Revolutionary Worker*, newspaper of the Revolutionary Communist Party, USA, published weekly by RCP Publications, Chicago.

WITBD? — *What Is To Be Done?*, by V.I. Lenin, FLP, Peking, 1975.

The arrest of Karl Marx in Brussels, Belgium during the revolutionary uprisings which swept Europe in 1848.

INTRODUCTION

"Oppression breeds resistance": this is a basic law of social development. Those who yearn for and dream of something higher, better, freer — those who want to fight for something more than the dog-eat-dog (and worse) world of today — know, or at least sense, that the key to "something better" lies precisely in the resistance of the masses. And while the intensity of that resistance ebbs and flows, there do occur crucial junctures at which, in the words of Marx, "all society is sprung into the air," and dreams can be realized in the clear light of day.

But resistance alone is not enough — not enough, at least, to carry through the truly fundamental change that is called for by the conditions of present-day society. For that to happen people must be armed with a scientific understanding of society, including a rigorous and critical grasp of the basic role of the resistance of the masses and the process of revolution itself. While this sort of understanding is hardly a prerequisite for mass resistance, the difference it can and does make lies in just what that resistance will accomplish: whether the slave chains will merely be rattled, or really shattered; whether the fortress of the old order will only be shaken, or new ground seized for the cause of emancipation; whether people will fight blindly (even if fiercely, for a while), or with head up and eyes fixed on the furthest horizon, prepared to *win*.

How is science key to that? And is there really such a thing as a "science" of revolution anyway? Or to take it from another angle, what is meant by saying that Marxism-Leninism, Mao Tsetung Thought is scientific — and what is the significance of saying so?

To begin with, the method forged by Marxism — materialist dialectics — is the most systematic concentration of the scientific method ever achieved, the most accurate and critical tool of inquiry into the world (indeed, the universe) and how it works. Marxism is materialist: it focuses on the material world for the ultimate causes and directions of every event and phenomenon in nature or society. And it is dialectical in that it comprehends all phenomena in their changingness and development and in their interaction with other phenomena, and because it studies the struggle of opposites within a thing or process as the underlying basis of its motion and change.

Based on this method, Marxism penetrates through the mystification of social life promoted by the bourgeoisie (and reinforced by bourgeois social relations) to reveal the real dynamics of social development and the laws governing it. Human beings, after all, are a form of matter; their interaction with their environment and with each other is a natural process, albeit a highly complex one, with its own particularities and laws. These laws, as we shall see later, are not ironclad or immutable — but they are laws nonetheless, and must be mastered in order to consciously change human society.

Some have attempted to deny the scientific character of Marxism because of the controversy surrounding it; but controversy alone cannot rule a theory unscientific. Darwin's theory of evolution, after all, touched off something of a cataclysm in the scientific community, as did Einstein's theory of relativity. Scientists, as well as much of the rest of society, divided into contending camps over these theories; in both cases the struggle and eventual triumph of the proponents of the radical new theories had profound social ramifications. Marx was correct to regard science as an "historically dynamic, revolutionary force" (Engels' "Speech At The Graveside of Karl Marx"), and if, of all the overarching scientific theories ever developed, Marx's has most deeply divided society — and most affected it — that alone cannot make it unscientific. That a scientific theory directly hitting the tenderest nerve of bourgeois society — its exploitative class relations and its tendency toward proletarian revolution — causes the most unprecedented and far-reaching controversy is hardly surprising!

Marxism is a living science, and as such has found that many of its ideas once considered to be basic truths, or even fundamental theses, have been proven by history to be either mistaken in certain aspects, or basically wrong. Marx and Engels, for example, believed that proletarian revolution would occur first in the most advanced countries, and — if the revolution were to win — in several countries simultaneously. But with the development of imperialism at the turn of the century, the contradictions in the advanced countries were temporarily ameliorated; proletarian revolution broke out first in the more backward (though imperialist) country of Russia, and (some 30 years later) in China (and other oppressed nations) which as yet had not even fully consolidated capitalism. Further, the Soviet proletariat carried through the revolution and consolidated the first socialist state despite the fact that there were no other successful revolutionary attempts at the time. In this case the particular thesis of Marx and Engels turned out wrong; but the Marxist *method* enabled Lenin to analyze how and why conditions had changed, what new factors accounted for this unforeseen development and — most important — what it meant for present and future practical *action*.

Such a process of development is quite consistent with genuine scientific character. To return to the example of Darwin, today some scientists — in light of new phenomena and data, and continuing struggle over Darwin's (and others') interpretations and theoretical framework — believe that certain of Darwin's points, and even major theses, are mistaken. For instance, Darwin's emphasis on the gradual character of evolution is currently challenged by those who propose a pattern of periods of relative stasis punctuated by radical breaks and leaps in development. Yet the leaders of this school emphatically and correctly uphold and build off of the foundation and overall framework developed by Darwin.

Likewise, the science of revolution has not been, and cannot remain, unchanged, unmodified, unchallenged — that is to say, it cannot be stagnant and still be scientific. New challenges force its continual development and growth, the sharpening of its critical edge, the irreverent weeding out of what's been proven wrong (and/or become stale) and the further development of its correct kernel. But all this has to proceed and build off of the foundation laid by Marx and Engels, and deepened since them.

This book is intended as an introduction to this foundation, a bridge and a guide to the basic principles and body of Marxist theory. We are entering a time in which training in these principles is urgently required — a period when the imperialist system is being wracked by a severe crisis, one which *may* offer unprecedented opportunities and will surely pose tremendous challenges. The ability to identify and analyze the seed of the new straining beneath the surface, and to grasp its dynamics of development, will then be especially crucial. The extent to which revolutionary feelings and aspirations are deepened into revolutionary science *now* and how far that science is applied towards transforming spontaneous resistance into conscious revolution, has everything to do with what will be made of those opportunities and challenges, and how much of the future will be wrenched from the rubble of the old.

*****

Such training is not easy. Scientific theory, including Marxist theory, is typically mystified in bourgeois society. Its connection to the social practice of the masses is concealed, and it is treated as the exclusive product and province of geniuses and the elite. As for the masses — in the words of Alfred Lord Tennyson, Victorian England's poet laureate, "Theirs not to reason why,/Theirs but to do and die."

But this breach — while real enough in class society, and constantly reinforced by the educational system and the conditions of the masses — is not founded in "human nature." It can and must be overcome, and struggled against from the very start, in order to make revolution. *Everyone* who undertakes to scientifically understand society must wage this battle.

"There is no royal road to science," Marx wrote, "and only those who do not dread the fatiguing climb of its steep paths have a chance of gaining its luminous summits." (*Capital*, Vol. 1, preface, p. 21)

The development of Marxism itself reflects materialist dialectics. The centrality of struggle to progress and the foundation of theoretical struggle in the practical questions facing society can be seen in examining the actual contributions and lives of the foremost Marxists.

Karl Marx was born in Germany, in 1818, and became active in the revolutionary movement there in the late 1830s; by the early '40s he had been exiled, and soon after began his lifelong collaboration with Frederick Engels. The two started by thoroughly criticizing German philosophy — in the movement's beginnings, Engels once noted, political differences expressed themselves through contending philosophical schools — and in the process synthesized the foundations of materialist dialectics and the materialist conception of history. Marx and Engels also set about organizing a revolutionary international workers' organization, the Communist League, during this period; the League's Manifesto, published in 1848 and now known as the *Communist Manifesto*, was the first (and still most concentrated) expression of the principles of communism, laying out the materialist conception of history, including the necessity for the proletariat to overthrow the bourgeoisie and ''organize itself as the ruling class'' to carry through the transition to classless society.

1848 also witnessed a revolutionary wave that swept through Europe, an upsurge in which both Marx and Engels played active roles. But when the tide ebbed, the two agreed that the main task for the time being was to forge more deeply the foundations of communist theory. Hence Marx gave himself over to his main life's work, his study of capitalist political economy, which later bore fruit in the three volumes of *Capital*. *Capital* goes into the very bowels of the capitalist system, but dissects those murky and tangled entrails with the lofty sweep of science and history. Marx laid bare the inner dynamics of capital and analyzed its metamorphoses and development, and in doing this further developed the method of materialist dialectics.

But Marx and Engels also continued to participate in and give guidance to the revolutionary movement. They led in founding the First International, the first organization of workers' parties and groups around the world, and their works on various events of the day — and most especially on the Paris Commune, as published in *The Civil War in France* — were invaluable for both the period at hand and future generations as well. In *The Civil War in France*, the basic Marxist view of the bourgeois state, and of the proletarian dictatorship which must replace it, were developed for the first time. And while neither Marx nor Engels lived to see the proletarian revolution (besides the short-lived Commune), their work bore direct fruit only a few decades after they died.

The next phase in the development of Marxism and the proletarian revolution was led by V.I. Lenin. Lenin was born in 1870 in Russia, then a country still emerging from feudalism. Lenin's older brother had been executed for involvement in revolutionary activities, and Lenin turned to Marxism a few years later. While Lenin sought to apply Marxism to the conditions of Russia, his work was fundamentally grounded in the stand of the *international* proletariat and retains its value today. *What Is To Be Done?*, written a few years before the Russian Revolution of 1905, broke new ground on the nature of the party, its relation to the masses and the contradictions involved in building a *revolutionary* (as opposed to *reformist*) movement — ground which is still being fought for (and on) today. In the ebb that followed the 1905 Revolution, when the philosophical foundations of Marxism came under wide attack, Lenin defended and further developed those foundations in *Materialism and Empirio-Criticism*.

But the world had changed in profound ways since the deaths of Marx and Engels; capital had entered a new (and final) stage of development, with new phenomena and an all-around intensification of its contradictions. This found its sharpest expression in the eruption of the first interimperialist war in 1914. To the initial shock of Lenin, and the rest of the world, virtually the entire ''official'' socialist movement capitulated to their governments, vociferously supporting the war, or else going along with (and apologizing for) such support. Lenin's articles polemicizing against this collapse charted the basic course for revolutionaries facing the unprecedented challenge, and opportunities, posed by the war. Beyond that, his major work *Imperialism* uncovered the real significance and material roots of the war, and for the first time analyzed the dynamics of imperialism as the newest and highest stage of capitalism. And when, as Lenin had anticipated, the war began to produce revolutionary situations in a number of countries, his *State and Revolution* — a major summation and deepening of the Marxist view of the state, written in the summer of 1917 — proved invaluable to the proletarian seizure of power in Russia that autumn.

Lenin led the Soviet state in its early, difficult years, and also led in the formation of the Third International; but his life, cut short by disease induced by an assassin's bullet, came to an end in 1924. Nevertheless, the Soviet state, led by Joseph Stalin, continued on the socialist road for 30 years, providing important aid for the international communist movement and accumulating invaluable experience, both positive and negative, in actually constructing the new society.

Meanwhile, in the words of Mao Tsetung, the "salvoes of the October Revolution" had carried Marxism around the world. Mao himself was born in China in 1893, and took part in the anti-imperialist rebellions that reached a peak in 1919, in the May Fourth Movement. During the long, arduous revolutionary wars in China, lasting from 1921 to 1949, Mao developed Marxism to a qualitatively higher level in such areas as revolution in colonial countries, military strategy and culture. And his important philosophical works in this period — "On Practice" and "On Contradiction," written in 1937 during a major struggle within the Chinese Communist Party against dogmatist political and military lines — also raised Marxist philosophy to a higher plane.

After the victory of the Chinese Revolution in 1949, and later in the face of the restoration of capitalism in the USSR and the collapse of the international communist movement following the death of Stalin, Mao led further important advances. Foremost among these was his theory of *continuing the revolution under the dictatorship of the proletariat*, which for the first time uncovered and analyzed the continued existence of the bourgeoisie under socialism, and the means and method for waging the struggle against it. It was a breakthrough which guided the Great Proletarian Cultural Revolution, a landmark in world history on the level of the Paris Commune and the October Revolution. As part of carrying all this through, Mao made still further advances in philosophy and in political economy as well, both as they apply to the specific problems of socialist society and more generally.[1]

---

[1] For various reasons Mao's contributions in the period after socialism are not concentrated in any one or two particular works by him; the best single summary of his developments of Marxism — both in that period and overall — can be found in *Mao Tsetung's Immortal Contributions,* by Bob Avakian, Chairman of the Central Committee, RCP, USA.

This, of course, does not bring the development of Marxism to an end; how could it? As Mao was to say in his "Reading Notes on the Soviet Text *Political Economy*," "Any philosophy is in the service of its contemporary tasks." (*A Critique of Soviet Economics*, Monthly Review, 1977, p. 114) And so it is today: the science must be studied, and then used to bring alive the new. This book, again, is an *introduction* to the science of revolution; it aims to provide a foundation and context for going deeper into the theory of Marxism, in order to understand and change the world, and to rise to the challenges posed to this generation by events worldwide. The basic foundation laid out here is a point of departure, an aid to that further necessary development, a plateau from which to help carry forward the ascent to new peaks and greater heights.

1
PHILOSOPHY

In the play *Galileo*, by the revolutionary dramatist Bertolt Brecht, there is a pivotal scene between Galileo and his assistant, a monk. The Church has begun to attack Galileo, and the monk's loyalties are divided. He appeals to Galileo to renounce his work with the telescope, work that has borne out the heretical theory of Copernicus that the earth spins around the sun (and not vice versa, as the Church held); and in arguing, the monk invokes the unsettling effects of this theory on the peasantry, including his own parents:

> They scrape a living, and underlying their poverty there is a sort of order. There are routines. The routine of scrubbing the floors, the routine of the seasons in the olive orchard, the routine of paying taxes. . . . They draw the strength they need to sweat with their loaded baskets up the stony paths, to bear children, even to eat, from the sight of the trees greening each year anew, from the reproachful face of the soil, which is never satisfied, and from the little church and Bible texts they hear there on Sunday. They have been told that God relies upon them and that the pageant of the world has been written around them and that they may be tested in the important or unimportant parts handed out to them. How could they take it, were I to tell them that they are on a lump of stone ceaselessly spinning in empty space, circling around a second-rate star? What, then, would be the use of their patience, their accep-

tance of misery? What comfort, then, the Holy Scriptures, which have mercifully explained their crucifixion? The Holy Scriptures would then be proved full of mistakes. No, I see them begin to look frightened. I see them slowly put their spoons down on the table. They would feel cheated. (Reprinted by permission of Grove Press Inc., *Galileo*, © 1966 by Eric Bentley, © 1940 by Arvid Englind, © 1952 by Bertolt Brecht)

When Galileo didn't heed this sort of appeal, the Holy Fathers threatened him with torture. Other scientists were burnt at the stake, and *all* who fought for this theory were hounded and suppressed.

Beneath the fury of this struggle over scientific theory lay a conflict between classes. The Church and its ideological authority served as a bulwark of the feudal landlords, protecting (and partaking in) the exploitation of the peasantry; to challenge it, and its myth of a divinely ordered universe, implied an attack on an earthly constellation of economic and political interests. What made Galileo's experiments so threatening was the rise of the merchants, manufacturers and others in the growing cities who were straining against the bonds of feudal society. They supported scientific investigation both as an economic aid[1] *and*, more generally, as an important part of the rebellion against the feudal stranglehold over every sphere of society, including science and culture, as well as politics and economics.

Over the next few centuries, as the conflict intensified and spread, the terms of the struggle increasingly took in more than this or that particular scientific theory, and ranged over philosophy and world outlook generally. Materialist philosophy went into battle against the idealism fostered by the Church.[2] This too

---

[1] The Copernican theory, which showed that the earth revolved around the sun and not the other way around, was necessary, for example, as a basis to correctly navigate the oceans to new markets in Asia, Africa and America. Science generally was needed to advance production and manufacture — the discovery of air pressure came about through studying why suction pumps could not draw water out of flooded mines beneath a level of 33 feet.

[2] Materialism holds that matter exists independently of and in fact gives rise to consciousness (rather than the reverse), and that the answers to problems are to be sought in investigating the material world and discovering its laws; idealist philosophy maintains that consciousness, or even a supposed spiritual realm, transcends matter. Idealism looks to contemplation of "divine" laws, etc., for truth. These conflicting world outlooks are examined in greater depth later in the chapter.

went along with and served the rise of the bourgeoisie, again not only or even mainly as a stimulus to production, but also as a tremendous influence for rebellion in politics. The Peasant War in Germany in the 1520s, the English Civil War in 1660, the French Revolution in 1789 — all these went against feudal political domination, and (despite the influence of religious ideas, even religious fanaticism, among the masses involved) necessarily went against the Catholic Church's ideological and philosophical hegemony as well. This whole volcanic period of bourgeois revolution impelled materialist philosophy forward, and was itself in turn spurred forward by it.

Such interpenetration between class struggle and philosophy was far from unique to that period. Philosophy has always been profoundly partisan, and still is. Take the ancient philosopher Plato. He opposed physical experimentation and investigation, holding that truth could only be discovered through logic and the contemplation of perfect forms; the only sciences he allowed among his students were geometry and other higher mathematics (while covering over the source of their seemingly perfect forms in material reality). This was no quirk of Plato's, but flowed from his position as ideologue of the slaveholding class of his day, which was locked in struggle against forces relying more on sailing and trade (the Ionians, whose philosophers were the first materialists and the greatest of the Greek scientists). Plato justified and promoted the subjugation and enslavement of one class to another in his "classic" philosophical work, *The Republic*. There he advises the rulers of his proposed perfect order to "tell one genuine lie worthy of the name":

> [That] the training and education we were giving them [i.e., the education of the common people by the guardians] was all a dream, and they only imagined all this was happening to them and around them; but in truth they were being moulded and trained down inside the earth, where they and their arms and all their trappings were being fashioned. When they were completely made, the earth their mother delivered them from her womb. . . . "So you are all brothers in the city," we shall tell them in our fable, "but while God moulded you, he mingled gold in the generation of some, and those are the ones fit to rule, who are therefore the most precious; he mingled silver in the assistants, [i.e., the soldiers]; and iron and brass in farmers and the other craftsmen." (cited in J.S., "Plato: Classical Ideologue of Reaction," *The Communist*, No. 5, RCP Publications, Chicago, May, 1979, p. 153)

But if class interests and class struggle play a determining role in philosophy so long as society is divided into classes, what exactly is the importance of philosophy to the class struggle? To begin with, let's sharpen up what we *mean* by philosophy. Unlike particular bodies of knowledge concerning specific categories of things (e.g., astronomy, biology, economics, etc.), philosophies are comprehensive world outlooks, systematic ways of analyzing and understanding the various phenomena and events of the universe.

In that light, philosophy has a twofold importance. First, no matter how consciously or consistently they may do it, *everyone* applies one method or another — that is, a philosophy — to understanding the world. The world outlook that views life on earth as a vale of tears and seeks meaning and salvation in submission to a mythical god off in heaven, tends to reinforce one sort of behavior; the idea that individuals confront the universe alone and wrench what meaning they can out of "the moment" reinforces another. And those who say "I have no philosophy, I just do what works," express (and act on) a philosophy even as they deny it — the philosophy of *pragmatism*, the dominant one in the U.S. The concentrated struggle over world outlook and method that goes on in philosophy, then, has far-reaching effects on peoples' spontaneous and seemingly *un*philosophical everyday thinking . . . and thus on their actions, including their political actions.

Beyond its broad effect on the masses, though, philosophy is critically important to forging and guiding a genuinely revolutionary movement. No movement can transform the world — *fundamentally* transform it — without a method to correctly understand it. The revolutionary advances led by Marx, Lenin and Mao in both practice and theory were achieved — and could only have been achieved — on the basis of forging, deepening and applying materialist dialectics, and waging struggle against various attacks on the philosophical front by the bourgeoisie. By the same token, the influence of pragmatism on the revolutionary movement — which has often taken the form of downplaying the struggle over philosophy (as well as struggle over ideological and political line generally) — has led to a narrow obsession with what "seems to work" in the short run, and has played no small part in the movement's seduction by illusory and momentary concessions, and even at times its abandonment of the revolutionary goal.

Further, the very character of the proletariat and the proletarian revolution, as opposed to all previous revolutions and rising
forces in society, demands the conscious mastery of philosophy.
The *Communist Manifesto* points out that:

> All the preceding classes that got the upper hand, sought to fortify
> their already acquired status by subjecting society at large to their
> conditions of appropriation, and thereby also every other pre-
> vious mode of appropriation. The proletarians cannot become
> masters of the productive forces of society, except by abolishing
> their own previous mode of appropriation. They have nothing of
> their own to secure and to fortify; their mission is to destroy all
> previous securities for, and insurances of, individual property.
> (*Manifesto*, 45)

The implications of this for the world outlook characteristic of
this class and its revolution are also made clear:

> The Communist revolution is the most radical rupture with tradi-
> tional property relations; no wonder that its development involves
> the most radical rupture with traditional ideas. (*Manifesto*, 57)

Particularly in those countries where it has long ruled, and
reflecting a general historical trend, the revolutionary days of the
bourgeoisie have long since given way to unbridled reaction, and
its philosophy has travelled a parallel course. The search for truth
has given way to apologies for exploitation and Plato-like
homilies; the fresh spirit of seeking and welcoming the changingness in all things has been turned stale by the priestly odor of those
who think they defend eternal, foreordained orders. Today the
task of changing, and knowing, the world rests most fundamentally with the revolutionary proletariat. And unlike all previous
rising forces in society and all other social classes, the proletariat
cannot allow philosophy to become calcified into another dogma,
another set of ideas that justifies the world as it is instead of explaining it, and that papers over contradictions instead of uncovering them. Any philosophy that assumes the trappings of a
divine order or state religion — whatever the heaven promised or
the icons worshipped — is worse than useless.

The revolutionary proletariat must be armed with a critical
philosophy which correctly reflects the world as it is (which includes most essentially as it is changing), and which enables the
proletariat to penetrate to the essence behind the appearance and

grasp the inner thread of complex events and chaotic upheaval in order to influence and determine their outcome. It needs philosophy in order to *win*, in both the broadest and most all-encompassing sense and — linked to that — at the crucial cross-roads and junctures of battle. This weapon, this philosophy, is *materialist dialectics*.

Dialectics

Contradiction: Key to Existence and Change

Galileo, and before him Copernicus, surely struck a blow for scientific truth, but they only began to uncover how volatile and explosive the universe really is.

Let's look a little deeper at the sun itself. What "holds the sun together" — "what it is" — is a process of mindbogglingly massive and continuous thermonuclear explosions on the order of thousands of hydrogen bombs a second. These reactions transform hydrogen at the sun's core into helium, thereby radiating heat and light. This entire complex of physical and chemical reactions — contradictions — "making up" the sun will in billions of years likely be superseded by different ones, until the sun itself dies or is wiped out — even as new stars arise, in part synthesized from the broken down mass and dispersed energy of what *was* the sun.

Constant development and transformation, explosiveness and changeability, all based on the struggle of opposites, drives forward not only the sun but the entire material universe; and this fundamental law forms the basis of materialist dialectics. "Marxist philosophy," Mao wrote, "holds that the law of the unity of opposites is the fundamental law of the universe. This law operates universally, whether in the natural world, in human society, or in man's thinking." ("On the Correct Handling of Contradictions Among the People," *MSR*, 442-443)

To grasp the contradictory properties within a phenomenon and the character of their constant struggle and mutual transformation, to understand how that struggle in turn gives rise to qualitatively new things — that is the heart of the dialectical method.

But this method doesn't "come naturally," any more than the internal dynamics of the sun are apparent to people through the warmth on their skin. In fact, to judge only from everyday perceptions, the sun would indeed seem solid, revolving around a flat earth. The struggle and interpenetration of opposites that actually give a thing or process its character generally goes on beneath the surface. Dialectics uncovers the hidden mainsprings not apparent to "sound common sense," which as Engels once remarked, while a "respectable fellow . . . in the homely realm of his own four walls, has very wonderful adventures" when he enters "the wide world of research." (*Anti-Dühring*, 26)

Lenin summed up the basic law of dialectics in opposition to the *metaphysical*, "common-sense" conception of development as follows:

> The identity of opposites . . . is the recognition (discovery) of the contradictory, *mutually exclusive*, opposite tendencies in *all* phenomena and processes of nature (*including* mind and society). The condition for the knowledge of all processes in the world in their "*self-movement*," in their spontaneous development, in their real life, is the knowledge of them as a unity of opposites. Development is the "struggle" of opposites. The two basic (or two possible? or two historically observable?) conceptions of development (evolution) are: development as decrease and increase, as repetition, *and* development as a unity of opposites (the division of a unity into two mutually exclusive opposites and their reciprocal relation).
>
> In the first conception of motion, *self*-movement, its *driving* force, its source, its motive, remains in the shade (or this source is made *external* — God, subject, etc.). In the second conception attention is chiefly directed to knowledge of the *source* of "*self*-"movement. ("On the Question of Dialectics," *MEM*, 341)

Note that Lenin underscores "*all* phenomena" in his opening sentence. Can this be true? Is everything driven forward by internal contradiction?

Every living organism exists and develops through breaking down (or "dividing into two") certain entities (food, air, carbon dioxide, water, etc.), expelling the waste and transforming the rest into constituents of a new and qualitatively different form. Motion and relative rest, flushing out the dead and reconstituting the new, rapid growth and periods of relative stability — these are all contradictory processes that make up the life activity of any plant or animal. Reproduction proceeds through contradiction and splitting into two: from the simple cell division of amoebae to the sexual process in higher organisms that synthesizes a wholly new offspring from half the chromosomes of each parent. And when the temporary and relative stability that characterizes these processes eventually breaks down, the organism dies and disintegrates. . .and in its decay generates the basis for new things or processes to be synthesized.

Societies, too, advance through the struggle of opposites. "The history of all hitherto existing [class] society is the history of class struggles," Marx and Engels stated in the *Communist Manifesto*.

> Freeman and slave, patrician and plebian, lord and serf, guild-master and journeyman, in a word, oppressor and oppressed, stood in constant opposition to one another, carried on an uninterrupted, now hidden, now open fight, a fight that each time ended, either in a revolutionary re-constitution of society at large, or in the common ruin of the contending classes. (*Manifesto*, 30, 31)

Knowledge, contrary to conventional (bourgeois) wisdom, does not advance through a gradual accumulation of facts alone, but even more importantly through the *struggle* between fiercely contending theories, as established views of the world are challenged and eventually broken down by newer (and usually truer) ones. Einstein's theory, for example, first overthrew and then subsumed the accepted view of the universe developed by Isaac Newton. The clash between opposite ideas and the struggle to resolve these contradictions is the lifeblood of knowledge.[3]

Contradiction is universal, propelling every process and thing. But *universality* also means that in the development of each thing, a movement of opposites goes on from beginning to end. The growth of a child, for instance, unfolds in contradictions between bursts of rapid growth and periods of relative consolidation, dependence and independence, learning the old ways and forging and trying out (their own) new ideas. Where, at any point in the process, is there *not* contradiction and struggle?

Cataclysmic earthquakes have their source in the mounting and finally untenable pressures beneath the earth's surface, caused

---

[3] The word *dialectics* itself comes from the Greek *dialego*, meaning to discourse and debate — the early dialecticians believed truth was discovered through the debate between opposed ideas.

by the huge plates that make up the structure of the earth's underlying crust pressing against one another and finally erupting (and at times shifting direction — which has led, in fact, to the wide shifting and formation of continents over millions of years).

Unforeseen crises of all sorts have their roots in ongoing contradictory struggle. The class struggle, as the *Manifesto* states, may indeed be "now hidden, now open" — but it is *continual*, whatever its form. And the relatively "hidden" revolutionary elements that exist and struggle during nonrevolutionary periods, the germinating contradictions pushing up below the surface, form the basis for and interpenetrate with eruptions of revolutionary upsurge.

Lenin lays great stress on *internal* contradictions as the "driving force" of development; but this does not mean that external causes play no role at all. Ice, when heated enough, changes into water, which is certainly a change in *quality*, and not just degree (as one can test by diving into a swimming pool full of ice cubes, or pouring water into a Coke). Still, this does not make external causes principal; no amount of heat can transform ice into chocolate milk, or molten lead. The ability of ice to undergo certain qualitative changes and not others results from its internal contradictions, in this case the contradictory properties of hydrogen and oxygen in their simultaneous interdependence and struggle with each other.

Yet that example alone doesn't sufficiently address the question of the relation between internal and external contradictions. Can it not be said, for example, that the transformation of water into steam is the result of the contradictory struggle between heat and water — in other words, that on a different level (e.g., considering a steam engine) the contradiction between water and heat is internal and not external? And that ultimately the very concept of external cause is meaningless?

No, it is not meaningless. . . but it *is* relative. This is bound up with the fact that there are qualitatively different levels to the structure of matter (speaking here of *all* matter, whether subatomic particles, human societies or galaxies). Water molecules, for example, contain atoms. These atoms, however, are not "mini-molecules," but qualitatively different organizations of matter with distinct contradictory characteristics, properties and structures. Their combination into a molecule is conditional —

and in the absence of certain underlying conditions, the molecule will break down. But, at the same time, the behavior of these atoms when they *are* integrated into the structure of a molecule will be more determined by the contradictions of the molecule than by their own internal particularities as atoms.

To take another example, let's look at the relation between the organs of the body and the body as a whole. The various organs, tissues and cells that make up the body have their own particular contradictions which define them and must be understood in their own right. On the other hand, and more fundamentally, the human organism is an integral whole, and its various organs do not basically have an independent existence (and history of development), but function and develop as a subordinate part of the whole organism. The body is not an "alliance of cells"; neither the cells, nor the larger organs, can function as such if the body overall is dead, while the body itself sheds millions of dead cells a day, and can even get along without certain vital organs.

While contradiction goes on in each organ, and while "local diseases" develop within organs — influencing, even at times determining, the health of the organism as a whole — this again only takes on meaning in terms of its relation to the rest of the body. Heart disease, for example, cannot be correctly understood separately from the diet, activity, mental outlook and strength of the body as a whole and its other organs.

Of course, the argument could be made in turn that since the health of different individuals is largely determined by their status in society, that *this* is the level on which disease should be studied and treated; and indeed for certain purposes (massive prevention programs, epidemics, etc.) it *is*. But the body of an individual person is not related to society in a way analogous to the relationship between different organs and the body as a whole. To cure a sick person, the internal contradictions in this case (i.e., the systems, organs, cells of a person) are principal over the external ones (environment, society, etc.).

The point here is that the *concrete character* of the process or thing being analyzed must be kept to the forefront. There are different levels of structure to matter, and any level is both relatively autonomous and at the same time linked to and influenced by other levels. Therefore clarity on what exactly is under study, and on that basis which contradictions should be considered internal and which external, and how they relate, is critically important to dialectical analysis. Mao emphasized understanding the "law of contradiction in things in a concrete way." ("On Contradiction," *MSR*, 90) The actual opposites which constitute and push forward the development of a thing or process must be ascertained, their interaction and struggle studied and understood.

Identity and Struggle and the Leap to the New

How do mutually exclusive opposites actually coexist within a single process or thing? And why does this concept of the unity, or *identity*, of opposites, in the words of Lenin, "furnish the key to the 'leaps,' to the 'interruption of gradualness,' to the 'transformation into the opposite,' to the destruction of the old and the emergence of the new"? ("On the Question of Dialectics," *MEM*, 341-342)

To begin with, identity has both a popular and a philosophical meaning. Philosophically, the identity of opposites does *not* mean that the two aspects of a contradiction are the same as each other, or can't be told apart; it refers instead both to the coexistence of opposites within a single entity, and to their property under certain circumstances of transforming into each other, thereby qualitatively transforming the character of the thing or process at hand.

To begin with the first aspect of the philosophical meaning of identity, the coexistence of opposites: while every entity or process is a contradiction composed of opposing forces, through most of their existence entities exist in a relatively stable state. To put it another way, within any entity or process there are new and rising forces struggling against the framework of the thing, striving to negate its character and bring something new into being; nevertheless, at any given time a thing is still more itself than "not itself." An egg, while containing a developing chicken, remains an *egg* — a hard, white shell surrounding an embryo. Capitalist society, while containing elements of future socialist society (in the form of socialized production, the proletariat, its party, etc.) which continually struggle within and against the dominant capitalist framework, is still nevertheless *capitalist* society. The opposites in a contradiction coexist with one another, and this (temporary) coexistence is one aspect of what is meant by the "identity of opposites."

Such coexistence, however, is not static; it's more in the character of a relatively stable framework within which the ceaseless struggle of opposites goes on. And this ongoing struggle of opposites partially alters the character of the identity itself even before it reaches a point of intensity which fundamentally ruptures the identity (or the framework).

Let's look at a few other cases of mutual coexistence and interdependence of opposites. Life is obviously diametrically opposed to death — but really, wouldn't the very concept of life be meaningless without death, and vice versa? Death only has meaning as a limit to life, and life itself only continues so long as organisms break down and synthesize elements from dead plants and animals (and simultaneously expel the dead cells and toxic waste from their own selves).

Or take war; war is qualitatively different from peace — still the two have identity as well. Peace treaties turn out to be nothing but the framework within which rival bourgeoisies compete with each other and prepare for new wars, while war itself is not conducted for its own sake, but to set the terms for new (and more favorable) peaceful arrangements. And there is identity and struggle in the contradiction between just and unjust wars, too — as when the Russian proletariat transformed the unjust, imperialist war waged by its own bourgeoisie in World War 1 into a revolutionary civil war in Russia. Further, wars waged by oppressed classes and nations for their liberation develop as a qualitative leap out of the — relatively — nonmilitary struggle of the oppressed against the oppressor.

But the matter does not end with the dependence of opposites upon each other for their existence. As Mao wrote:

> . . . what is more important is their transformation into each other. That is to say, in given conditions, each of the contradictory aspects within a thing transforms itself into its opposite, changes its position to that of its opposite. This is the second meaning of the identity of contradiction. ("On Contradiction," *MSR*, 119)

While the struggle between its two aspects goes on throughout the life of the contradiction, and both aspects undergo partial transformations through different stages as a result of this (as well as other contradictions influencing the process), there inevitably comes a point when the old identity can no longer comprehend the contradictory aspects in their changed character. The subordinate aspect bursts forth, overcomes the formerly principal aspect, and brings a qualitatively new and different entity into being. The shell of the egg is destroyed and replaced by *its* opposite, the chicken; the shell of capitalist society is ruptured by the proletarian revolution and a new society begins to be created.[4]

These are *leaps* to the new — not gradual and obvious transitions by degree — but leaps in which really new things suddenly present themselves through the destruction, or at least overcoming, of the old. World war does not develop through a gradual mounting of hostilities until it has one day imperceptibly become war, but, as the bourgeois military experts themselves say, arises out of critical flashpoints. Nor does water pass through a paste-like state before turning to ice.

This applies, for instance, to the rise of the bourgeoisie, which was generated within the pores of feudal society, from among its merchants, traders, artisans and independent peasants. They facilitated exchange and some improvement of the productive forces within feudal society, and for several centuries these nascent bourgeois forces developed. But *as* they developed and grew, the very conditions and social relations that had earlier fostered their rise began to be felt as constraints on further growth, while at the same time the growth of commodity exchange gradually corroded those feudal relations. The conflict and pressure grew; at a certain point, the bourgeoisie began to mount all-out revolutionary assaults against the feudal order,

---

[4] Obviously, the replacement of one entire form of society by another on a global scale is more complex and tortuous than the birth of a single chicken; any single proletarian revolution does not destroy capitalist society worldwide *or* even the bourgeoisie in the country where the revolution occurs (as will be explained in Chapter 4), though it constitutes an important leap in that process. Taken over a long historical epoch, however, it *is* true that capitalist relations and capitalist society *are* totally destroyed, and an entirely new entity brought into being, as a result of the struggle between opposites. As Marx described this entire process in a compressed and concentrated way: "Centralisation of the means of production and socialisation of labour at last reach a point where they become incompatible with their capitalist integument. Thus [the] integument is burst asunder. The knell of capitalist private property sounds. The expropriators are expropriated." (*Capital*, Vol. 1, 763)

and bourgeois society could only come into being on the basis of a definite break and rupture with that order. It's important to note here that this break occurred during a time when the bourgeoisie (and the relations it embodied and represented) still existed in quite rudimentary form. Only with the breaking apart of feudal society, and the clearing away of a certain amount of "rubble," could the *new* social relations really take root and grow.

The new rising aspect must rupture the old identity in order to really blossom, or fully come into its own; and this has even greater (and qualitatively different) implications for the proletarian revolution, as will be discussed later.

In contrast, one thing that stands out in the reformist programme of a transition to socialism by means of gradual reform is its denial of development through leaps, its denial of the emergence of the qualitatively new through the rupture with the old. Thus this erroneous political line has a profoundly wrong philosophical outlook at its root. As long as the old identity of a contradiction fundamentally "holds" — as long as things stay in the "same ballpark" — no modifications by degree can themselves fundamentally change things. The new must negate the confines and bounds of the old identity in which it occupies a subordinate, suppressed position; the very underpinnings of the old must be *ruptured* for the new to become the principal aspect and to fully reveal itself, develop and flourish.

The identity of opposites in the preceding examples resides not only in their coexistence, but also in their change of place in their relationship within the contradiction. In the leap from water to ice, the contradictory identity between the energy of the individual molecule (which tends to random motion) on the one hand, and the bonding force *between* molecules on the other, goes from a state in which the molecular energy is dominant enough to permit a degree of fluidity to one in which the molecular bonding force becomes principal, and the molecules are frozen. Between the proletariat and the bourgeoisie, the bourgeoisie (as noted) does not vanish immediately after the socialist revolution but continues to exist and wage struggle (speaking here specifically of the internal makeup of socialist countries) as a dominated and subordinate aspect of the contradiction (as long as the society remains on the socialist road); what has changed is the respective position of the two aspects in the contradiction. This transformation of opposites into each other changes the qualitative character of the entity as a whole and the forms assumed by its contradictory aspects — from water to ice, or capitalism to socialism. In the latter case, the period in which the bourgeoisie is dominated (first in various countries, later on a world scale) will eventually result in its full disappearance — at which point the proletariat itself will also go out of existence (after all, how could there be a proletariat without its opposite?) and another new entity, communist society, with its own contradictions and struggle, will arise.

Identity, to sum up, is contradictory: opposites both coexist and transform themselves into one another. Their coexistence is itself a process of mutual transformation, and their transformation into each other is generally not absolute but goes on in wavelike, or spiral-like, development (more on this later). For this reason both Lenin and Mao in their works emphasized the *fluidity* and interpenetration in the relationship between the opposite aspects of a contradiction, with Mao writing in "On Contradiction" that:

> The fact is that the unity or identity of opposites in objective things is not dead or rigid, but is living, conditional, mobile, temporary and relative; in given conditions, every contradictory aspect transforms itself into its opposite. Reflected in man's thinking, this becomes the Marxist world outlook of materialist dialectics. It is only the reactionary ruling classes of the past and present and the metaphysicians in their service who regard opposites not as living, conditional, mobile and transforming themselves into one another, but as dead and rigid, and they propagate this fallacy everywhere to delude the masses of the people, thus seeking to perpetuate their rule. The task of Communists is to expose the fallacies of the reactionaries and metaphysicians, to propagate the dialectics inherent in things, and so accelerate the transformation of things and achieve the goal of revolution. (*MSR*, 121-122)

At the same time, not every imaginable pair of things in the world actually constitutes a unity of opposites, nor do things which under certain conditions form a unity of opposites always exist as such. The key here, again, is concreteness. Chickens do not emerge from stones; water does not freeze into lead.

Further, in the relationship between the opposite aspects of a contradiction, identity and struggle do not exist on a par. Struggle is principal over identity. Identity, or relative order, is a temporary condition, but struggle never ceases; it permeates a process from beginning to end and leads to the transformation of opposites and the eventual annihilation of the process (and its replacement by something new). In fact, when struggle ceases, identity goes out of existence as well, since the process itself has come to an end.

In *Communists Are Rebels*, Bob Avakian writes that:

> For all these reasons, all ideas of stagnation, permanence — and permanent order — of unchanging absolutes, are contrary to nature and its laws and to humanity's struggle with the rest of nature, through society, and to the laws of social development (and of thought). In political expression, these ideas are reactionary and serve reactionary social forces. (*Communists Are Rebels*, Revolutionary Communist Youth pamphlet, 1980, p. 18)

The stars, the planets, different organisms — all are forms of matter in motion in which the constituent opposites coexist for a time in one form, only to eventually be severed through struggle and dissolve (and become in different forms the elements of new entities). Each individual person, for example, is nothing but a particular and conditional combination of matter...matter which existed in different forms previously and will exist in other forms in the future.

Take the ecology of natural environments. This is often portrayed as a somewhat static and unchanging thing (often in response to the anarchic and destructive activities of capital in tearing up the environment). Yet environments are conditional unities of many different sets of opposites, which exist and develop in constant flux and change. Today's ecology is not that of the ice age, nor does it resemble the epoch of the dinosaurs. Go back far enough and the atmosphere of the earth contained almost no oxygen, which itself was generated through the development of algae and the photosynthesis necessary to its existence, and which — as it became more predominant — caused the massive extinction of species which could not exist in an oxygen-rich environment.

It is particularly important to apply this understanding to socialism, to grasp it not as an unchanging order but a society teeming with contradictions, and advancing through upheavals and turmoil to qualitatively higher stages, and eventually to its own extinction and replacement with something higher. This is even true of communism. An opposite view, putting the main emphasis on "socialist order," or "consolidating the socialist system," inevitably entails the attempt to smother the new and arising, which by nature takes shape through struggling against the principal aspect of the identity in which it arises. Socialism can only advance — and beyond that, communism can only be realized — through pushing through and beyond social relations which at one point may have genuinely signified something new and progressive but which if clung to become ossified and lifeless and must be overthrown. And indeed, the entire transition period to communism is made up of struggles between the revolutionary proletariat, which wants to advance, and those forces who cling to and defend what has become outdated and restrictive.

Again, Lenin's warning to take the identical opposites in a thing or process "not as dead, rigid, but as living, conditional, mobile, becoming transformed into one another" ("Conspectus of Hegel's Book *The Science of Logic*," *LCW*, Vol. 38, 109) rings home; and his characterization of socialism (in another work) as a combination of dying capitalism and nascent communism is an important application of just this principle of the identity and struggle of opposites.

Universal and Particular

How is one to grasp the essence of any given process or phenomenon, the actual character of the contradiction pushing forward its development? In this, the contradictory relationship between the universal and the particular is critical. Mao wrote in "On Contradiction" that:

> In considering each form of motion of matter, we must observe the points which it has in common with other forms of motion. But what is especially important and necessary, constituting as it does the foundation of our knowledge of a thing, is to observe what is particular to this form of motion of matter, namely, to observe the qualitative difference between this form of motion and other forms. Only when we have done so can we distinguish between things. Every form of motion contains within itself its own particular contradiction. This particular contradiction constitutes the particular essence which distinguishes one thing from another. It is the internal cause or, as it may be called, the basis for the immense variety of things in the world. There are many forms

of motion in nature, mechanical motion, sound, light, heat, electricity, dissociation, combination, and so on. All these forms are interdependent, but in its essence each is different from the others. The particular essence of each form of motion is determined by its own particular contradiction. This holds true not only for nature but also for social and ideological phenomena. Every form of society, every form of ideology, has its own particular contradiction and particular essence. (*MSR*, 96)

For example, in studying chemistry, it is essential to know that chemical compounds are composed of atoms which combine (and dissociate) on the basis of their contradictory characters. On the other hand, this general knowledge — this grasp of the *universality* of certain contradictions in chemistry — obviously cannot by itself get us past the threshold of understanding why elements combine in some combinations but not others; what the properties of various elements are, both singly and in combination with other elements in a compound; or how they can be used and transformed.

Similarly, in studying (class) society the point of departure should be the class relations and the class struggle. But again, this in and of itself does not resolve the problem of the different forms that class struggle takes in vastly different societies — for example, feudal, capitalist or socialist society — nor does it reveal the underlying particular contradictions compelling classes to act in various ways. Finally, it does not reveal in what direction society must be transformed and how to do this.

Even once those questions *are* addressed, the particular character of contradictions must be studied still more deeply. While it is indispensable to understand that this is the age of imperialism, and that the task of the proletariat worldwide is to lead revolution and overthrow the capitalist mode of production and push forward the transition to communist society, this is only the first step. What is further required is the analysis of the tremendously complex and varying tasks before the international proletariat in differing and ever changing stages of development of the process worldwide and in different kinds of countries (imperialist powers, oppressed nations, or socialist countries — when they exist), and beyond that the elucidation of the different contradictions in each particular country.

Here it is important to return to Mao's statement in the

passage cited above that the particular is the "foundation of our knowledge." How is this so and what is its importance? In the first place, it is only through the experience with and study of many different particulars that the broad patterns universal to a given set of phenomena can be discovered. There was much experimentation with chemistry and chemical compounds before the general principles on which atoms combined were discovered, and Marx and Engels' famous statement on the centrality of class struggle to history was not an inspired hunch but the product both of their first-hand experience in a period of concentrated revolutionary struggle in Europe and of their sweeping and detailed study of history. These universal principles were the *abstraction* of many different particulars.

The relationship between the universal and particular is vitally important to the development of human knowledge. Mao explained that:

> As regards the sequence in the movement of man's knowledge, there is always a gradual growth from the knowledge of individual and particular things to the knowledge of things in general. Only after man knows the particular essence of many different things can he proceed to generalization and know the common essence of things. When man attains the knowledge of this common essence, he uses it as a guide and proceeds to study various concrete things which have not yet been studied, or studied thoroughly, and to discover the particular essence of each; only thus is he able to supplement, enrich and develop his knowledge of their common essence and prevent such knowledge from withering or petrifying. These are the two processes of cognition: one, from the particular to the general, and the other, from the general to the particular. Thus cognition always moves in cycles and (so long as scientific method is strictly adhered to) each cycle advances human knowledge a step higher and so makes it more and more profound. ("On Contradiction," *MSR*, 97)

Note that Mao does not treat the universal as simply the sum total of particularity; in fact, elsewhere (in the essay "On Practice") he cites Lenin's statement that "the abstraction of *matter*, of a *law* of nature, the abstraction of *value*, etc., in short, *all* scientific (correct, serious, not absurd) abstractions reflect nature more deeply, truly and *completely.*" (*MSR*, 69-70) Correct abstractions concentrate the essential character underlying the many particulars, reveal the relationships between various phenomena and aspects of things, and discard what is mainly superficial and inessential. There is both universal and particular character residing in any process or phenomenon, and these aspects are at the same time linked and mutually exclusive; grasping their contradictory struggle and interaction is (to again cite Mao) "the quintessence of the problem of contradiction in things; failure to understand it is tantamount to abandoning dialectics."[5] ("On Contradiction," *MSR*, 109)

Politically, the error of focusing only on the universal and severing it from its connection to the particular generally takes the form of dogmatism. Useless, damaging attempts are made to force the complex and many-sided character of reality to fit into preconceived and usually simplistic ideological straitjackets. And while in times of upsurge this may lead to rashly trying to advance without taking the particular character of the situation into account, more frequently it comes out in failing to grasp the real revolutionary opportunities at junctures which don't conform to some bookish notions of what a revolutionary situation is "supposed to" look like.

To cut the link from the other side — that is, to take every new particular change and development as justification for departing from and basically throwing out the universal principles of Marxism — amounts to one of the philosophical underpinnings of revisionism.[6] The individual trees are set against comprehending the overall character of the forest. At bottom, the revisionist and dogmatist both deny the relationship between universality and particularity and share a common approach to the world (if from opposite sides); both demand that reality "go by the book" (in the most narrowly conceived way) and when (inevitably) that doesn't happen, the dogmatist denies

---

[5] Lenin discussed the concept as follows in "On the Question of Dialectics": ". . .the particular exists only in the connection that leads to the universal. The universal exists only in the particular and through the particular. Every particular is (in one way or another) a universal. Every universal is (a fragment, or an aspect, or the essence of) a particular. Every universal only approximately embraces all the particular objects. Every particular enters into the universal incompletely, etc., etc." (*MEM*, 343)

[6] Revisionism refers to any trend which claims the mantle of Marxism while propagating ideas and carrying out actions directly opposed to the spirit, goals and fundamental principles of Marxism — and the practice of genuine Marxists.

reality, while the revisionist throws out the book.

In fact, there is no such thing as typical, or textbook, examples of *anything*...outside of textbooks! Up close all phenomena present anomalies and deviations; ironically, however, these particular deviations can only be understood after a certain point on the basis of a firm grounding in the universal and abstract — knowledge which does not pretend or attempt to perfectly reflect every particular aspect of a thing, but which alone can dig into its essentials. Especially in studying the experience of previous revolutions, the point and stand must not be to vainly try to fit today's events into replays of the past, but, as Bob Avakian put it in *Conquer The World?...*, "to combine a sweeping historical view with the rigorous and critical dissecting of especially crucial and concentrated historical experiences, and to draw out as fully as possible the lessons and to struggle to forge the lessons as sharply as possible as weapons for now and for the future." (*Conquer The World?...*, 9)

Lenin, for example, had to wage a tremendous struggle during the revolutionary upsurge that took place in Russia from 1905 to 1907 over the question of guerrilla warfare. Before the 1905 revolution, this had been advanced by some revolutionaries as a substitute for the work of raising consciousness through broad agitation and propaganda, a line which in an imperialist country (which Russia was) would lead to a dead end, and which Lenin fought against. But by 1905-1907, when things overall had reached a revolutionary situation and a struggle for power was actually on the agenda, guerrilla warfare took on more of a mass character and a different meaning; now Lenin had to battle against those who saw it as wrong *per se* in every conceivable situation. Lenin began his essay "Guerrilla Warfare" by stating that:

> Absolutely hostile to all abstract formulas and to all doctrinaire recipes, Marxism demands an attentive attitude to the *mass* struggle in progress, which, as the movement develops, as the class-consciousness of the masses grows, as economic and political crises become acute, continually gives rise to new and more varied methods of defence and offence. Marxism, therefore, positively does not renounce any form of struggle. Under no circumstances does Marxism confine itself to the forms of struggle that are possible and that exist at the given moment only, recognizing as it does that new forms of struggle, unknown to the

participants of the given period, *inevitably* arise as the given social situation changes. In this respect Marxism *learns*, if we may so express it, from mass practice, and makes no claim whatever to *teach* the masses forms of struggle invented by "systematizers" in the seclusion of their studies. We know . . . that the coming crisis will bring us new forms of struggle that we are now unable to foresee. (*MEM*, 185-186).

And he concludes the same essay as follows:

> We have not the slightest intention of foisting on practical workers any artificial form of struggle, or even of deciding from our armchair what part this or that form of guerrilla warfare should play in the general course of the civil war in Russia . . . But we do regard it as our duty as far as possible to help to arrive at a correct *theoretical* assessment of the new forms of struggle brought forward by life. We do regard it as our duty relentlessly to combat stereotypes and prejudices which hamper the class-conscious workers in correctly formulating a new and difficult problem and in correctly approaching its solution. (*MEM*, 198-199).

Was Lenin here dismissing the importance of the universal? No, he was analyzing the particular case of guerrilla warfare in connection with the overall revolutionary struggle, and uncovering beneath this particular form what was universal in it as a method of *revolutionary* struggle. Using Marxism as a guide to action, as a method for understanding the new and its connections to the struggle for communism, he revealed the link between the particular and universal.

This method can be seen in Lenin's work *Imperialism, the Highest Stage of Capitalism*. By the 20th century, some twenty years after the death of Marx, qualitatively new phenomena had emerged in capitalist countries. This did not outdate Marx, as some suggested, but neither was it sufficient to rest with what Marx had accomplished in *Capital*. Lenin analyzed the development of capitalism into a new stage with its own particular contradictions, a higher stage which had not resolved the earlier contradictions but had changed them in certain respects and overall intensified them. Through analysis of the principal imperialist powers Lenin showed the various ways that imperialism had unfolded out of the contradictions of capitalism, and from the tremendous variety manifest in the handful of imperialist powers he abstracted certain common essential features — even as he noted where and how and why the various countries deviated from this or that "typical" characteristic.

Lenin's elucidation of these contradictions in turn was not "the last word," but a new point of departure for a deeper understanding of imperialist society both in his day and today as well, when imperialism has developed in many new and inevitably unanticipated ways while retaining the underlying character that Lenin had shown to be universal to it.

Mao pointed out that "because the range of things is vast and there is no limit to their development, what is universal in one context becomes particular in another. Conversely, what is particular in one context becomes universal in another." ("On Contradiction," *MSR*, 107) Imperialism, in one light, is a particular contradiction (or set of contradictions) in the context of capitalist society generally, or even more universally, in the context of the contradiction between productive forces and relations of production (and the economic base and superstructure) in society; in another context, imperialism's contradictions form the universal framework in which the particular character of different aspects or different stages of its development must be analyzed. The link between particular and universal is key to understanding the development of things from one stage to another, and the overall significance of any given process or stage of a process.

Stages of Development and the Process Overall: Fundamental and Principal Contradictions

The process of stage-like development is marked by the relationship between the *fundamental* contradiction of a process, which at bottom characterizes and underlies it from beginning to end, and the *principal* contradiction, that contradiction which at any given stage most influences the development of all the many particular contradictions in a process and which determines the character of the particular stage as a whole.

Mao discussed the stage-like development of the fundamental contradiction in "On Contradiction," writing that:

> The fundamental contradiction in the process of development of a thing and the essence of the process determined by this fundamental contradiction will not disappear until the process is

completed; but in a lengthy process the conditions usually differ at each stage. The reason is that, although the nature of the fundamental contradiction in the process of development of a thing and the essence of the process remain unchanged, the fundamental contradiction becomes more and more intensified as it passes from one stage to another in the lengthy process. In addition, among the numerous major and minor contradictions which are determined or influenced by the fundamental contradiction, some become intensified, some are temporarily or partially resolved or mitigated, and some new ones emerge; hence the process is marked by stages. If people do not pay attention to the stages in the process of development of a thing, they cannot deal with its contradictions properly. (*MSR*, 102)

But in any process or phenomenon (which is marked by a fundamental contradiction) the key to grasping the character of a specific stage and determining the key link in the transition to the next (and as Mao notes, more intensified) stage lies in locating the principal contradiction. Mao lays stress on this point as well:

. . . [I]f in any process there are a number of contradictions, one of them must be the principal contradiction playing the leading and decisive role, while the rest occupy a secondary and subordinate position. Therefore, in studying any complex process in which there are two or more contradictions, we must devote every effort to finding its principal contradiction. Once this principal contradiction is grasped, all problems can be readily solved. (*MSR*, 111-112)

The principal contradiction in a process does *not* determine the essence of the process *as a whole*; it is *not* the same thing as the fundamental contradiction, although the fundamental contradiction finds expression in it. Again, what distinguishes it as principal is that it is most critical to the unfolding of the fundamental contradiction and overall determines and influences the development of the other contradictions *at that given stage* of the process. While the principal contradiction may not have to be thoroughly resolved for the fundamental contradiction to advance, still, the unfolding of the principal contradiction at the given stage to a certain point is necessary to the overall working out of the fundamental contradiction.

Take, for example, chess, a game whose fundamental contradiction focuses on the capture of the opposing king. This fundamental goal, however, is generally only accomplished in the working through of three distinct phases of the game: the opening, in which the player strives to develop the mobility of all his pieces while setting up a stable defense for the king; the middle game, in which complicated combinations and concerted attacks are mounted with the aim of hamstringing the opponent's mobility and smashing his defenses; and the end game, when the opponent's king is finally brought under direct attack. Each succeeding phase — with its different aims and consequently different sorts of moves and combinations — can only be undertaken when the necessary basis has been laid through the earlier stage; on the other hand, should a player tarry too long in the opening or middle phase of the game, attempting to somehow "fully develop" each stage, defeat is just as likely. In political struggle this becomes far more complex.

During the Chinese Revolution, after China was directly invaded by Japan, Mao struggled for the strategy of uniting with the Communist Party's former bitter foes, the ruling Kuomintang Party, to fight Japanese imperialism. Why? In Mao's analysis the fundamental contradiction of the overall process of the Chinese Revolution was between the masses of Chinese people and imperialism and feudalism. This was determined by China's semi-feudal and semi-colonial character, and made unity with the national bourgeoisie possible, at least at certain points. What made such a temporary alliance correct and necessary at the time was the emergence of a new principal contradiction. Before the Japanese armed invasion, the fundamental contradiction principally found expression in the civil war between the Chinese Communist Party and the Kuomintang, which was essentially tied to U.S. and British imperialism. With the invasion, and given the actual situation in China (in particular the relative strength of the different class forces) and the world overall (including Japan's necessity to go all out to seize China and oust other, rival imperialists as part of *its* need for a redivision of the world, as well as the necessity and freedom of U.S. and British imperialism, the existence of the Soviet Union, its policies [correct and incorrect], etc., etc.), this contradiction was superseded by another: that between the Chinese nation and Japanese imperialism (and its lackeys). Thus it became both possible and necessary to temporarily unite with (even if only to somewhat neutralize) the Kuomintang and focus efforts on armed struggle against the Japanese Army, in order to resolve the new principal contradiction. The Chinese Revolution passed from the stages of the first and second revolutionary civil wars to the period of the war of anti-Japanese resistance.

But throughout that stage of the revolution, Mao also fought for the orientation of treating it *as a stage*, and a preparatory period for the point when the contradiction between the Kuomintang and Chinese Communist Party would again become principal. After the defeat of Japan in 1945, a struggle did ensue within the Communist Party over whether to renew and intensify the struggle against the Kuomintang, or to maintain at all costs the unity conditioned by the Japanese invasion. Those who fought for the latter, erroneous line would have ended up negating the fundamental contradiction — between the Chinese masses and imperialism and feudalism — by denying that it had advanced to a new stage, expressed in a new principal contradiction. Only by dint of the fiercest struggle, and a thoroughgoing application of dialectics, was the third revolutionary civil war launched and led to victory.

These different stages themselves were far from static, but constantly shifted and were further divided into substages in which different contradictions in turn could be identified as principal (in the context of that substage), and different tactics and policies undertaken to resolve them and advance things to a higher stage.

Must the principal contradiction at any stage be fully or even basically resolved in order to advance to the next stage? Not necessarily; while the principal contradiction is indeed principal, it is not the *sole* contradiction in a complex process, and its very workings (and those of the fundamental contradiction) may intensify other contradictions to the point where one of them emerges as principal. Often the necessary level of resolution cannot be predicted.

The Communist Party of China correctly analyzed, for example, that in the 1960's the principal contradiction in the world was between imperialism (headed then by U.S. imperialism) and the oppressed nations, or "third world" (as it is commonly referred to).[7] This contradiction found its most concentrated expression in the Vietnam war, which profoundly influenced all the other contradictions in the world. But while the contradiction between imperialism and the third world reached a certain level of resolution, it can hardly be said that it was in any sense completely resolved! It did, however, unfold far enough and influence the other contradictions in such a way as to give rise to an overall intensification of the underlying fundamental contradiction, and to help lay the basis for and give way to a shift in the principal contradiction to that between the imperialist blocs headed respectively by the U.S. and the USSR.

In fact, over the last few years the contradiction between imperialism and the nations it oppresses has become *sharper* (witness Iran, Afghanistan, Central America, Eritrea, etc.). But this does not mean that it influences the other contradictions and the process overall in the same decisive way it did in the '60s, for instance. Its current sharpness occurs in an overall context which is more set by the intensifying principal contradiction between the Western and Eastern imperialist blocs, with the consequent strain on the whole imperialist fabric both creating fissures through which those (and other kinds of) struggles erupt and at the same time causing frantic moves by both imperialist blocs to keep those eruptions from "getting out of hand," and to maneuver within them on the basis of the looming showdown.

The link between the principal contradiction at a stage and the fundamental contradiction underlying the process as a whole is an important aspect of dialectics. The tendency to become so immersed in the particular stage of a process as to lose sight of the overriding and fundamental contradiction (of which it's a particular and temporary expression) has historically proven to be a powerful pull away from a sweeping and dialectical view, and towards revisionism. At the same time, of course, neither will it do to gloss over or negate the task of analyzing key junctures, stages and turning points in a process, or to misassess those stages and junctures. The point is to grasp and master the dialectical method overall, including the links between the fundamental and principal contradictions.

---

[7]Cf. *Whence the Differences?* (n.p., n.d.), esp. "More on the Differences Between Comrade Togliatti and Ourselves," and *The Polemic on the General Line of the International Communist Movement* (Red Star Press, London, 1976), esp. "Proposal Concerning the General Line. . . ."

Analysis and Synthesis
and the Spiral of Development

The importance of grasping the stage-like development of a process lies in being able to push forward a struggle through various stages and to eventually fully resolve its fundamental contradiction — and thus give rise to a new process, with new contradictions. This is the process of *synthesis*, the creation of the new, which can only proceed through struggle against and eventual overcoming of the old. Mao wrote:

> We often speak of "the new superseding the old." The supersession of the old by the new is a general, eternal and inviolable law of the universe. The transformation of one thing into another, through leaps of different forms in accordance with its essence and external conditions — this is the process of the new superseding the old. ("On Contradiction," *MSR*, 113)

Mao then goes on to emphasize the centrality of *struggle* to this; that is, the new supersedes the old on the basis of repeated and intensifying struggle, and qualitatively new processes and things really only come into being on the basis of overcoming and fundamentally vanquishing the old.

Synthesis (especially in complex processes) doesn't proceed in some sort of predetermined or cut-and-dried way. It's a spiraling process full of advance and setback, destruction and construction, decay and reconstitution, all of which interpenetrate; the resolution of a fundamental contradiction in any complex process entails the emergence of new contradictions at different stages, as well as the intensification of some, mitigation of others, etc. This spiral nature of development can be seen throughout nature and society.

This is shown, for example, in the evolution of the universe. Contemporary theory holds that after the Big Bang,[8] the now-known universe contained only hydrogen and helium. But as the first generation of stars to coalesce out of the form of matter created by the Big Bang themselves exploded in massive supernovas, the tremendous heat generated in those explosions broke

---

[8] A titanic explosion of matter and energy occurring roughly 18 billion years ago, and the farthest point back in the history of the known universe to which science has thus far penetrated.

down the atoms of these elements and then fused them back together in new ways, thus creating new elements (such as carbon, oxygen, etc.). The matter and energy given off in that round of explosions eventually synthesized itself in another "generation" of stars, this time with a qualitatively more complex chemical structure. In this light, the exploding supernovas were at one and the same time an incredibly massive destruction of the old order *and* the basis for *synthesis* on a qualitatively new level. Of course, the generations referred to here are extremely approximate; it is not as if the entire first generation of stars after the Big Bang exploded anywhere near simultaneously, or as if they (and their "descendants") did not (and do not) vary in many ways from one another. But that's precisely the point; while processes do not proceed in orderly or predetermined ways, packaged in nice little categories instantly amenable to human understanding, they do in fact approximate spirals which have their own (particular and conditional) "laws" (or better, contradictory characteristics) which broadly mark them off from other periods of development despite the interconnections.

At the same time, contradictions do not necessarily develop in a predetermined path; different processes and things interpenetrate and influence one another, and relatively external contradictions (in one context) can alter a process' direction of development and even eliminate it altogether. Further, while things tend to develop in spirals, there is no "great spiral" that comprehends all matter; i.e., it is not the case that *all* matter is moving in a certain direction (as if in a god-like plan), but only that individual processes, things, entities, etc., do tend to develop in spirals — and that this is an important, if relative, law of matter and facet of the dialectical method.

Let's look at the evolution of species on earth. This is often portrayed as an extremely gradual process in which each generation improves upon the last and, over time, a new species gradually and imperceptibly emerges. Actually, evolution has been marked by periods of tremendous extinctions followed by incredibly rapid development of new species in a concentrated period of time. The dinosaurs, which dominated the animal kingdom for 140 million years, were wiped out in an extinction that eliminated between 25% and 50% of the species on earth at that time. Interestingly, there is a lot of speculation, and more than a little evidence, that dinosaurs were continuing to develop at the time they became extinct, and that the cause of the extinction was a severe change in the earth's climate due to an externally-caused cataclysm; some think a huge meteor crashed into the earth and the dust that filled the atmosphere blocked out the sun's rays enough to drastically alter the temperature, a change to which the dinosaurs, along with many other species, could not adapt.

The little tree-dwelling animal which became the prototype for the mammals was not an improved edition of the dinosaur but a form of animal which differed qualitatively from the dinosaurs (e.g., its heating system, method of reproduction, etc.) in ways enabling it to survive the wipe-out and begin to take root, flourish and branch out on various paths of development in the (temporarily) "species-depleted" world. And the fossil record does not show humans developing out of four-legged monkeys via a series of stooped-over intermediaries, but reveals instead a sudden emergence of upright walkers.

Just to sum up this example and put it in the context of spiral development, the point here is both that the epoch of dinosaurs and that of mammals form distinct spirals of development with their own fundamental contradiction and particular characteristics, *and* that this development did not proceed in a straight line but in a zig-zag, spiraling development, through which the fundamental contradiction of the process unfolded (until, in the case of dinosaurs, it was ended, perhaps by a dead end in development, perhaps by the intervention of a higher process, or maybe by a combination of the two).

Spiral-like development also characterizes the history of societies. There was nothing predetermined as to where, when and how capitalist society would develop, for example; it happened to have emerged from the particular contradictions confronting European society at a certain point. Its *particular* form of emergence was not somehow set in motion centuries earlier (and still less was it inherent in some "European" qualities). Further, its emergence was not at all orderly but full of revolution and counter-revolution, false starts and anomalies.[9] At the

---

[9] An example of a false start can be seen in Renaissance Italy. There commodity production and trade developed to the point where merchant capital was beginning to

same time, while capitalism was not predestined to develop in the particular place and shape that it did, it is also true that the contradiction between commodity production and the production for use characteristic of feudal society would continually assert itself in the decay, stagnation and/or dissolution of various feudal societies (as had been happening since the first feudal societies in Egypt) until inevitably, in some place, a new mode of production based on the ascendancy of commodity production and commodity relations (i.e., capitalism) would achieve dominance. [10] In other words, and more generally, while all processes contain within them the tendency for contradictions to come to a head, the exact content and working out of that change is not at all inevitable; it's not "automatic." As Mao remarked about water, "only after I don't know how many tens of millions of years was [it] formed; hydrogen and oxygen aren't just transformed immediately in any old way into water. Water has its history too." ("Talk on Questions of Philosophy," *Chairman Mao Talks to the People*, ed., Stuart Schram, Pantheon Books, N.Y., 1974, p. 221)

To look at this from a different angle, what's being pointed to is a universal unity in all processes between *analysis* and *synthesis*. These categories, customarily used in human thought, have their roots in and correspond to the material world. Analysis is the breaking down and differentiation of an entity into its constituent opposites, their polarization, and struggle; synthesis is the overcoming of the old aspect by the new through that struggle, the conquering of the formerly principal by the formerly secondary, and the emergence of a qualitatively new process. These two processes interpenetrate through all stages; that is, while there are periods of development of a process in which

---

be transformed into industrial capital, but for various reasons — including advances in navigation developed as a result of the Renaissance, but which allowed Northern Europe to bypass the Italian trading cities en route to the East — this did not come to fruition, and the bourgeois revolution did not take place there for another several centuries.

[10] Commodity production is production for exchange, and capitalism is distinguished from all other systems by the preeminence of this form of production. Feudalism is marked by production for use, in which the production of the peasants goes in the main for the direct use of either the peasants themselves or their landlords. For more on why and how these two forms of production clashed, see Chapter 2.

struggle and polarization are principal, and periods of relative identity, there is still synthesis going on within periods of analysis, and vice versa. For example, as applied to thought (to be addressed more deeply later) while one is *analyzing* a problem he or she must at the same time carry on some synthesis, in the form of advancing overall (or partial) hypotheses, testing them, evaluating results, etc., as part of that process of analysis; and when analysis is relatively complete and a solution or concept synthesized, this too is never absolute and contains within it many unsolved and/or new problems. Still, with the development of a new concept, theory, etc., a certain level of synthesis can be said to have been achieved.

Similarly, the proletariat synthesizes the bourgeoisie. Analysis goes on in the revolutionary struggle between the two, and (partial) synthesis with the victory of socialist revolution; but this synthesis is still partial, and in another light is a different form or stage of analysis, because the bourgeoisie has yet to be vanquished or fully "eaten up" until the full elimination of bourgeois production relations, social relations, and ideas on a world scale — at which point both the proletariat and bourgeoisie will have been fully synthesized in *communist society*, a new entity with new contradictory aspects.

This conception of synthesis was forged by Mao after the victory of the revolution in 1949, when the class struggle in China took on new and more complex forms characteristic of socialism (forms which had not yet been correctly analysed). At one point a revisionist philosopher, Yang Hsien-chen (Yang Xianzhen), postulated that the economic base of the revolutionary society served both capitalism and socialism in what *he* called a synthesis of the two. Yang claimed synthesis to be the *combination* of the two contradictory aspects. (Applied to the earlier examples, according to Yang synthesis of a concept might mean a melding of two opposed theories; synthesis of proletariat and bourgeoisie would mean the indefinite preservation of each.) Mao argued against this:

> You have all witnessed how the two opposites, the Kuomintang and the Communist Party, were synthesized on the mainland. The synthesis took place like this: their armies came, and we devoured them, we ate them bite by bite. It was not a case of two combining into one . . . it was not the synthesis of two peacefully

coexisting opposites. They didn't want to coexist peacefully, they wanted to devour you.... For his part, Yang Hsien-chen believes that two combine into one, and that synthesis is the indissoluble tie between two opposites. What indissoluble ties are there in this world? Things may be tied, but in the end they must be severed. There is nothing which cannot be severed.... ("Talk on Questions of Philosophy," *Chairman Mao Talks to the People*, 224-225)

While the complex conditions following the victory of the Chinese Revolution had necessitated some cooperation with certain capitalist producers, and while the conditions had also made possible a nonantagonistic (i.e., relatively nonviolent) struggle between the victorious revolution and these producers, Mao nonetheless correctly insisted that the proper orientation was one of gradually overcoming the elements of capitalist production in new China through *struggle* — lest the then-secondary aspects spontaneously grow in strength and seize back power.[11]

In discussing Mao's conception of synthesis and the struggle against Yang Hsien-chen in particular, Bob Avakian wrote that:

The difference here, the heart of this struggle in the realm of philosophy, is no mere academic debate but the struggle between two fundamentally opposed lines, the revolutionary line of resolving contradiction through struggle versus the reactionary line of attempting to reconcile contradiction through the subordination of the progressive to the reactionary, the advanced to the backward, the new to the old, the correct to the incorrect, etc. (*Immortal*, 181)

Beyond opposing the idea of the new arising through a combination of opposites, Mao's theory of synthesis also represents a leap beyond (and rupture with) the earlier Marxist conception of development as concentrated in the concept of the "negation of the negation."

What is meant by "negation of the negation"? To understand this, we must first analyze what it arose in opposition to. Before the forging of dialectics, the dominant notion of development was the mechanical model of the universe expressed most notably by the English scientist Isaac Newton and also by the

---

[11]Mao's struggle against Yang Hsien-chen, and his particular conception of synthesis, is outlined in the important pamphlet, *Three Major Struggles on China's Philosophical Front* (FLP, 1973).

French philosopher René Descartes in the 17th century. They both conceived of all change as analogous to the change of place undergone by the different parts of a complex mechanism in the course of an endlessly cyclical process; Newton correctly saw the solar system, for example, as involving the change of place of the different planets at different points in their cyclical orbits but did not grasp the fact that the solar system and the orbits of the various planets had arisen from previous forms of matter in motion, had undergone stage-like development and would be superseded by still other forms. In the view pioneered by Newton and Descartes — *mechanical* materialism — once God set a certain process in motion there could be nothing but change of place, or increase and/or decrease, occurring in regularly determined cycles. Applied to society this conception yields a picture in which the pendulum may swing between progress and reaction, but certain "eternal" characteristics — e.g., exploitation, division between mental and manual labor, political domination, etc. — endure.

But as study in different spheres of natural science gradually revealed the limitations of this mechanical view, and as society itself underwent increasingly drastic change, the dialectical view (first really developed into a systematic philosophical method by Hegel) arose to challenge the incorrect notion of endlessly cyclical development. Hegel posed a pattern of development in which entities, or elements of entities, once negated by their opposites return again to negate their original negations — but on a higher level.

Engels (and Marx) laid out a number of examples illustrating this concept in various works, though the most important exposition of it is in the chapter of *Anti-Dühring* entitled "The Negation of the Negation." There Engels called the "negation of the negation" "an extremely general, and for this very reason extremely far-reaching and important, law of development of nature, history and thought...."(*Anti-Dühring*, 179) For instance, primitive communism is negated by class society, but class society in its turn is negated by communism — which contains elements of the first-negated primitive communism, but now on the qualitatively higher plane of humanity's (relatively) conscious mastery over nature and its own social relations. A barleycorn grain is negated by the plant which germinates out of it; this plant is negated by its seeds, now much more numerous than the original one. Primitive materialism is negated by idealism; but idealism also gives rise to dialectics, and thus the synthesis — dialectical materialism — carries with it elements of primitive materialism transformed to a higher level.

Marx in *Capital* cites as an example of this process the small producers or artisans who owned their own means of production individually. They were negated by the capitalists who expropriated them and exploited them as proletarians. But these capitalists will then be negated by the proletariat, who will expropriate the capitalists and transform the now massive and collectively worked means of production into means of production again owned by the producers — but now by the producers constituted as a collectivity.

The first thing wrong with the "negation of the negation" is that this "law" does not correctly describe how things *actually* change; while the new most certainly arises from the old, the "negation of the negation," to put it bluntly, doesn't exist. There is such a multitude of phenomena that in no way correspond to "negation of the negation" that it cannot accurately be called any sort of general law. Capitalism negated feudalism and socialism will negate capitalism; but how is socialism a resurrection of certain elements of feudalism? Einstein's physics negated Newton's; can it be said that Einstein resurrected certain elements of Ptolemaic (pre-Copernican, earth-centered cosmology) in doing that (let alone as an essential part of the process)? The Vietnam war was a critically important watershed in the recent development of imperialism; in what way did it constitute a "negation of the negation"? Was it such in relation to World War 2? Imposing such a method on reality would inevitably lead away from a correct and concrete understanding of the Vietnam war's real roots and the particular (and tremendously important) role it actually did play.

The heart of the problem, though, can be seen even more clearly in examining those things that the "negation of the negation" does in fact seem to describe. Take for instance the process of primitive communism-class society-communism. Will communism then be negated in turn by some higher level of society containing important elements of class society? No, obviously not. But is it possible that communism *won't* teem with contraditions? That it won't be transformed at some point into something qualitatively different? The method embodied in the "negation of the negation" closes off the path of future development and instead tends to pose communism as an end point.

In criticizing the concept of the "negation of the negation," Bob Avakian raises the question of "Why, and who said, that everything has its 'characteristic' way of being negated?" And then he continues:

> This to me smacks of predetermination and of the notion of the unchanging essence of things. Mao opposed this kind of thinking when he pointed out that heredity and mutation are a unity of opposites. Engels even says several sentences later that it is not possible to "grow barley successfully" without learning how to do it — which is true, but who says that growing barley is "characteristic" of it and the proper way it should be negated, while crushing it is not? Mankind and nature (apparently) have done more of the former to the barley grain than the latter, so far, but is that something which could not change? Or could not the barley grain change in some other way? In short, when Engels insists that "I must therefore set up the first negation in such a way that the second remains or becomes possible. . . . [a]ccording to the particular nature of each individual case," he has included an element of metaphysics in this explanation of dialectics. He goes on to say that "If I grind a grain of barley, if I crush an insect, it is true that I have carried out the first act, but have made the second act impossible." *The* second act, as if there is one required, necessary, "characteristic," proper, predetermined "second act." Here we can see how the concept of the "negation of the negation" comes into antagonism with the actual fundamental law of materialist dialectics, the unity of opposites (contradiction). (Bob Avakian, "More on the Question of Dialectics," *RW*, No. 95, March 6, 1981)

The dialectics forged by Marx and Engels represented overall a tremendous and unprecedented leap in human knowledge, a critical synthesis of all that had gone before. This synthesis, however, did not result from the "negation of the negation" in the realm of philosophy (an explanation advanced at one point by Engels), but (as Engels, and Marx, point out in other places) was forged in response to capitalist production relations and large-scale industry (with the constant flux and changingness it introduced into society), the polarization between the proletariat and the bourgeoisie and eruption of class struggle between the two, developments in natural science and dialectical-

ly related developments in the realm of human thought (including, in the historical context, the limitations reached by bourgeois ideology in philosophy, political economy and history),
and the struggle to break through and resolve those limitations
and contradictions.

In this, too, there is no end point (as might be implied by the
"negation of the negation" model). Are there after all no further
negations necessary in materialist dialectics as a method or
philosophy? Thought can only imperfectly reflect how the world
constantly develops and changes, and people must struggle to
develop more accurate pictures of reality and solve new problems. But the further emergence of contradictions within Marxist philosophy will not result in the negation of Marxism by a
"higher form" of metaphysics or idealism, but can only be
resolved through reforging the method of materialist dialectics
to a higher level of synthesis — as has in fact gone on since Marx
and Engels.[12]

In line with all this, it is necessary to lay stress on and go
more deeply into the *tortuous character* of spiral development.
The failed revolution of 1905, Lenin once noted, served as a
dress rehearsal for 1917. The years between the two attempts,
however, did not witness a gradual accumulation of forces by
the revolutionaries, but a wave-like motion of ebb and upsurge,
depression and resurgence. The revolutionaries had to go
through remarkable twists and turns and wage different sorts of
struggles, including in the period from 1908 to 1912 a crucial
series of inner-party struggles: against ideological onslaughts to
combine Marxism with religion or other anti-Marxist ideologies,
against a revisionist political line, and against a liquidationist
organizational line which called for the dissolution of the party
altogether. These struggles tempered the Bolshevik Party and in
large measure laid the basis for its ability to take a revolutionary
stand at the outbreak of World War 1 and to later successfully

---

[12] The tendencies toward a linear, one-two-three notion of development that exist in *Anti-Dühring* assume yet more concentrated form in the book, *Dialectical
and Historical Materialism*, by Stalin. This book, while containing some correct
material and intended as a concise (and thus necessarily a bit simplified) summary, nevertheless errs so much on this and some other scores that it has done
significant damage precisely in the form of training people in mechanical, rather
than dialectical, materialism.

carry out the October Revolution.

Similarly, the proletarian revolution as a worldwide process has not followed a model of the gradual addition of countries to a "socialist column," eventually leading to a "tipping of the balance" and a communist world. Instead it has been marked by periods of revolutionary advance for the proletariat, in which important parts of the globe have been seized and/or important historical experience accumulated (e.g., the periods directly following the two world wars, and the late 1960s), alternating with times of lull, of consolidation and sometimes of real setback. As discussed in depth in Chapters 3 and 4, however, the overall motion involved has been one of increasing ripeness of the material conditions for revolution and a deeper ideological and political tempering of the vanguard forces of the proletariat. One byproduct, in fact, of the 1956 revisionist coup and restoration of capitalism (albeit in state-capitalist form) in the Soviet Union was the deepened philosophical understanding of the principle of spiral development forged by Mao as part of his grappling with that experience.

Before this period both the "negation of the negation" and the "law of the transformation of quantity into quality" had generally been put on a par with the unity and struggle of opposites — all as "three laws" of dialectics. Mao not only showed the essentially invalid character of the "negation of the negation," but pointed out that the transformation of quantity into quality — while an important principle of development — is basically a case of the unity of opposites, in this case the unity (and struggle) between quantity and quality.

The unity of opposites between quantity and quality relates to two contradictory forms of motion of a thing or process. There is gradual, or quantitative change, in which the contradictions of a thing or process may intensify (or be mitigated), while its qualitative character remains essentially the same; and there is qualitative change, in which the struggle of opposites comes to a head and results in a fundamentally new entity. Water, for example, in changing to steam, goes through a period of quantitative buildup of heat, in which its fundamental qualitative character as water does not change as it gets hotter — until, that is, it reaches the boiling point and makes a leap to the qualitatively new entity of steam. In society, too, the contradictions mount and intensify until the old identity can no longer comprehend them, and a period of open revolutionary struggle begins. If the new revolutionary forces are victorious, society is then reorganized on a qualitatively new basis. The new entity or process, in turn, gives rise to a new period of quantitative and gradual change, but on a new qualitative basis with new contradictions and opposites; then, eventually, comes a new period of qualitative change, and on and on.

But it's important that this principle 1) not be construed arithmetically or mechanically, and 2) not be put on a par with the fundamental law of the unity and transformation of opposites. To take one example of mechanical interpretation of this law, there is the idea that evolutionary change in species results from millions of micro-mutations over an extraordinarily long period of time leading at last to qualitative change. But this is now challenged by the theory that one or several mutations can have a qualitative and overall effect on an organism.[13] Politically, among Marxists, this problem has shown itself in the at-

---

[13]The limitations of a simple arithmetic view of quantity into quality as a law of nature come out fairly sharply in the examination of subatomic particles. In the article "Matter is Infinitely Divisible," written by Chinese physicist Bian Sizu before the 1976 coup, the division of *wavicles*, the smallest unit of matter currently known to man, is discussed as follows:

"In what way will wavicles be divided? It can't be a routine way, and blindly applying the old experience. The molecule is divided into atoms, gravitational field and electromagnetic field; the atom is divided into atomic nucleus, electromagnetic field, and electron; the atomic nucleus is divided into proton, neutron and nuclear field. On every level they all are the new form of unity between particle and field; they all are new nodal points, and they are all qualitatively different. Into what forms will wavicles be divided? It is possible it will be the current form of unity between particles and fields. It is also possible a big qualitative change will take place, giving rise to a new discrete material form and a new continuous material form; they would be new things different from both the particles we know by now and the fields we know by now. It is possible that they will be divided smaller and smaller, but it is also possible that they will be divided bigger and bigger. What will be pulled out of wavicles may possibly 'grow fatter,' become bigger than when it was inside. This might lead to a new development of the relationship between the part and the whole. What would it turn out to be? This is a concrete scientific question. Matter has infinite diversity, the concrete division of matter also has infinite diversity. 'Marxism-Leninism has in no way exhausted truth but ceaselessly opens up roads to the knowledge of truth in the course of practice.' (Mao Tsetung, "On Practice") Dialectical materialism never issues forth into other spheres to give orders; it doesn't draw conclusions on this question, substituting itself for natural science." (in *RW*, No. 122, Sept. 18, 1981, p. 23) •

tempt to measure progress, or the preparations of conditions for a qualitative leap, in basically quantitative terms. This comes out crudely, for example, in the all-too-common practice of measuring *how many* workers follow the banner of the party at any given time as the yardstick for judging both the correctness of its line and the revolutionary potential of the near future — by which method the Democratic Party in the U.S. is the most proletarian of all, and the sudden eruption of revolution after years of relative lull would be simply inexplicable.

While the party's links to the masses are vital to its ability to carry out the tasks and rise to the challenges of *any* period, and are particularly critical in taking advantage of revolutionary opportunities, this cannot be *reduced* to a question of numbers — as, again, the previously-cited example of the Bolsheviks shows. (The Bolsheviks, incidently, because of the ideological and political cohesiveness of their organization, were able to grow by ten times in the period of a few months when a revolutionary situation did emerge, without fundamentally diluting that political cohesiveness, and were able to forge the necessary links to be able to assess the development of the situation into an insurrectionary one and then take advantage of it.)

However, the more mechanical view of the quality/quantity contradiction increasingly came to the fore during the period of Stalin's leadership. This led to an obsession with "how many masses were grouped around the party" (rather than putting in first place the *quality* and political character of those links), and an emphasis within the Soviet Union on how many new productive forces were developed under socialist ownership (with little or no emphasis on the transformation of the relations between people working, narrowing the gap in distribution relations, or the transformation of the superstructure). All this gave ground to a view opposed to the dialectical understanding of qualitative transformation through the struggle between opposites.

Here the danger of raising this contradiction (quantity/quality) to the same level as the fundamental law of dialectics begins to become clear. For if it is made coequal to the unity and struggle of opposites, then essentially what is being done is a Yang Hsien-chen-style two-into-one of dialectical and mechanical materialism, which ultimately means the domination of *mechanical* materialism. Change tends to be viewed mechanically, as if it were basically due to the gradual addition of strength to the secondary aspect of the contradiction and at a certain point a sort of tipping of the balance toward it. This is not a dynamic, dialectically materialist view of the process of change, including synthesis. Change does not proceed by simple addition, nor simply from within a given process. While internal causes are principal over external, contradictions cannot be viewed simply as "things unto themselves." Rather, change proceeds through a complex process in which there is internal development as well as external influence, and some of the external processes are in fact incorporated into the original contradiction. *All* of this can, in that sense, be considered part of the quantitative stage of a given process. Then, through all this, the process reaches a point at which a leap takes place (the stage of qualitative change). Clearly, this is more than mere arithmetic.

Again, it *is* both true and important that the struggle of opposites goes on in a more or less gradual form and — related to that — in concentrated periods of crisis in which qualitative leaps become possible. But listen to how Lenin dialectically applies and elucidates this:

> Motion, in its turn, is regarded not only from the standpoint of the past, but also from the standpoint of the future, and, at the same time, not in accordance with the vulgar conception of the "evolutionists," who see only slow changes, but dialectically: "in developments of such magnitude twenty years are not more than a day," Marx wrote to Engels, "although later there may come days in which twenty years are concentrated." At each stage of development, at each moment, proletarian tactics must take account of this objectively inevitable dialectics of human history, on the one hand utilizing the periods of political stagnation or of sluggish, so-called "peaceful" development in order to develop the class-consciousness, strength and fighting capacity of the advanced class, and, on the other hand, conducting all this work of utilization towards the "final aim" of the movement of this class and towards the creation in it of the faculty for practically performing great tasks in the great days in which "twenty years are concentrated." ("Karl Marx," *MEM*, 38-39)

Here, indeed, is an exposition of the method and application of materialist *dialectics* to the task of understanding and changing history — to make revolution.

Marxist Materialism

"There are rifts and rifts," wrote Pisarev concerning the rift between dreams and reality. "My dream may run ahead of the natural
march of events or may fly off at a tangent in a direction in which no
natural march of events will ever proceed. In the first case my
dream will not cause any harm; it may even support and augment
the energy of the workingmen. . . . There is nothing in such dreams
that would distort or paralyze labour power. On the contrary, if
man were completely deprived of the ability to dream in this way, if
he could not from time to time run ahead and mentally conceive, in
an entire and completed picture, the product to which his hands are
only just beginning to lend shape, then I cannot at all imagine what
stimulus there would be to induce man to undertake and complete
extensive and strenuous work in the sphere of art, science and practical endeavour. . . . The rift between dreams and reality causes no
harm if only the person dreaming believes seriously in his dream, if
he attentively observes life, compares his observations with his cas-
tles in the air and if, generally speaking, he works conscientiously
for the achievement of his fantasies. If there is some connection between dreams and life then all is well." (*What Is To Be Done?*, 211)

So quoted the dreamer Lenin, further remarking that "of this kind
of dreaming there is unfortunately too little in our movement."
Lenin continued: "And the people most responsible for this are
those who boast of their sober views, their 'closeness' to the 'concrete'. . . ." (*WITBD?*, 212)

The problem pointed to by Lenin in 1902 still permeates most
of what passes for communism and Marxism. Marxism is nothing
if not the transformation into reality of the loftiest dreams known
to humanity; and yet this is exactly what is lost sight of, dismissed
or downright opposed, all too often in the name of upholding
materialism and opposing idealism.

Marxism, it is true, is materialist and *not* idealist. But these
terms have both a popular meaning and a specifically philosophical one, which are generally at odds. The philosophical doctrine of
materialism holds that the material world exists *objectively*, i.e.,
independent of human (or any other) consciousness. Human
consciousness is itself a product of the material world, and the
activity of a specific material organ — the brain and central nervous system. And the ideas of the brain are more or less accurate
reflections of the objectively existing material world.

Idealism, on the other hand, refers to those philosophies which maintain that the material world is ultimately the creation of consciousness. This may take the form of *objective* idealism, in which god, the absolute idea, spirit, or whatever, is conceived of as having created the world and/or in which the world is nothing but reflections or manifestations (however imperfect) of abstract ideals (e.g., justice, beauty, etc.) which exist on another plane in a perfect state; or it may be *subjective* idealism, in which reality is believed to be nothing more than the experiences of each individual and that nothing beyond these experiences can be verified as actually existing.

These are obviously quite far from the vulgar definitions of materialism and idealism, i.e., that materialists are set off by their lust for worldly goods while idealists look to the loftier things in life. Wide of the mark as these cliches are, it is not only the distortions of the bourgeoisie which account for their widespread currency — the revisionists, who constantly promote mechanical materialism and gross economic determinism, must also share the blame.

But back to the central point — the opposition of materialism to idealism. The basic split between idealism and materialism concerns the nature of the contradiction between matter and consciousness. Matter has existed eternally, in an infinite and ever-changing variety of forms; but through it all it *exists*, whether as mass or energy, a block of steel or an exploding supernova. As life on earth developed, matter began to give rise to its opposite, consciousness. The rudiments of this are found in the earliest, most primitive organisms and their ability to respond to environmental stimuli. This reaches a qualitatively higher state in the more intelligent animals, who can draw conclusions about their immediate environment and make decisions, and it takes another leap with *human* consciousness. Humans have the capacity to analyze their experience, dream up different ways the future might be, and work to make reality conform to their ideas and dreams, constantly comparing one to the other. Still, developed as it is, consciousness is nevertheless based on material reality and the product and property of a highly organized form of matter, the brain. This much is basic to all materialism.

But "this much" does not really lay bare *how* matter gives rise to consciousness, or how people gain knowledge. Nor does it uncover the basis for consciousness to transform matter. Lacking that, the doctrine of materialism becomes one-sided and lifeless, in which the opposites of matter and consciousness are conceived of statically, and the leap from one to the other is shrouded in mystery.

Marx's Leap —
The Centrality of Practice

And that was the state of things before Marx and Engels synthesized materialist dialectics in the 1840s. Hegelian dialectics, in which they both had been trained, had led to a dead end because of its overriding idealism. Though Hegel's dialectical method reflected the flux and changingness of the material world — and indeed arose on the basis of the tumultuous changes going on in society at the time — he still postulated that the material world was only the working out or manifestation of a preexisting ideal. According to Hegel, humanity's goal was to become conscious of this, at which point both humanity and history would reach their conclusion in an ideal state, perfectly corresponding to the Absolute Idea. However, the upheaval in society which had inspired Hegel's dialectics in the first place did not cease but intensified, in turn bringing forward a section of radical Hegelians, most notably Marx, who rejected Hegel's conclusions while maintaining his contributions to the dialectical method.

In the meantime, materialism was also revived. As with dialectics, it was spurred on by the rapid developments in natural science and production bound up with the rise of capitalism. But this materialism was essentially *mechanical*. It viewed all development as cyclical, or as extensions in quantity rather than changes in quality. Beyond that, it still could not fully come to grips with the relationship between conciousness and matter. The materialists of the day saw consciousness as the passive product of environment, which reached its highest state in reflecting or contemplating nature in thought. These limitations in materialism grew out of, first, the state of natural science, in which mechanics was still the principal focus of study and a process was studied either in isolation, in a static state or as a cyclically repeating process. Beyond that, these limitations also arose out of the development of society overall, which had witnessed the gradual increase in the strength of the bourgeoisie but not yet (except for England) the total and qualitative transformation of a society by the capitalist mode of production.

Marx and Engels, however, came into their own in the midst of (and as active participants in) the most far-reaching series of bourgeois revolutionary movements that had yet developed, and at a time when the proletariat was first beginning to mount the political stage. Further, natural science was on the verge of historical breakthroughs in cell biology, in the understanding of the transformation of energy and in the theory of evolution, all of which tended to support a more dialectical view of nature. But Marx and Engels did not merely passively reflect these developments and try to modify the already existing philosophies, nor did they somehow take the best of materialism and combine it with the best of dialectics. They analyzed and criticized the limitations of all previous philosophy, stepped back to look at history and science with new eyes, brought to bear the lessons of the class struggle raging at that time, and then made a leap in forging something qualitatively new: materialist dialectics. The heart of this leap in the realm of philosophy rested on their insight into human practice as the decisive link between matter and consciousness, and the mutual and continuous transformation of the one into the other.

This is concentrated in Marx's 1845 "Theses on Feuerbach," which, as Engels put it, contains the "brilliant germ of the new world outlook." In this brief but profound essay, Marx unfolds a number of ideas around the centrality of practice to consciousness.

Before Marx, materialism held that the task of cognition was to reflect objective reality, or to contemplate it. But how had people come to know anything at all about the objective world, or even begun to reflect on it, except through active practice with it and in it? Reflection (and hence knowledge) arises from the struggle over the contradictions that come up in various realms of human practice. The main spheres of practice, as summed up later by Mao, generally encompass the struggle for production, the class struggle and scientific experiment. The view of the world that predominates in any given epoch, and the character of the questions of the day that generate the most intense debate, do not arise by chance, or merely as the further working out and refinement of ideological problems grappled with by the preceding generation. Rather they reflect and concentrate the contradictions encountered by real, historically concrete people engaged in changing the world. Their practice, of course, is conditioned by the level of understanding reached by previous generations; but practice is the basis for the spiral-like interpenetration between changing and knowing the world.

Further, Marx asserted that practice is not only the ultimate source of ideas and consciousness, but also serves as the criterion of the truth of a given idea. "The question whether objective truth can be attained by human thinking is not a question of theory but is a *practical* question," Marx wrote in the "Theses." "In practice man must prove the truth, that is, the reality and power, the this-sidedness of his thinking. The dispute over the reality or non-reality of thinking which is isolated from practice is a purely *scholastic* question." ("Theses on Feuerbach," *MESW*, Vol. 1, 13) Practice is the key link in the contradiction between matter and consciousness, and in the spiral of knowledge. Contending ideas arise out of practice, and their truth can only ultimately be determined by the results of their application to practice. [14]

Turning to society, Marx exposed the essential fallacy in the materialist notion of the day that grasped the ultimately determining role that people's conditions of life play in their thinking, but which from there set out to create all sorts of utopian schemes to impose a preplanned, worked-out ideal model on society and which took for granted that the reorganizer stood above or outside of the society he or she aspired to change. This forgot, as Marx powerfully (and dialectically) put it, "that men themselves change circumstances and that the educator himself must be educated." The only way in which the changing of people's environment and of their own activity (and consciousness) could be

---

[14] Of course, "results" and their summation involve *struggle*, and especially in class society this struggle is far from "disinterested" or above the fray, but profoundly influenced by the relative strength of different class forces upholding different ideas. Mao pointed out that "In social struggle, the forces representing the advanced class sometimes suffer defeat not because their ideas are incorrect but because, in the balance of forces engaged in struggle, they are not as powerful for the time being as the forces of reaction...." ("Where Do Correct Ideas Come From?," *MSR*, 503) This applies to natural science, too, where new and higher truths do not automatically win out but only gain hegemony through struggle. Truth is objective and not determined by human will, but the struggle to grasp truth is very much influenced by the relations and struggle in society.

carried through lay in linking the two through the "revolutionizing practice" of the people themselves. The people had to be both changer and changed, subject and object; as Marx was to continually emphasize throughout his life, the emancipation of the working class would have to be the work of the working class. But at the same time, the proletariat would have to make revolution both to remove the old foundations of society *and* to rid "itself of all the muck of ages and become fitted to found society anew." (*The German Ideology*, Chap. 1, *MESW*, Vol. 1, 41)

Human practice, Marx went on to point out in the "Theses," could not be approached abstractly, and he criticized Feuerbach for not seeing "that the 'religious sentiment' is itself a *social product*, and that the abstract individual whom he analyses belongs in reality to a particular form of society."

"Social life is essentially *practical*," Marx wrote, and at the same time all human practice concretely takes place within a given society at a specific level of development. All human ideas and consciousness, then, had to be rooted in the *practice* that historically concrete people engaged in as members of a specific society; as he wrote earlier in "Theses," ". . . the human essence is no abstraction inherent in each single individual. In its reality it is the *ensemble* of social relations." (*MESW*, Vol. 1 , 14-15)

Finally Marx thrust philosophy itself onto the barricades, in his famous conclusion on the purpose of the struggle for truth: "The philosophers have only *interpreted* the world, in various ways;" he wrote, "the point, however, is to *change* it." (*MESW*, Vol. 1, 15)

To sum up, Marx located the source of all human ideas and knowledge in practice, and the test for truth in returning ideas to practice; further, he showed that practice (and hence the struggle for truth) takes place in a definite social context, and that the process of changing society (and thus the ideas, and practice, of humanity) requires that the masses themselves "revolutionize practice." For the first time, the real dynamics of knowledge and change were revealed.

The Marxist Theory of Knowledge:
The Unity of Knowing and Doing

What then is the process through which people come to know and change the world? Knowledge develops through two stages, the perceptual and the rational. Perceptual knowledge arises from people's direct experience in their interaction with the material world. In the first stages of practice people principally assimilate raw experience and form impressions, and begin to develop rough ideas of the relations between things. Through the course of repeated and unfolding experience, as people constantly compare and contrast it with earlier experience, stack it up against previously held ideas, analyze it from many different angles, and try out new ideas, the basis is laid for a leap to a qualitatively deeper level of knowledge: *rational* knowledge. In this stage the key element is *synthesis* (though analysis continues within it) of accumulated raw impressions, rough ideas, partial and beginning bits of understanding and insight into *concepts* which — as Mao put it — "grasp the essence, the totality and the internal relations of things."

Anyone who's had experience with an unfamiliar culture or country, or even a new city, knows this process: the initial period of being bombarded with impressions of totally new experience, thinking things over in light of previous experience and expectations that may come from books, movies, etc., talking to new people...even the routine things usually taken for granted become something of a challenge and a source of learning and speculation. Only after a while, and only after a number of false or partially true conclusions and ideas, does one make the leap to a more all-around and accurate understanding.

Or take the scientist, who on the basis of work in a specific field begins to run across certain repeated contradictory phenomena in practice. This is at first perceptual knowledge. After a while an hypothesis is formed to account for these contradictions; then this hypothesis is tested in practice, the results summed up and struggled over, and the hypothesis itself either discarded, refined or deepened. And the same process is familiar as well to every revolutionary activist whose understanding of a task at hand has gone from the primitive to the more developed and more correct through the course of repeated practice and summation of perceptual experience.

Social movements and society as a whole also follow this process; to take only one example — but a sweeping and crucial one — the revolutionary proletariat's understanding of the contradictions involved in the transition to communism has only (and *could*

only have) proceeded to deeper levels through the scientific summation of the historical *experience* of making and carrying through
revolution (though, of course, the exact path of this process has
not been inevitable). Only the revolutionary experience of the
Paris Commune in 1871 (summed up by Marx in *The Civil War In
France* and returned to by Lenin in *State and Revolution*) revealed
the necessity for the proletariat to decisively shatter the bourgeois
state machine and constitute its own dictatorship; and only the experience of Soviet society in forty years of building socialism, and
later of socialist China (especially the Great Proletarian Cultural
Revolution), enabled Mao to discover the continued existence of
classes and class struggle throughout the transition to communism, and to elucidate the necessity (and fundamental
method) for fighting against the attempts of a newly engendered
bourgeoisie in socialist society to restore capitalism.

Perceptual and rational knowledge form an integrated process of cognition. Mao remarks that:

> The perceptual and the rational are qualitatively different, but are
> not divorced from each other; they are unified on the basis of prac-
> tice. Our practice proves that what is perceived cannot at once be
> comprehended and that only what is comprehended can be more
> deeply perceived. Perception only solves the problem of
> phenomena; theory alone can solve the problem of essence. ("On
> Practice," *MSR*, 70)

And later, reemphasizing this point:

> The rational is reliable precisely because it has its source in sense
> perceptions, otherwise it would be like water without a source, a
> tree without roots, subjective, self-engendered and unreliable.
> ("On Practice," *MSR*, 74)

The richer the experience, the more possible it is to reconstruct
concepts which deeply and truly reflect reality and are thus able
to powerfully change and affect it.

But there is, of course, a *leap* involved here; the sheer accumulation of experience itself does not result in rational
knowledge. Experience must be subjected to analysis and synthesis,

> . . . to reconstruct the rich data of sense perception, discarding the
> dross and selecting the essential, eliminating the false and retaining
> the true, proceeding from the one to the other and from the outside

> to the inside, in order to form a system of concepts and theories....
> Such reconstructed knowledge is not more empty or more
> unreliable; on the contrary, whatever has been scientifically
> reconstructed in the process of cognition, on the basis of practice,
> reflects objective reality, as Lenin said, more deeply, more truly,
> more fully. ("On Practice," *MSR*, 75)

Experience must be torn apart and critically assimilated. This process is linked closely to the contradiction between particular and universal in dialectics, in that perceptual knowledge consists in large part of the acquaintance with a host of particulars while rational knowledge reveals what is universal and essential to particulars.

This does not yet complete the spiral of practice and theory, for the whole point of knowing the world lies in changing it. But if the leap from experience to ideas and concepts involves struggle, this is still more true in the leap back to practice and the struggle to apply those ideas to changing reality. For one thing, even the most tempered and tested idea can only partially reflect reality. This is because people engaged in practice and in developing theories are finite beings, working in a concrete so⌐ al context with a given level of science and technology, and at a specific (and perhaps very early) stage of a process — while reality is infinitely complex, inexhaustible and ever changing. Generally, ideas and theories have to be altered and modified or perhaps discarded (if they are wrong) in the course of struggling to put them into practice, as the two stages of doing and knowing constantly interpenetrate. Further, as Mao puts it,

> ...in many instances, failures have to be repeated many times
> before errors in knowledge can be corrected and correspondence
> with the laws of the objective process achieved, and consequently
> before the subjective can be transformed into the objective, or in
> other words, before the anticipated results can be achieved in prac-
> tice. ("On Practice," *MSR*, 78-79)

Such failures do not necessarily prove an idea is essentially wrong — though they might — but may just mean that the heart of the idea must be further reshaped, or persevered in; and especially in class society, the reason for failure may not be the correctness or incorrectness of the idea, but the relative balance of class forces. The defeat of the Paris Commune after two-and-a-half months did not prove the wrong-headedness of proletarian revolution; on the contrary, that experience was the source of invaluable lessons that must still guide the proletariat in its revolutionary struggle. As Marx said at the time, it achieved a new "point of departure." At the same time, the defeat of the Commune also revealed that some of its particular guiding ideas were mistaken, and some still in relatively primitive stages, needing development, further testing and recasting — and, more principally, that the bourgeoisie at that point was too strong to be decisively defeated in France, no matter how correctly the Parisians had battled.

It's important here to grasp that the process of "practice-knowledge-practice on a higher level" can never be fully completed. In a certain sense, the more fully an idea corresponds to reality the more *un*predictable will be the ways in which it changes that reality. This is certainly true in the class struggle, when an idea can become a tremendous material force in the hands of the masses who wield it in totally unexpected ways, and who are unleashed to create new ways of doing things. It is also true in natural science, when an inspired insight may open up a hitherto unexplored sphere with absolutely new results; no one, for example, could predict the character of the subatomic structure when the atomic nucleus first was split. So as practice transforms the world, new ideas and theories must be developed and old truths reworked and recast in the light of new knowledge so as to keep pace.

Freedom and Necessity

But people don't just know and change the world at will, or engage in any sort of practice they please. The reason that no one before Marx and Engels discovered the laws particular to capitalist development has everything to do with the objectively given limitations of human practice before them. And the further development of Marxism, including in the realm of philosophy, has been bound up with the unfolding of human practice since then.

Here the answer to the perennial question of whether people have "free will" begins to take shape, in the form of another question: "free" in relation to what? To begin with, imagine a society and its members at any given stage of development you like. They live in a particular material environment with a certain climate, raw materials, etc. They must produce food, shelter, etc., with a set of productive forces (that is, means of production, skills, etc.) handed down from previous generations. And they do this within a certain set of social relations which face them as objective necessity; that is, these social relations are also encountered as a set of compulsions and limits, whether explicitly understood as such, or unspoken (and at times even un*felt*). Their understanding of both the material environment and their own social relations must take off from (and therefore again to an extent be limited by) the level of understanding of these things that has already been achieved, and the degree to which as processes they have unfolded. Freedom, then, only has meaning within a certain framework; it exists relative to its opposite, *necessity*.

On the other hand, within necessity there *is* indeed freedom — but here what is meant by "freedom" is crucial. The bourgeoisie defines freedom as the *absence* of any and all compulsion. Leaving aside for now the utter hypocrisy of the bourgeoisie in this, the fact is that there is *always* some form of compulsion or necessity. On just the most basic level, there are objective laws that govern natural processes — can humanity free itself, for example, of the laws of electricity, etc.? The political ideal of bourgeois freedom, which basically translates into being "left alone to do what you want," makes about as much sense. [15]

In truth, as Engels pointed out, freedom consists in *understanding* necessity and, as Mao most importantly added, in its transformation, too. That is, the freedom of any individual, class, social movement, etc., consists first, in their understanding of the inner laws of the necessity they confront: e.g., if people basically *understand* (through practice, scientific experiment, etc.) the inner dynamics of a flooding river and its currents, and the way in which electricity is generated, *then* the possibility to transform that destructive flood into a source of power opens up

---

[15] The question of bourgeois notions of freedom is a deep and important one, which cannot be fully examined without some discussion and analysis of bourgeois production relations, and the bourgeois state; we will return, therefore, to this question in later chapters. Here our point more concerns the philosophical categories of freedom and necessity.

(through the construction of a hydroelectric dam); and second, in their actual *acting* on reality on the basis of that understanding, since the abstract comprehension of the laws that *might* enable one to do something is only half the battle in transforming necessity (raging floods) to freedom (in this case, electric power). To put it simply, mere understanding of the causes of floods won't prevent you from getting washed down the river, and still less will it give you electric power — without first doing some *work*.

Freedom and necessity interpenetrate. Exercising freedom reveals hitherto unknown aspects and depths to the necessity one faces and simultaneously *changes* the limits of necessity. Only through attempting to build dams did people find out the complications and contradictions involved; and *through* their construction the very environment which made dams necessary was in part transformed. At the same time, this transformation — *any transformation* — did not and cannot *eliminate* necessity, freedom creates new necessity, new terms for the struggle to know and master the world, in an unending spiral. And the creation of new necessity through freedom occurs both in the partial (or quantitative) altering of the terms of the old necessity, *and* in its rupture and the emergence of qualitatively new necessity (with qualitatively different kinds of freedom demanded — and possible).

Why is it only now that humanity has the freedom to eliminate classes and class distinctions?[16] It's not as if people never dreamed of such a thing; they did, and there are, for example, numerous peasant revolts down through history which set up egalitarian orders. But these societies never lasted long, and inevitably fragmented and repolarized into rich and poor. Only in modern society — in which production and scientific knowledge have reached a level capable of underlying a whole new relation between human society and nature; in which production has become socialized on a truly unprecedented scale; in which the proletarian class has emerged carrying out that socialized production, and class polarization and struggle make more

---

[16]Leaving aside here primitive communism, which existed and could only exist on the basis of relatively undeveloped productive forces; see Chapter 4 for more discussion of this.

evident the real relations in society — is there the potential to construct a world in which, as Mao said, "all mankind consciously and voluntarily changes itself and the world." Of course, this freedom too can only really exist on the basis of the proletariat going forward to scientifically know and change society through revolution.

Absolute and Relative Truth

Knowledge, then, has proceeded from a lower to a higher level in relationship to and in accordance with the parallel and interpenetrating development of production (and other forms of practice). But while the understanding of objective reality is then conditional on the level of development of practice and therefore *relative*, at the same time it contains aspects of the unconditional and *absolute*. It is the character of matter as objective (i.e., independent of consciousness) that gives truth its absolute character, for ideas do not just refer to themselves or each other but to the objectively — and absolutely — existing external world, and they do so more or less accurately or inaccurately.

To put it another way, human knowledge — which is all ultimately relative, conditional, incomplete — has proceeded *toward* deeper knowledge of the objective world without ever reaching absolute truth. Consciousness can never fully and totally reflect an infinite and ever-changing material world, but through an endless succession of generations and development of relative truths its reflection of the world does become deeper and truer. Mao, in "On Practice," wrote that:

> Marxists recognize that in the absolute and general process of development of the universe, the development of each particular process is relative, and that hence, in the endless flow of absolute truth, man's knowledge of a particular process at any given stage of development is only relative truth. The sum total of innumerable relative truths constitutes absolute truth. The development of an objective process is full of contradictions and struggles, and so is the development of the movement of human knowledge. (*MSR*, 80)

Engels examined this contradiction in an important section of *Anti-Dühring* (Chapter IX, Morals and Law. Eternal Truths.). Dühring was a metaphysical materialist who wanted to enshrine certain truths as absolute and eternal. He reasoned from the existence of "eternal truths" in mathematics or other spheres of physical science that such truths must exist also in social sciences, and that in fact he had hit upon them. This mechanical materialism was fundamentally idealist, as Engels showed.

Engels pointed out that human understanding had certain inherent limitations in comprehending the inexhaustible and constantly changing world, including the fact that while human thought as a whole is unlimited in its *capacity* for knowledge, this is only realized through practice in societies at limited stages of development.

And what of those truths which people discover that *are* unconditionally true? Even in the "exact sciences," as Engels calls them — mathematics, chemistry, physics — the more that they develop, the *more rare* "final and ultimate truths" become. He discusses the example of Boyle's Law, which states that if the temperature of a given volume of gases remains constant, the volume will then vary inversely with the pressure to which the gases are subjected. And in fact countless cases have demonstrated that if the pressure is increased, the gases contract, and if it lessens, they expand.

But Engels then immediately pointed out that Boyle's Law does not hold good in certain cases, and that any physicist would say rather that it holds good within certain limits of pressure and temperature and for certain gases; and even within these more restricted limits he would not exclude the possibility of a still narrower limitation or altered formulation as the result of future investigations. This is how things stand with final and ultimate truths in physics, for example.

At the same time, Engels also stressed that those scientists who began to discover the limitations of Boyle's Law did not on that account throw it out altogether; had they done so, they "would have committed an error far greater than the one contained in Boyle's Law" (*Anti-Dühring*, 114), for they would have thrown out an idea that amounts to a tremendous advance in more correctly and deeply reflecting the nature of the behavior of gases whatever its — inevitable — particular and conditional limitations.

But if scientific laws in physics contain this element of relativity, "eternal truths are in an even worse plight in . . . the historical [group of sciences]." (*Anti-Dühring*, 111) Not only is society extremely complex and ever changing, but unlike the physical sciences, no social process ever repeats itself in anywhere close to precisely the same way. Beyond that, a tremendous amount of practice is necessary with any particular social formation to deduce its laws of development; but especially when that practice is *revolutionary*, it tends to eliminate the very form or expression of the contradiction that it set out to grasp! Engels concluded that:

> Therefore, anyone who sets out here to hunt down final and ultimate truths, genuine, absolutely immutable truths, will bring home but little, apart from platitudes and commonplaces of the sorriest kind — for example, that generally men cannot live without working; that up to the present they have for the most part been divided into rulers and ruled; that Napoleon died on May 5, 1821; and so on. (*Anti-Dühring*, 112)

Ironically enough, Marxism's emphasis on the relative character of most truths brings out from another angle the importance of the struggle to develop, defend and deepen correct theory. Marxism conceives of the struggle for truth as an *active* and never-ending process, in which humanity arrives at deeper and deeper levels of cognition (though not in a linear way since reverses, setbacks and the [temporary] victory of wrong ideas are part of this spiral process). The spirit of dogmatism, in which truth is turned into a set of frozen lifeless explanations which do nothing but lend the faithful a measure of certainty in a head-breakingly complex and defiantly changing world, is absolutely inimical to genuine Marxism and real theoretical struggle. It cuts truth off from its source and its purpose, the transformation of reality through practice, and breaks the cycle described by Mao:

> Discover the truth through practice, and again through practice verify and develop the truth. Start from perceptual knowledge and actively develop it into rational knowledge; then start from rational knowledge and actively guide revolutionary practice to change both the subjective and the objective world. Practice, knowledge, again practice, and again knowledge. This form repeats itself in endless cycles, and with each cycle the content of practice and knowledge rises to a higher level. Such is the whole of the dialectical-materialist theory of knowledge, and such is the dialectical-materialist theory of the unity of knowing and doing. ("On Practice," *MSR*, 81-82)

Lenin's Struggle Against Agnosticism

But this is a far cry from the view that all truths are relative — and nothing more. Such is the theory of truth that finds concentrated expression in *agnosticism*. Agnosticism questions and ultimately denies the ability of theory to correctly know the world.

Basically the agnostic argues that the *only* reliable knowledge is perceptual knowledge, and that therefore any attempts to abstract from that experience and get behind appearances to the essence and direction of things are mere guesswork — inspired guesswork, perhaps, but guesswork all the same. And where guesses are concerned, your guess is as good as mine (as the agnostics —at least the more bourgeois-democratic of them — carry equality into the sphere of theory).

To put it another way, the agnostics seize on the fact that all theory is rooted in experience in order to maintain that theory can only describe experience itself, and not any sort of reality independent of and greater than any (and all) human experience. The very existence of such reality cannot be logically proved, by their lights.

Agnosticism as it first rose to prominence reflected the exigencies of a bourgeoisie that still needed science but was increasingly threatened by the spread of a materialist world view. On the one hand, it conceded the necessity for studying the world and advancing science; but on the other it reduced science to a set of hypotheses which could lay claim to describing certain limited experience, but could *not* draw definite conclusions about underlying reality and hence could not legitimately advance any overall and really scientific critique of society. This agnostic trend later developed into *positivism*, which openly opposed materialism for supposedly "creating" a reality which existed independently of human experience. The fact that the existence of such a reality is proven by people's daily practice in production, not to mention in eating food, lying down in a bed to sleep, etc., was of no account to these academic acrobats.

By the early 1900s agnosticism (and positivism) began to gain influence within the Marxist movement. This was concentrated in the Russian movement, particularly after the defeat of the 1905 Revolution, when a number of erstwhile Marxists called for a reexamination of Marxist philosophy, and a recasting of it along positivist lines. And it led to a milestone in the struggle to defend and develop Marxist philosophy, one waged by Lenin against the agnostics.

The agnostics, borrowing much of their thinking from the good physicist but poor philosopher Mach, argued that, with certain advances in physics since Marx and Engels, and in particular since experiments with radium had shown that matter seemed to spontaneously disappear, then the concept of matter itself was outdated. And if matter could be shown to disappear, then how could anything certain be said about the world, how could anything but very conditional statements on what our senses *seemed* to experience be advanced?

But there was more to the crisis of faith of these former Marxists than experiments in radium. The defeat of the 1905 Revolution and the inevitable ebb in the movement which followed it had led many of these intellectuals to doubt the prospect and even possibility of the revolution which they had only so recently thrown themselves into (or generally supported at least); for if the revolution did not succeed, did this not throw Marxism into serious question? — as if Marxism "promises" or guarantees instant success.

At the same time, capitalism was developing into the qualitatively higher stage of *imperialism*. Much of the particular analysis in *Capital* no longer applied. And based on the superprofits extracted by imperialism from the colonies and oppressed nations, in the advanced countries the bourgeoisie had been able to make concessions to significant sections of the working class.

This formed the social basis for a line that saw as an open question the insolubility of capitalist contradictions (within the framework of capitalism) and the need for socialist revolution. The influence of agnosticism within Marxism thus arose with and fed the grossest sort of chauvinism. It confined itself to the experience and conditions of the working class in the imperialist countries only (and even there of a privileged minority of the proletariat), and ignored the tremendously increased immiseration in the colonies that made possible the spreading of crumbs to workers in the advanced countries.

The agnostic trend, then, gained momentum on the basis of real developments in the world and seemed to speak to the changes that were happening (including the defeat of the 1905 Revolution in Russia). This made the line all the more damaging, and made the necessity to refute it all the more urgent. Here was a case where sharp political contradictions had found their main expression within Marxism in a struggle over philosophy. Lenin summed this up in the article, "Certain Features in the Historical Development of Marxism." There he wrote that:

> It is precisely because Marxism is not a lifeless dogma, not any final, finished and ready-made, immutable doctrine, but a living guide to action, that it was bound to reflect the astonishingly abrupt change in the conditions of social life [referring here to the pronounced ebb that followed 1905-1907 — LW]. That change was reflected in profound disintegration and disunity, in every manner of vacillation, in short, in a very serious *internal* crisis of Marxism. The need resolutely to resist this disintegration, resolutely and persistently to uphold the *foundations* of Marxism was again placed on the order of the day. In the preceding period [again, 1905-1907 — LW], extremely wide sections of the classes that cannot avoid Marxism in formulating their aims had assimilated Marxism in an extremely one-sided and mutilated fashion — they had learned by rote certain "slogans," certain answers to tactical questions, *without having understood* the Marxist criteria underlying these answers. The "revaluation of all values" in the various spheres of social life led to a "revision" of the most abstract and general philosophical foundations of Marxism.... (*MEM*, 304-305)

Defending Marxist philosophy had become *central*:

> Nothing is more important than to rally *all* Marxists who have realized the profundity of the crisis and the necessity of combating it for defence of the theoretical foundations of Marxism and its basic propositions, which are being distorted from diametrically opposite sides by the spread of bourgeois influence to the various "fellow-travellers" of Marxism. (*MEM*, 306)

And Lenin carried through this struggle in the classic work *Materialism and Empirio-Criticism*.

For one thing, Lenin exposed that the agnostics were pulling a sleight-of-hand by confounding the philosophical concept of matter (its property of existing independently of consciousness) with its meaning in physics, in which it had been treated as interchangeable with the concept of *mass* (the property of specific physical bodies in offering resistance to acceleration). The transformation of matter, as *mass*, into energy confirmed rather than refuted materialism — *dialectical* materialism, that is. Lenin explained:

> "Matter is disappearing" means that the limit within which we have hitherto known matter is vanishing and that our knowledge is penetrating deeper; properties of matter are likewise disappearing which formerly seemed absolute, immutable, and primary (impenetrability, inertia, mass, etc.) and which are now revealed to be relative and characteristic only of certain states of matter. (*Materialism*, 311)

But this change in knowledge did not invalidate materialism, "[f]or the *sole* 'property' of matter with whose recognition philosophical materialism is bound up is the property of *being an objective reality*, of existing outside our mind." (*Materialism*, 311)

To materialist dialectics there was nothing strange about the ability of matter to transform itself into apparently opposite states; in fact the discovery of the mutual transformation of the opposites of mass and energy was a *corroboration* of dialectical materialism and made possible its deepening. Dialectical materialism, Lenin wrote,

> . . . insists on the approximate, relative character of every scientific theory of the structure of matter and its properties; it insists on the absence of absolute boundaries in nature, on the transformation of moving matter from one state into another, which is to us apparently irreconcilable with it, and so forth . . .
>
> The electron is as *inexhaustible* as the atom, nature is infinite, but it infinitely *exists*. And it is this sole categorical, this sole unconditional recognition of nature's *existence* outside the mind and perception of man that distinguishes dialectical materialism from relativist agnosticism and idealism. (*Materialism*, 312-314)

Further, while Dühring had insisted one-sidedly on the absolute character of certain truths, the agnostics seized on the opposite aspect of the contradiction to deny absolute truth in general. They were just as wrong, and Lenin went into their one-sidedness to penetrate deeper into the relationship between relative and absolute truth.

> From the standpoint of modern materialism, *i.e.*, Marxism, the *limits* of approximation of our knowledge to objective, absolute truth are historically conditional, but the existence of such truth is

unconditional, and the fact that we are approaching nearer to it is also unconditional. The contours of the picture are historically conditional, but the fact that this picture depicts an objectively existing model is unconditional. When and under what circumstances we reached, in our knowledge of the essential nature of things, the discovery of alizarin in coal tar or the discovery of electrons in the atom is historically conditional; but that every such discovery is an advance of "absolutely objective knowledge" is unconditional. In a word, every ideology is historically conditional, but it is unconditionally true that to every scientific ideology (as distinct, for instance, from religious ideology), there corresponds an objective truth, absolute nature. (*Materialism,* 152-153)

It's only this dialectical understanding of the relationship between absolute and relative truth that prevents science from becoming frozen into a dogma on the one hand, or being diluted with all sorts of bourgeois, quasi-religious and generally antiscientific junk on the other, in the name of "all truth is relative." The heart of relativism is not so much the recognition of the relativity of knowledge — Marxism recognizes *that* — but, as Lenin puts it, its "denial of any objective measure or model existing independently of humanity to which our relative knowledge approximates." (*Materialism,* 154)

Finally, some important agnostics of this period — especially the positivists and pragmatists — distorted the criterion of practice in the theory of knowledge. They based their theory of truth on whether an idea allows them to achieve the results that they desired in practice. But what is it that determines those "desires"? The Ptolemaic (earth-centered) theory of the solar system is useful within certain bounds. So, for that matter, is Catholicism. Neither, however, is true. Rejecting an objectively existing reality, the agnostic has no choice but to put the individual at the center of determining truth, and turn away from the question of social practice generally and its role in the overall motion of the contradiction between reality and human understanding of it (and ability to transform it). Some of those Lenin was dealing with tried to get around this by proposing that if a majority of people found an idea to be true, *that* made it so — by which standard, Lenin pointed out, elves and hobgoblins would have to be classed as real in certain places. The mere fact that a majority thinks an idea to be true or even finds it useful does not in itself have anything to do with whether that idea really is true.

By limiting the true to that which is immediately useful without questioning the overall structure of reality, this strain of agnosticism limits the quest for truth to tinkering within the parameters of the status quo and makes impossible an all-encompassing critique of that status quo on the basis of its underlying contradictions. On this question of truth and usefulness, this variant of agnosticism provides the ideological underpinnings for the particularly American brand of positivism, *pragmatism*. Pragmatism openly declares that truth is *created* by its usefulness, and further states — in the words of its chief ideologue, William James — that those theories are most true which are most useful in "effecting the transition from a relatively conflicting experience to a relatively integrated one" (cited in J.S., "Against Pragmatism," in *The Communist*, Vol. 2, No. 2, 1978, p. 9) — in other words, cooling out and reconciling contradictions.

Pragmatism's impact in the revolutionary movement has taken the especially damaging form of divorcing the evaluation of the immediate results achieved in practice from the overall critique developed by Marxism on the essential character of class society and the contradictions involved in the transition to classless society. What counts, then, is *how many* people are mobilized rather than the line around which they're mobilized, or — to take a common form of this under socialism — how *much* production is boosted rather than how deeply (and whether) it serves the overall advance to communism worldwide and, more broadly, how that advance is being carried out. Immediate experience becomes unmoored from the dialectical and historical materialist framework necessary to evaluate it, the task of "discarding the dross and selecting the essential" (as Mao put it) is made unpracticable, and results can only be measured in quantitative and inevitably bourgeois terms.

Yes, the 1905 Revolution in Russia had been defeated; yes, in the advanced countries capitalism had developed in unforeseen ways into a qualitatively new stage, imperialism. Faced with that, the agnostic line tried to wriggle out of the challenges posed — both theoretical and practical — and sought objectively (at least) to make peace with the bourgeoisie. But for the dialectical materialist this crisis posed the necessity to dig deeper for a more all-sided and fluid understanding of reality, and to grasp the fundamental principles and method of materialist dialectics *more* profoundly in order to rise to the new demands posed by a complex and changing reality. In doing so, Lenin forged further along and broke new ground on the path first hewed by Marx and Engels. As he wrote:

> The sole conclusion to be drawn from the opinion of the Marxists that Marx's theory is an objective truth, is that by following the *path* of Marxist theory we shall draw closer and closer to objective truth (without ever exhausting it); but by following *any other path* we shall arrive at nothing but confusion and lies. (*Materialism*, 162)

2

POLITICAL ECONOMY

"Tools are made by men. When tools call for a revolution, they will speak through men . . . ." So spoke Mao, graphically and poetically. But how is it that *tools* demand revolution?

To begin with, while people create tools there is another sense in which tools create — and created — people. When some time close to four million years ago a species of prehuman primates went from carrying and utilizing found objects to refashioning them into tools, natural selection (and other evolutionary pressures) favored development of a bigger, more complex brain which could further enhance the advantage provided by the hand's new versatility and freedom to make tools. Later, as labor became more complex and these beings had ideas too complex to communicate by simple calls, evolution similarly favored the development of the apparatus for speech in humans. With labor as the key link, this spiraling dialectic — through many as-yet uncharted phases and twists and turns — led to the emergence of modern humanity some 50,000 years ago.[1]

It may be hard today to think of labor as the foundation for

---

[1] This process is discussed in depth in Engels' "The Part Played By Labour in the Transition from Ape to Man."

humanity — especially in class society where mental and manual labor have been torn asunder, and these spheres are themselves in varying degrees further chopped up and reduced in the greatest part to anti-human drudgery. But this condition of class society — in which the masses of people hate their basic life-activity, experiencing it as something alien to their will — this condition, which seems so "eternal" and inherent in human labor today, will be transformed and shown to be temporary with the completion of the communist revolution. Then the further development of society and the overcoming, as Marx put it, of the "enslaving subordination of the individual to the division of labor" will make labor "life's prime want" as well as its basic necessity.[2] ("Critique of the Gotha Programme," *MESW*, Vol. 3, 19)

For Marx, what makes labor *labor* — as opposed to mere instinctive interaction with the environment — is precisely its con-

---

[2]Labor assumes its most hideous character in that very society in which the potential for an unprecedented lightening of labor first presents itself: capitalism. In *Capital*, Marx describes in depth the effects of capitalist production on the labor process; for instance: "Machinery is put to a wrong use, with the object of transforming the workman, from his very childhood, into a part of a detail-machine. In this way, not only are the expenses of his reproduction considerably lessened, but at the same time his helpless dependence upon the factory as a whole, and therefore upon the capitalist, is rendered complete.. . .In handicrafts and manufacture, the workman makes use of a tool, in the factory, the machine makes use of him. There the movements of the instrument of labour proceed from him, here it is the movements of the machine that he must follow. In manufacture the workmen are parts of a living mechanism. In the factory we have a lifeless mechanism independent of the workman, who becomes its mere living appendage. 'The miserable routine of endless drudgery and toil in which the same mechanical process is gone through over and over again, is like the labour of Sisyphus. The burden of labour, like the rock, keeps ever falling back on the worn-out labourer.' (Engels) At the same time that factory work exhausts the nervous system to the uttermost, it does away with the many-sided play of the muscles, and confiscates every atom of freedom, both in bodily and intellectual activity. The lightening of the labour, even, becomes a sort of torture, since the machine does not free the labourer from work, but deprives the work of all interest. Every kind of capitalist production, in so far as it is not only a labour-process, but also a process of creating surplus-value, has this in common, that it is not the workman that employs the instruments of labour, but the instruments of labour that employ the workman. But it is only in the factory system that this inversion for the first time acquires technical and palpable reality. By means of its conversion into an automaton, the instrument of labour confronts the labourer, during the labour-process, in the shape of capital, of dead labour, that dominates, and pumps dry, living labour-power. The separation of the intellectual powers of production from the manual labour, and the conversion of those powers into the might of capital over labour, is, as we have already shown, finally completed by modern industry erected on the foundation of machinery." (*Capital*, Vol. 1, 422-423.)

scious character. In *Capital* he points out that:

> A spider conducts operations that resemble those of a weaver, and a bee puts to shame many an architect in the construction of her cells. But what distinguishes the worst architect from the best of bees is this, that the architect raises his structure in imagination before he erects it in reality. At the end of every labour process, we get a result that already existed in the imagination of the labourer at its commencement. (*Capital*, Vol. 1, 178)

Labor, and the tools which it implies, pushed forward not only the evolution of humans, but of human society as well. Because labor is conscious practice, because, that is, people critically reflect on and alter what they are doing, they tend to constantly improve and develop new tools and methods, and to acquire a deeper understanding of the world. The leaps through history from hunting and gathering to agriculture, from draft animals to steam engines, and from internal combustion machines to computers all demonstrate this advance.

This process, however, has hardly been smooth and without contradiction. People not only use and develop tools, but must enter into certain social relations in order to do so. Who owns the means of production? What are the relations between people in the productive process? How is the product distributed? These are the three main spheres of production relations (the sum total of which form the economic base of a society). Of them ownership is generally principal — though the other two react back on and can influence ownership, and at times assume even greater importance than ownership itself.

In general, different ensembles of production relations arise on and correspond to different levels of development of the productive forces (tools, raw materials, natural resources and people's abilities to use them). Slave relations, for example, have generally arisen in conditions in which the means and forces of production were advanced enough to yield a surplus, but were still relatively crude, demanding tremendous physical exertion but little mental effort from the producers.[3] In the famous slave

---

[3]In the case of slavery in the U.S., in which slave relations existed within an overall capitalist society, and production was overwhelmingly for the capitalist world market, the sort of production in which the slaves were engaged — large-scale plantation production of cotton, tobacco, etc., requiring huge masses of laborers — was for a long time more economically carried out by slaves. This was true despite

societies of Greece and Rome, the owners owned the major means of production including, of course, the slaves themselves. The relations between people in the labor process were marked by extreme violence and coercion (as slaves were literally worked to death under the lash) and the slave was given only enough to subsist on, oftentimes being fed worse than the owners' beasts of burden.

But the slave mode of production in these ancient societies made possible the accumulation of huge surpluses. A leisure class arose, which engaged in scientific experiment. Artisans and traders also developed in slave society's pores, and the productive forces advanced. But the relations of slavery which had made possible that advance soon worked against its further development. Facing brute coercion and likely to be worked to death in a year or two, the slave had no incentive to use technically more developed tools. On the contrary — the slaves' constant resistance, including sabotage and breaking of tools, precluded the further sophistication of tools and tended to freeze production at the level of the cruder, more coarse, less breakable ones. Further, the stamp of slavery itself began to put all manual labor in disrepute, and this fostered the decay of slave societies generally.

The tools — to return to Mao's image — thus needed badly to speak. Speak they did: through massive slave revolts and through the struggles of the "barbarians" against Roman domination. These, of course, were obviously not mechanical actions characteristic of tools, but the conscious and heroic actions of people who refused to tolerate enslavement and sensed the potential for something greater for humanity. But the very ideals and visions that led to revolt after revolt were rooted in the contradictions between the productive forces, needing to constantly advance, and the production relations, which had become a straitjacket upon the forces and a source of decay for society as a whole. These struggles among people (no matter how unconscious the actors)

---

the fact that the resistance in the form of sabotage carried out by the slaves kept the tools at a crude level. In this case, the slave owners were compelled to hold back the development of production — and to keep the slaves in ignorance through measures calling for severe punishment and even death for those slaves who learned or taught reading — in order to preserve slave relations. Especially with the development of capitalist industry and agriculture in the rest of the U.S., this became a very sharp contradiction, which was only resolved with the Civil War.

proved to be the *agent* through which the productive forces dissolved the by-then restrictive economic relations.

This points to another important principle: the contradictions in society's mode of production find their concentrated expression (and can only ultimately be resolved through struggle) in the superstructure — the political institutions, ideas, art, philosophy, etc. — that arises upon the economic relations. The superstructure is like a shell that grows up around and protects the economic base.[4] As a superstructure it is more "visible" than the foundation on which it rests: the ideas, politics and so on are what immediately come to mind in thinking about a society, and are the main ways in which a society thinks about itself. But the contradictions between the economic base and the forces of production lie at the foundation of this edifice, and give rise to the cracks and fissures that rip through its walls. At the same time — to pursue the metaphor just a bit further — to lay new foundations ultimately involves shattering the shell and clearing away the rubble.

Of course, this is a fairly rough sketch of the relations of the different main elements in the totality of society, and these categories are not only mutually exclusive, but also fluidly interpenetrate and transform into each other. While the forces of production are generally principal over the economic base, sometimes transformations in the base are necessary to advance the forces, and hence become principal; and while the base is generally principal over the superstructure, again, sometimes the superstructure becomes decisive and principal.

The importance of studying political economy — which focuses on the economic relations of society — lies in the need to grasp the underlying developments that set the terms of the class struggle. Political economy reveals the material basis for the tasks that historical development has put on the revolutionary agenda. While the economic relations alone don't make up the totality or sole determining element of society (any more than political economy constitutes the totality of Marxism), they *are* basic and

---

[4]In reality, the relationship between base and superstructure is more fluid and less mechanical than this metaphor would imply; we use it here to give a *basic* sense of the relationship involved, with the caveat that the actual analysis of a concrete society must approach this contradiction (as well as that between the forces and relations of production) as one with a great deal of interpenetration, complexity and fluidity — as will be seen in Chapters 3 and 4.

their study is integral to any deep understanding of society and revolution.

The Rise of Capitalism

The economic mainsprings of political struggle first began to become clear during the struggle of the rising bourgeoisie against feudal society in Europe.[5] While all feudal societies were enmeshed in contradictions, and marked by antagonistic struggle between peasant and lord, it was Europe where those contradictions first ripened enough and in such a way as to allow the emergence of a new form of society (over the course of centuries). Within Europe, England in particular provided the most developed example of a capitalist economy (and society), and for that reason was taken by Marx as his focus in *Capital*. At the same time, this development of capitalism in Europe was neither the result of some imagined "inherent superiority of white Europeans," or — alternately — a form of aberrant behavior unique to them; had such development been for some reason aborted there, it would have eventually taken place in some other feudal society, for capitalism is the only resolution to the contradictions of feudalism.[6] Mao, for example, notes that capitalist factors were developing in the decaying feudal society of China shortly before it was "opened up" by Europe — an "opening" which then largely determined China's future development.[7]

The feudal economy of Western and Northern Europe, especially after the 10th century, developed as a unity of opposites between production for the direct use of the producers (and their

---

[5] Although even this conflict was first fought out in other, mainly religious, forms — cf. Engels' *Socialism: Utopian and Scientific*, which is part of a larger work, *Anti-Dühring*, as well as his *Peasant War In Germany*.

[6] This refers not to each and every individual feudal society, but to the process of world-historic development. Once capital becomes qualitatively dominant on a world scale, drawing all peoples and societies into its web of social relations and determining the basic course of development of those societies, then the contradictions of the various particular pre-capitalist societies can only be resolved as part of the world-historic process of resolving the contradictions of *capitalism*. In other words — and this will be analyzed more deeply in Chapter 3 on imperialism — the resolution of the contradictions of feudalism in those countries can now become an important part of the resolution of the more overriding contradictions between the oppressed nations and imperialism.

[7] For more on the particular causes of Europe's early development of capitalism, see Engels' *The Origin of the Family, Private Property and the State*.

lords), and production for exchange. The serfs and peasants either
directly consumed what they produced, or handed it over to their
landlords (or the Church) who would directly consume it. The
landlord exploited the peasant either directly through appropria-
ting the goods produced by the peasant, or through obliging the
peasant to work a set number of days on the landlord's lands.
These were the dominant relations of society. The landlord
owned the land, the peasant in most cases owned the implements
of his labor. The peasant was not owned outright[8] but was assumed to be bound to the lands of his lord as part of the natural
order of things — an assumption backed up by codes, laws and
their enforcers. Correspondingly, the peasants often had the right
to use certain communal lands (for timber, grazing, etc.) and the
right to stay on the land.

At the same time, as a secondary aspect in feudal society, commodity production also went on — that is, production not for the
direct use of the producer (though of course it had to be ultimately
useful to someone), but for exchange for other products. At first
this commodity production in feudal Europe was carried on by independent artisans, or by guilds,[9] which specialized in ironwork-
ing (for plows, horseshoes, etc.), leather (harnesses, shoes), etc.
And it was also fostered by the merchants, flourishing within the
fabric of feudal society, traveling from estate to estate, or region to
region, trading the goods from one area to another.

Within this early commodity production there was an important contradiction between the small producer and the merchant.
The artisan produced commodities in order to get other commodities for his use. He did fine if he merely broke even. The merchant, however, purchased commodities with money in order to
sell them for *more* money to someone else; his whole *raison d'etre*
was to get more money at the end of the circuit than he had at the
beginning. This latter form of circulation is restless and incessant;
it pushed production forward to serve that trade, and hence pushed
forward commodity relations. Trading and manufacturing towns

---

[8]Serfs in many cases were owned outright, essentially, and the lord had power of
life and death over them; still, serfdom was not marked by the large-scale trade in
human flesh and the extreme and killing conditions of labor characterizing the
slave empire.

[9]Hereditary orders of different trades which monopolize the right to carry out certain types of skilled production.

began to spring up on the seacoasts of Europe (unlike the earlier towns which directly served and were dominated by specific feudal estates), and strained against the subordination of the town to the feudal countryside.

Slowly at first, the bonds of feudal society were corroded. Focusing on the way this worked itself out in England, by the mid-1400s the development of the Flemish wool manufactures in Belgium created a tremendous demand for raw wool from England. In response to that, the feudal nobility — already in an unstable state due to a series of wars and the rise of an independent small-farmer peasantry — began to take by force what had been the allotments of land to the peasantry and turn them into grazing areas for sheep. Tens of thousands of peasants were driven from the land. At the same time — and this was also an important factor spurring on the turn to wool production for exchange instead of general production for use — the lords had become deeply indebted to the merchants in the towns, due both to feudal wars and to their purchases of the luxury items beginning to flow into the trading towns. In order to economize, the lords began to drive off their retainers (the hangers-on, advisers, soldiers and servants of the feudal courts which had originally reflected the power and status of the lord).

A mass of dispossessed potential laborers began to drift through England.[10] It now became possible for the merchants and moneylenders to set up shop with primitive means of production, gather a number of these propertyless vagabonds together under one roof, and hire them to work these means of production. This was the internal basis, in England, for capitalist production to take root: the dispossession of large masses of people from any means with which to support themselves, and the emergence of a class with the money necessary to purchase means of production and hire the dispossessed to work for them. Their propertyless character made it possible for these masses to be forged into a *proletariat*; and this propertyless character remains the essential mark of the proletariat.

But all this — though crucial and necessary — was not suffi-

---

[10] To discipline these drifters and forge them into a malleable workforce, the rulers of the time resorted to incredible brutality; Henry VIII, for instance, had 72,000 vagabonds hanged during his reign.

cient unto itself to usher in the dominance of capital and the flowering of the bourgeoisie. Colonization, slavery and genocide were the external conditions necessary for this new mode of production to get started. Marx, discussing the genesis of the industrial capitalist, makes this clear:

> The discovery of gold and silver in America, the extirpation, enslavement and entombment in mines of the aboriginal population, the beginning of the conquest and looting of the East Indies, the turning of Africa into a warren for the commercial hunting of black-skins, signalised the rosy dawn of the era of capitalist production. These idyllic proceedings are the chief momenta of primitive accumulation. On their heels treads the commercial war of the European nations, with the globe for a theatre. It begins with the revolt of the Netherlands from Spain, assumes giant dimensions in England's Anti-Jacobin War, and is still going on in the opium wars against China. . . . (*Capital*, Vol. 1, 751)

Thus the bourgeoisie was born in the throes of the creation of the world market, and came into the world "dripping from head to foot, from every pore, with blood and dirt." (760)

The merchants and traders, along with some of the guild-masters, former artisans, more commercially-minded feudal lords and better-off peasants, were transformed into the bourgeoisie. But the old feudal relations under which this bourgeoisie had first arisen had now become intolerable fetters on its further development. The feudal system, for example, forced merchants to pay tariffs as they traveled between feudal estates; it bound the peasants to the land, when the largest possible mass of *free* labor (in the double sense of free from feudal obligation, and "free" from the ability to support and feed itself) was needed by the capitalists; and it divided areas into decentralized principalities or provinces, when the nascent bourgeoisie needed strongly centralized nation-states to fight its wars and carry out its colonization.

Thus developed the long and stormy period of bourgeois revolution and feudal counter-revolution, of war and upheaval, and of the development of the productive forces pushed on by these transformations. The bourgeoisie, and capitalist production, developed through phases of simple cooperation, manufacture and industry over the course of several centuries.[11]

---

[11]See *Capital*, Vol. 1, Part IV.

With the development of capitalism, its antagonist — the proletariat — developed too. As the *Manifesto* put it:

> In proportion as the bourgeoisie, *i.e.*, capital, is developed, in the
> same proportion is the proletariat, the modern working class,
> developed — a class of labourers, who live only so long as they find
> work, and who find work only so long as their labour increases
> capital....
> The essential condition for the existence, and for the sway of the
> bourgeois class, is the formation and augmentation of capital; the
> condition for capital is wage-labour. Wage-labour rests exclusively
> on competition between the labourers. The advance of industry,
> whose involuntary promoter is the bourgeoisie, replaces the isola-
> tion of the labourers, due to competition, by their revolutionary
> combination, due to association. The development of Modern In-
> dustry, therefore, cuts from under its feet the very foundation on
> which the bourgeoisie produces and appropriates products. What
> the bourgeoisie, therefore, produces, above all, are its own grave-
> diggers. Its fall and the victory of the proletariat are equally in-
> evitable. (*Manifesto*, 39, 46)

It was only in the late 18th century, however, that industrial
capitalism fully came into its own, with the French Revolution,
and what is euphemistically known as the "industrial revolution"
in England. "Euphemistically" because this "revolution" entailed
the brutal immiseration of the English proletariat, the intensification of slavery in the American South, and the subjugation of India
and starvation of literally millions through the breaking of the
native economy.[12]

By 1825 the capitalist world was shaken by its first great
economic crisis. For the first time millions went hungry not
because too little had been produced, but because too *much* had —
too much, that is, to allow for the profits necessary to continue
production. It was the first open rebellion of the new and massive
productive forces against the relations they were bound in.

The next decade witnessed the first great proletarian struggles in England and France. In 1846 the most severe economic
crisis yet rocked England and then spread to all of continental Europe. In February, 1848 virtually the whole of Europe erupted in
revolutionary struggle.

---

[12] See Marx's *Capital*, Vol. 1, as well as his article "The Future Results of British
Rule in India," *MESW*, Vol. 1, and Engels' *The Condition of the Working Class in
England*.

The 1848 revolutions — whose opening volleys coincided with the publication of the *Communist Manifesto* — were an important turning point. "Everywhere that revolution was the work of the working class," wrote Engels, "it was the [proletariat] that built the barricades and paid with its lifeblood." He went on:

> Only the Paris workers, in overthrowing the government, had the very definite intention of overthrowing the bourgeois regime. But conscious though they were of the fatal antagonism existing between their own class and the bourgeoisie, still, neither the economic progress of the country nor the intellectual development of the mass of French workers had as yet reached the stage which would have made a social reconstruction possible. In the final analysis, therefore, the fruits of the revolution were reaped by the capitalist class. In the other countries, in Italy, in Germany, in Austria, the workers, from the very outset, did nothing but raise the bourgeoisie to power. ("Preface to the Italian Edition of 1893," *Manifesto*, 27)

Marxist Political Economy

Marx and Engels fought actively in these revolutionary upsurges; Marx founded and edited the key revolutionary newspaper in Germany, while Engels commanded a revolutionary army. Each wrote important works analyzing the lessons of the stormy revolutionary period. But by 1851 they had summed up that the high tide was subsiding, that the crisis — both economic and political — was temporarily over and that new tasks lay before communists.

Specifically, while the basis of materialist dialectics and communist politics had been forged by the publication of the *Manifesto* and in the works concerning the 1848-51 upsurge, the further development and application of the science was urgently needed. At the time, however, many of the defeated revolutionists opposed Marx and Engels and clung to the hope that the revolutionary situation would reoccur very shortly in much the same form; this could (and did) lead only to demoralization, since history does not repeat itself but moves in spiral-like motion.

On the other hand, in the wake of the revolutionary defeats and the temporary stabilization and renewed expansion of capital, a strong reformist trend also grew up among the proletariat. Already in 1849 the first organized conscious reformist trend developed in the proletariat, adopting the name of "social-democracy." Marx summed this up as a merging of the petty bourgeoisie and proletariat, under the leadership of the petty bourgeoisie:

> A joint programme was drafted, joint election committees were set up and joint candidates put forward. From the social demands of the proletariat the revolutionary point was broken off and a democratic turn given to them; from the democratic claims of the petty bourgeoisie the purely political form was stripped off and their socialist point thrust forward. . . . The peculiar character of the Social-Democracy is epitomised in the fact that democratic-republican institutions are demanded as a means, not of doing away with two extremes, capital and wage-labour, but of weakening their antagonism and transforming it into harmony. ("The Eighteenth Brumaire of Louis Bonaparte," *MESW*, Vol. 1, 423)

In England reformism took even deeper root, and all over Europe various schemes and gimmicks were pushed in opposition to revolution. All these trends made it even more necessary to really plunge into the depths of the capitalist system, fully uncover the contradictions at the base of the class struggle, and reveal their motion and development.

To do this, Marx focused his study on England, the country in which the capitalist mode was most fully developed and the course of that development the best documented. Beginning in 1851 Marx began to analyze the tremendous amount of raw data in the British Museum on economic development; at the same time he studied the entire run of bourgeois political economists and reexamined — now on a deeper level — Hegel's dialectics. After a number of different approaches, Marx fixed on the commodity as the key focus, as the basic cell of capitalist life.

Commodity production had been the seed of capital, as it had dissolved the old feudal relations and eventually brought propertyless workers face to face with property-owning capitalists; and capitalism itself was only the mature and highest form of commodity production. In 1867 Marx published one of the really fundamental works of revolutionary science — *Capital*. Lenin described its method and approach as follows:

> In his *Capital*, Marx first analyses the simplest, most ordinary and fundamental, most common and everyday *relation* of bourgeois (commodity) society, a relation encountered billions of times, namely, the exchange of commodities. In this very simple

phenomenon (in this "cell" of bourgeois society) analysis reveals *all* the contradictions (or the germs of *all* the contradictions) of modern society. The subsequent exposition shows us the development (*both* growth *and* movement) of these contradictions and of this society in the [summation] of its individual parts, from its beginning to its end. ("On the Question of Dialectics," *MEM*, 342)

And this will be the general approach of the chapter at hand, in beginning to dig into and lay bare the underlying contradictions and motion of capital.

Commodities and Capital

Value

What, then, are the contradictions involved in the "simple everyday relation" of the exchange of commodities? First, what is a commodity?

A commodity is a product which satisfies human wants, of whatever sort. But not all things satisfying human wants are commodities. A commodity is something not only *useful*, but produced specifically to be *exchanged* for other products. As such it has both *use value* and *exchange value* (or simply "value"). Thus in the very cell of the commodity there is the contradiction between use value and value.

If it were not useful, the commodity could not be exchanged. And yet the commodity itself has no real use for its producer, except insofar as it enables him or her to get other things in exchange. Thus while it must be useful to be exchanged, if it cannot be exchanged, for one reason or another, it will be of no more use than a heap of scrap. The use value and value are contained within the commodity as polar opposites, and there is a potential antagonism between the two implied in every commodity.

In earlier society exchange could have a purely "accidental" character — that is, different items might be exchanged in no particular proportion. Coastal tribes might have exchanged their fish surplus with inland tribes for animal hides. During the early phases of feudalism, when merchant capital was the main form of commodity exchange, this "accidental" character was due to the merchant's ability to monopolize a particular item, to carry out straight-up piracy and robbery, and so on. But as commodity production spread, the ratios in which different commodities exchanged became increasingly regular. Capitalism is the apogee of commodity production, a society in which virtually all production is for exchange; with its ascendancy the ratios of exchange for different commodities become basically consistent. Today a loaf of bread, for instance, generally has the same value as a light bulb.

But how do these more or less consistent proportions (which extend to literally millions of different items, and which are carried out billions of times a day) get set? What do two dissimilar commodities have in common that allows them to be equated — or what is the character which is universal to these many very particular things?

It's true, of course, that all these items have their usefulness in common. But can the quality of usefulness determine the proportions in which commodities exchange? Take light bulbs and bread. While both are generally useful (and necessary), how, by looking at or comparing the particular ways in which they are useful, can we determine in what measure to exchange the one for the other? We cannot — some other basis for determining this must be applied. Marx answered this: "If we then leave out of consideration the use-value of commodities, they have only one common property left, that of being products of labor." (*Capital*, Vol. 1, 38)

But how can labor — which involves the qualitatively different forms of, say, baking and weaving — serve as a uniform standard of measure? Because labor is itself contradictory. On the one hand, in creating a specific use value any one form of commodity-producing labor is qualitatively different from any other form — bread-baking being clearly distinct from shoemaking, as both are different from oil-refining. These forms of *concrete labor* create the qualitatively different use values in commodities. On the other hand, these particular forms of labor all share the universal character of being expenditures of human labor power. This quality, abstract (as opposed to concrete) labor, is measured by its duration (weeks, days, hours), and commodities themselves are exchanged on the basis of how great an expenditure of labor power — i.e., how much abstract labor — they contain. An hour of labor produces the same exchange value whether it is baking, foundry work, printing, etc.

Labor Theory of Value

This is the *labor theory of value*: the law that the value of the commodity is determined by the labor necessary for its production. Here we are not speaking of individual labor; a baker so slow that he takes twice as long to make the same loaf of bread as his competitor can hardly sell it at twice the price. It is the *average socially necessary labor time* which determines value: "[the time] required to produce an article under the normal conditions of production, and with the average degree of skill and intensity prevalent at the time," in Marx's formulation. (*Capital*, Vol. 1, 39) And while skilled labor produces a greater exchange value than unskilled labor in the same period of time, Marx also shows that "skilled labour counts only as simple labour intensified, or rather, as multiplied simple labour, a given quantity of skilled being considered equal to a greater quantity of simple labour. Experience shows that this reduction is constantly being made." (44)

What about the conventional wisdom which holds that value is determined by supply and demand? It is true that the prices of different commodities often fluctuate according to supply and demand. But this fluctuation goes on within given limits: generally whatever the relative supply and demand, bread, for example, does not sell for more than bicycles.[13] What then sets that center of gravity around which prices fluctuate? Again, it is the amount of abstract labor congealed in the products.

Actually the oscillation of the price of a product around its value is an important mechanism of the regulation (or domination) of the capitalist economy by the law of value. For one thing, when producers — due to high demand — can raise the selling price of an item above its value and thus rake in *extra* profits, other capitalists rush to invest in this now more profitable field. As the increased production rises to meet and eventually exceed the demand, and price begins to fall towards value and even below it, capital deserts it. The social division of labor is thus regulated through the blind workings of the law of value, although this is an anarchic "regulation," one proceeding in fits and starts, with

---

[13]And even if bread *might* be more expensive than a bicycle under certain *extreme* conditions, supply and demand is still not the basic factor in determining prices within commodity exchange.

unevenness and dislocation, and behind the backs and beyond the control of the commodity owners themselves.

The everyday relations of capitalist society may appear to be relations between things: commodities exchange for one another (generally through the medium of money). The rates at which they exchange appear to be either fixed by tradition or somehow in some unexplained way validated by the mass social practice of millions of buyers; in either event, those proportions appear to flow from some quality inherent in the commodity itself.

But on closer examination we find that what is expressed billions of times a day is not a mystical relation between things, but relations between different people or groups of people in which the underlying essence is shrouded by the commodity form. That is, the sale of a commodity expresses a relation between the labor of one person or group of people, and others. Here lies a critical and fundamental difference between Marxist and bourgeois political economy, as explained by Engels:

> Political economy [speaking specifically of the analysis of capitalism — *LW*] begins with *commodities*, begins from the moment when products are exchanged for one another — whether by individuals or by primitive communities. The product that appears in exchange is a commodity. It is, however, a commodity solely because a *relation* between two persons or communities attaches to the *thing*, the product, the relation between producer and consumer who are here no longer united in the same person. Here at once we have an example of a peculiar fact, which runs through the whole of economics and which has caused utter confusion in the minds of the bourgeois economists: economics deals not with things but with relations between persons, and, in the last resort, between classes; these relations are, however, always *attached to things* and *appear as things*. ("Karl Marx, *A Contribution to the Critique of Political Economy*," *MESW*, Vol. 1, 514)

Money, Commodity Circulation and Capital

Here a word on money is necessary. Briefly backtracking to the earlier example of direct barter of commodities, it's plain that if the coastal tribe did not want animal skins and needed baskets instead (which the inland tribe didn't produce), simple barter would prove inadequate. On the other hand, if the inland tribe could exchange a generally recognized form of wealth for the fish, which could later be used to buy something else, commodity exchange would be greatly facilitated.

A commodity was therefore needed to play the role of the generally recognized repository of value, with which all others could be exchanged. A number of commodities served this function in early societies: cattle, for example, were often used as a form of money in herding societies, with the value of all commodities being expressed in terms of so many head of cattle.

But the further expansion of commodity exchange and growth of merchant capital soon ran up against the limitations of this form as well. A merchant or trading party could not pack a ship with cattle to exchange at each port of call. And what happened if a particular commodity was not worth one head of cattle? The cow could not be divided into its various parts and still be worth anything (except as meat, or hides, etc., which would be different commodities than cattle *per se*). Gold and silver, because of their durability and great value relative to size, as well as their divisibility into smaller parts, eventually became recognized as universal equivalents in exchange.

While gold and silver functioned as money, their value in exchange, like that of all commodities, was still a reflection of their value as commodities, of the labor time congealed within them. But the substance of gold and silver was gradually worn away in passing from hand to hand in circulation. Further, the expansion of commodity production required a scale and ease of exchange that the nature and limited supply of the precious metals could not meet. Paper money began to be issued, backed up by reserves of gold and silver and the legal authority of the state.[14]

Money made easier the exchange of commodities among producers. The individual producer exchanged a product for money so that the money could be used (perhaps at a later date) to buy something else of equal value; production was no longer constrained by what any two producers could *directly* exchange, and hence commodity production as a whole received an impetus. Commodity circulation expanded and accelerated.

---

[14]Today as a reflection of both the further immense expansion of exchange and the sharpening of certain contradictions within the capitalist economy, gold is used almost exclusively in international transactions and there only as "backing" for

As noted earlier, the main protagonists of commodity circulation in the early period of feudalism were the merchants. Artisans and petty producers were also involved in commodity production and circulation, but it was basically limited by the scope of their own needs. Not so with the merchant. While the petty producer's circuit of exchange is C-M-C (that is, he sells his commodity [C] for money [M] to buy other commodities for his use [C]), that of the capitalist, including the merchant capitalist, is M-C-M; he aims not for a *different* commodity than the one he starts with (i.e., money), but only for *more* of it. It is not the personal wants of the capitalist for more use values that is his aim, but the constant self-expansion of capital.

As a capitalist, he is nothing but "the conscious representative of this movement," Marx wrote, and continued:

> His person, or rather his pocket, is the point from which the money starts and to which it returns. The expansion of value, which is the objective basis or main-spring of the circulation M-C-M, becomes his subjective aim, and it is only in so far as the appropriation of ever more and more wealth in the abstract becomes the sole motive of his operations, that he functions as a capitalist, that is, as capital personified and endowed with consciousness and a will. Use-values must therefore never be looked upon as the real aim of the capitalist; neither must the profit on any single transaction. The restless never-ending process of profit-making alone is what he aims at. (*Capital*, Vol. 1, 152-153)

The merchant often successfully completed the circuit through plunder, or cornering the market, etc.; but as commodity production came to subject the natural economy to its domination, *industrial* capital arose and eventually subordinated merchant capital (though in many cases it is merchants who have become the industrial capitalists). In both cases, the circuit M-C-M was still fundamental and had to be completed and renewed. But with industrial capital the self-expansion of capital could no longer mainly take place (or be explained) through thievery (at

---

such transactions. The convertibility of paper money into gold in the U.S. has been ended and check books (so-called "demand deposits") and credit have replaced even paper money as the principal means of exchange. But this money has no real value apart from the actual value produced by the economy. If the supply of money in circulation rises faster than the production of real values, the only result is a fall in the value of money itself — inflation.

least open thievery in the conventional sense), shrewdness or luck.

Why? Take a capitalist who buys $1,000 worth of commodities which he then sells for $1,100. He must have either bought the commodity at $100 below value, or sold it at $100 over value. Let's assume the latter. But now the capitalist must once more become a buyer, if he is to sell again. Does this next person from whom our capitalist purchases his commodities also enjoy the privilege of selling commodities at $100 above value? If so, then our first trader has immediately lost all the benefit of his earlier transaction; if not, how then does the latter capitalist make *his* profit and stay in business?

Or suppose that one shrewd trader is able to sell $1,000 worth of oil and use the money to buy not just $1,000 worth but $1,100 worth of grain. True, the first capitalist has made a killing. Nevertheless, there is still a problem: while before the exchange the sum of the values of the oil and grain was $2,100, afterward they total the same. One capitalist may have cheated another, but since the *total* value is the same you might just as well say that the first capitalist would have increased his value had he robbed the other of $100 straight-up. The particular capitalist may gain — at the expense of another — but capital as a whole does not. Yet, capitalist society as a whole *does* generally succeed in mounting up ever more wealth, and this cannot be explained by thievery pure and simple in the common usage of the word.

No, as commodity production ceases to be the exception and becomes the rule, the law of value asserts dominion over exchange, and commodities generally exchange according to the amount of abstract labor they contain. Under the domination of industrial capital, the conversion of money into capital and the self-expansion of value must be possible on the basis of the law of value, in such a way that the starting point is the exchange of equivalents. This means that a commodity possessing the peculiar property of being a source of value itself — a commodity whose use and consumption actually creates more value than it originally costs the buyer — must have arisen at some point.

It did: the commodity is the labor power sold by the property-less worker, the proletarian.

The Sale of Labor Power and Exploitation

As touched on earlier, the corrosive effects of merchant capital on feudal society were one of the main factors which wore away the bonds of that system and loosed tens of thousands of dispossessed peasants, serfs and others onto the English country-side and into the cities.[15] These proletarians could no longer produce to meet their own wants — and had nothing to exchange but their ability to work. In the cities, they encountered the owners of money and means of production, the merchants now setting up small manufacturing operations, to whom they sold their ability to work. Unlike the slaves, the proletarians sold this ability themselves of their own "free will," and not for life but by the day or week; unlike the serf or peasant, after the work was done and the wages paid, the proletarians owed no obligation to their master and were owed none in return.

The emergence of this social relation on a mass scale — the sale of labor power by propertyless wage workers to the owners of the means of production — marks off capitalism from all earlier commodity-producing societies. This relation lies at the heart of capital; in the sale of labor power at its value — not below it (necessarily) — lies the secret of capitalist exploitation.

How? As stated, the worker sells his or her labor power like any other commodity, at its value. And what is the value of labor power? Again, like every other commodity, its value is determined by the time it takes to produce it — that is, in this case, by the value of the clothing, food, shelter, etc., necessary during a given period of time to maintain the worker and allow him or her to provide for the raising of a new generation.

Only by selling *this* commodity can the worker live: the proletarian must *alienate* his/her "life activity," making it into an object separate from his/her existence and putting it up for sale. Marx powerfully lays this relationship bare:

> Thus his life-activity is for him only a means to enable him to exist. He works in order to live. He does not even reckon labour as part of his life, it is rather a sacrifice of his life. It is a commodity which he has made over to another. Hence, also, the product of his activity

---

[15] This mass dispossession is by no means unique to England but more or less typifies the transition from feudalism to capitalism.

is not the object of his activity. What he produces for himself is not the silk that he weaves, not the gold that he draws from the mine, not the palace that he builds. What he produces for himself is *wages*, and silk, gold, palace resolve themselves for him into a definite quantity of the means of subsistence, perhaps into a cotton jacket, some copper coins and a lodging in the cellar.... ("Wage-Labour and Capital," *MESW*, Vol. 1, 153)

Once the capitalist has purchased a day's labor power he uses it as he likes. The will of the worker no longer enters into it and his activity is subordinated to alien dictates.

Now the worker may well produce enough value in four hours to cover the cost of a day's wages — that is, it may in fact be the case that the necessities of life for the average worker (and family) for a day take only four hours of socially necessary labor to produce. But this in no way prevents the capitalist from working "his" worker for a full eight hours or more. And why should it? After all, he is not paying the worker for what he produces, but for the use of his labor power for a day. The difference between the two is the source of *surplus* value and capitalist profit.[16]

In practice, this could work out as follows: The capitalist purchases means of production, machinery, and raw materials. The value laid out for this is merely transferred to the finished products, either all at once or bit by bit, depending on the nature of the particular element of production. Suppose that a clothing manufacturer's cost for cotton and wear and tear on machinery during a day's work by each worker has a value equivalent to twelve hours of labor. Since money represents value, suppose one hour's labor time to be represented by $10. These means of production will then cost the capitalist $120 for the day, which he, correctly, counts as part of the final price of his product.

The capitalist also hires the worker and pays him the value of his labor power, the value of the day's necessities to maintain the worker and his family — say $40, or the equivalent of four hours labor. The capitalist puts the worker to work for eight hours, during which time the worker produces a certain number of shirts. The capitalist will sell the shirts at their value, which will be equal

---

[16]In practice this surplus value is divided up by the entire class of capitalists, including moneylenders and landowners as well as industrial capitalists. But this in no way alters the fact that the well-spring of the profit of the entire capitalist class is the surplus ripped from the working class at the point of production.

to the value transferred by the means of production (twelve hours labor) plus the eight hours added by the worker. The value of the shirts for the day then equals twenty hours labor time or $200. But the capitalist has only spent a total of $160 on means of production and wages. He makes $40 in surplus value.

Nothing in this example violates the law of exchange of equal values. No one was cheated of their "rightful due." It's just capitalism — fair and square. The labor power and materials were bought at their value and the shirts sold at their value — yet the capitalist still obtains a profit.

Why? Because though he paid the laborer the equivalent of four hours labor, he worked him for eight. The capitalist takes the value produced in the four hours of *unpaid labor* as his surplus value; thus profit is nothing but the expropriated labor of the working class. The capitalist's wealth grows with each passing day, while the worker must trudge between home and work each day to just keep his or her family's head above water.

Here, incidentally, the deceptive character of wages stands out. Wages — whether in hourly form or piece-rates — seem to pay the worker for the entire time or output on the job. The worker is being paid, says the capitalist, for the value of his labor. But labor is the *measure* of value, and "value of labor" has about as much meaning as the "poundage of weight." To put it simply, the proletarians *cannot* be paid the "value of their labor."

The workers are not ripped off, though, in the conventional sense; no, they are paid the value of the commodity they sell — labor *power*, the ability to work in general — which, once bought, is used by the capitalist according to his own needs and dictates.[17] The extraction of unpaid labor by the capitalist is built into the entire relationship; far from an aberration or malfunction, it's the very heart of the whole process. To leave the question of this inescapable exploitation at the level of a rip-off or swindle is tanta-

---

[17]In fact, with the transition to imperialism, there are huge sections of the proletariat in the oppressed nations who *are* paid less than the value of their labor power, and this super-exploitation is critical to the operation of imperialism; by the same token, there are workers in the advanced countries who are paid more than the value of their labor power, a calculated "bribe" of a sort that is also critical to imperialism's functioning (though in a different, more political, way). This doesn't change the basic character of the relationship between the bourgeoisie and the proletariat, though, and still less does it alter the essential conclusion to be drawn — as we shall see.

mount (and in practice inevitably leads) to acquiescing to exploitation, and demanding a mere loosening of the slave chains. Marx drew precisely this distinction when he insisted that:

> Instead of the *conservative* motto, *"A fair day's wage for a fair day's work!"* they [the proletariat — *LW*] ought to inscribe on their banner the *revolutionary* watchword, *"Abolition of the wages system!"* ("Wages, Price and Profit," *MESW*, Vol. 2, 75)

When they cannot deny that they have enriched themselves through exploitation of the proletariat, the capitalists and their apologists will then declare, even boast, that they deserve to enjoy the fruits of this unequal relationship because, after all, they "took the risk," they "put up the original capital," etc.

We already have begun to touch on what the hideous reality of the original capitalist accumulation was based on (and to what lengths they go to maintain their system). But let us even take the case of the fabled entrepreneur who saves his own earnings, begins a business, expands and finally becomes rich. As soon as this gallant knight of capital makes his first sally into the "business world" — that is, as soon as he invests his money — it is gone, transformed into machinery, raw materials *and labor power*. And more, the only way that original amount can be replaced, to say nothing of enlarged, is through the process of producing (and then selling) commodities. But who actually produces these commodities, and, most of all, who produces the surplus value which represents the expansion of the original amount? The workers, and no one else. In the example of the clothing manufacturer above, the capitalist would need $800 to begin production for a week, and to make a profit of $200. After four weeks he has amassed $800 profit, and would then carry on production entirely on the basis of the unpaid labor he has appropriated.

The capitalist could buy machinery, raw materials, etc., and then turn around and sell them. But then he would be no richer (unless he cheated) and would in reality be no capitalist (but at most a mere swindler). The only way for this capitalist to accumulate and grow rich is through the exploitation of labor power. And once again, so soon as his original money is invested and then replaced through the process of production (and exchange), from that time forward his capital no longer has its source in any action by him other than such exploitation.

Capital: A Social Relation

Having analyzed the implications of a single moment of capitalist production, it's important to step back and remember that we are not in fact dealing with isolated events, but with a social process encompassing billions of people and reproducing itself day in, day out. What is reproduced is not only massive profit, but a *social relationship* between capitalist and proletarian. Marx stressed this point over and over, and the following profound and compelling passage in *Capital* is worth deep study:

> On the one hand, the process of production incessantly converts material wealth into capital, into means of creating more wealth and means of enjoyment for the capitalist. On the other hand, the labourer, on quitting the process, is what he was on entering it, a source of wealth, but devoid of all means of making that wealth his own. Since, before entering on the process, his own labour has already been alienated from himself by the sale of his labour-power, has been appropriated by the capitalist and incorporated with capital, it must, during the process, be realised in a product that does not belong to him. Since the process of production is also the process by which the capitalist consumes labour-power, the product of the labourer is incessantly converted, not only into commodities, but into capital, into value that sucks up the value-creating power, into means of subsistence that buy the person of the labourer, into means of production that command the producers. The labourer therefore constantly produces material, objective wealth, but in the form of capital, of an alien power that dominates and exploits him; and the capitalist as constantly produces labour-power, but in the form of a subjective source of wealth, separated from the objects in and by which it can alone be realised; in short he produces the labourer, but as a wage-labourer. This incessant reproduction, this perpetuation of the labourer, is the sine quâ non [the basic prerequisite —*LW*] of capitalist production. (*Capital*, Vol. 1, 570-571)

Dead labor — that is, the labor time of previous workers congealed into means of production — dominates living labor, as an alien and antagonistic force. "Capital is dead labour," Marx writes elsewhere, "that, vampire-like, only lives by sucking living labour, and lives the more, the more labour it sucks." (*Capital*, Vol. 1, 233)

It is this *social relation*, constantly reproduced and extended, that is capital; the machinery, raw materials and even investment funds that are typically referred to as "capital" in bourgeois society only have that character in the conditions of that society. There is nothing inherent in a steel factory that makes it capital; it becomes such only within capitalist social relations, in which it serves as a means to the self-expansion of value, i.e., the sucking of surplus value from the proletariat for the bourgeoisie. This relation of production fetters the productive forces, while the proletariat creates its own chains anew every day. Only the destruction of those chains, those fetter-like relations, that system of wage-slavery and all the social institutions and ideas that arise from and serve it, can liberate the productive forces, and most especially the most important productive force of all — people.

The Accumulation of Capital

The constant production and reproduction of capitalist social relations moves in a spiral-like pattern. The surplus value produced by capital is not merely consumed by the capitalist but in the main is converted into (and reinvested as) greater amounts of capital. This process is the *accumulation of capital.*

Let's begin again with the process as it might go on in a single factory which produces, say, shirts. As in our earlier example, assume that the capitalist lays out $120 per day for means of production and raw material, and $40 in wages to cover the daily cost of the worker's labor power. Here too the $40 only forms the money expression of four hours of labor, and since the worker in this shop adds eight hours of labor per day to the value of the other commodities, we find that the capitalist is appropriating four hours of unpaid labor, which works out to a profit of $40. The sum total of the value laid out in means of production, etc., (and transferred to the new product in the course of the day) plus the value added by the worker in the paid portion of the day (which is covered by wages) plus the value embodied in the *unpaid* portion (which is profit clear and simple) amounts to $120 + $40 + $40, or $200. Finally, let's further assume that the worker produces forty shirts in an average day so that each shirt has its value expressed in a price of $5 (since $200/40 = $5).

Now, to give some life to this little equation, put the worker in the middle of a garment shop with 99 other workers, so that in one day this boss must lay out $12,000 for means of production and $4,000 for wages, while netting a profit of $4,000. The next day, as he prepares to begin the production process anew, suppose he already has in hand the extra $4,000 in surplus value from the previous day. The question then arises: what does he do with this profit?

He could, like the feudal lord of old, consume every bit of it in riotous feasts and tournaments for himself and his knights and retainers. But the feudal lord was supreme in his domain and within it more or less all surplus automatically flowed to him; not so the capitalist, who is neither limited to a single estate nor guaranteed his continued existence as capitalist by the social order. To remain a capitalist he must sell what his workers produce each day in the market, where he finds himself competing with other capitalists doing the same. He cannot consume the shirts produced by his workers in the way that the feudal lord used the grain and other goods made by his peasants; for the surplus value within them to be realized by the capitalist, they must be sold. This, after all, marks them as commodities. And it is this that in fact *compels* the capitalist to plow most of the surplus value into expanding his capital rather than personally consuming it. Should he refuse to do so he will eventually and inevitably be driven out of business and destroyed as a capitalist.

Why? Well, imagine that across the street there is a capitalist who begins with a set-up identical to the first. This capitalist, however, rather than consuming the entire surplus value produced by the workers decides instead to buy machinery that can double their productivity. He finds that while 100 workers with the old machinery could produce 4,000 shirts in a single day, they can turn out 8,000 with the new. Let's reexamine the equation in those terms.

This second capitalist has invested an extra $4,000 in machinery, which means that his investment in means of production, etc., totals $16,000 as opposed to the $12,000 of his competitor. Both pay out $4,000 in wages. But the second capitalist is selling double the amount of shirts. And while the *socially* necessary labor time for those shirts may still work out to a price of $5 a shirt, the value congealed in *his* 8,000 shirts is only $3 apiece. (Why? Because $16,000 in means of production + $4,000 in wages + $4,000 embodied in unpaid portion of working day = $24,000. $24,000/8000 shirts comes to $3 a shirt.)

At the same time, this capitalist who has invested the surplus produced by his workers in machinery now must dispose of 8,000 shirts instead of 4,000. If he decides to sell the shirts at $4 apiece he will be selling them below their social value (since value is determined by the *average socially necessary labor time*) but above their individual value. On the one hand he will be underselling his competitors and stealing their markets, and on the other he will be making a tidy profit over and above the surplus "normally" accruing to him. He leaps at the chance. Selling 8,000 shirts at $4 apiece amounts to a $32,000 gross on the daily product of his workers, a profit of $12,000 a day as opposed to the $4,000 of his competitors. Those competitors who do not keep pace will be ground down and cast aside, as no one will buy shirts at $5 when they can get them for $4. Thus the constant *compulsion* to put in new and more advanced machinery, to *accumulate* capital.

But there is a rub to this. The advantage of the frugal capitalist evaporates as soon as his competitors invest *their* surplus in new machinery. The new, lower amount of labor time per product, at first available to him alone, now becomes current across the board and the average socially necessary labor time lessens generally. As a result, the value of all shirts becomes lower, while many more must be sold to realize the surplus value.

In this sketch (admittedly oversimplified for purposes of clarity, but fundamentally accurate) the anarchy inherent in capitalist commodity production stands out. This anarchy on the one hand compels tremendous expansion and constant revolutionization of the productive process — compels, that is, the *extended reproduction* of capital. On the other it guarantees that that expansion proceeds irrationally and thus makes accumulation ever more precarious, as it becomes increasingly difficult to realize in sale the value of the commodities produced.

The capitalists in the above example cannot limit their production to what they think may be a reasonable market: if they do, some other capitalist will gobble up the market they are already producing for. Instead they must expand and go for more, and hope to find the markets for their commodities. Further, once the capitalist has invested the surplus value in the machinery (and though it may be his own or borrowed, it is surplus value nonetheless) he can still less afford not to press production to its very limit and throw as much as he possibly can on the market, since he must make good the investment. Yet the obstacles to realization continually assert themselves.

Engels described this contradiction in *Socialism: Utopian and Scientific*:

> We have seen how the capacity for improvement of modern machinery, which is pushed to a maximum, is transformed by the anarchy of social production into a compulsory commandment for the individual industrial capitalist constantly to improve his machinery, constantly to increase its productive power. The bare factual possibility of extending his field of production is transformed into a similar compulsory commandment for him. The enormous expansive force of large-scale industry, compared with which that of gases is mere child's play, now appears to us as a *need* for qualitative and quantitative expansion that laughs at all counteracting pressure. Such counteracting pressure is formed by consumption, by sales, by markets for the products of large-scale industry. But the capacity of the market to expand, both extensively and intensively, is primarily governed by quite different laws which operate far less energetically. The expansion of the market cannot keep pace with the expansion of production . . . . Capitalist production generates a new "vicious circle." (*Anti-Dühring*, 354-355)

This contradiction is not particular to a single industry, a single country, or to only a short period — the basic commandment, "Expand or Die," is universal to capital. During the period of capital's struggle against the fetters of feudal relations it formed a powerful motive force for the progress of society. The bounds of the feudal estates were broken, scattered individual producers were gathered into large concentrations and their labor coordinated on the basis of constantly developing instruments of labor, and nations were welded into integral economic entities with different sectors of production linked to one another; all this was spurred on by the establishment of the world market, and in turn fueled the further expansion of that world market. As the *Manifesto* states:

> Modern industry has established the world market, for which the discovery of America paved the way. This market has given an immense development to commerce, to navigation, to communication by land. This development has, in its turn, reacted on the extension of industry; and in proportion as industry, commerce, naviga-

tion, railways extended, in the same proportion the bourgeoisie developed, increased its capital, and pushed into the background every class handed down from the Middle Ages. (*Manifesto*, 32)

Concentration and Centralization of Capital

This dynamic leads to a concentration of capital. Individual capitals grow in size, and so does the aggregate social capital which together they constitute. Marx wrote:

> Every individual capital is a larger or smaller concentration of means of production, with a corresponding command over a larger or smaller labour-army. Every accumulation becomes the means of new accumulation. With the increasing mass of wealth which functions as capital, accumulation increases the concentration of that wealth in the hands of individual capitalists, and thereby widens the basis of production on a large scale and of the specific methods of capitalist production. The growth of social capital is effected by the growth of many individual capitals. (*Capital*, Vol. 1, 624-625)

Competition between capitals leads to the expropriation of capitalist by capitalist and to still further concentration. This latter form of concentration is not the simple concentration of means of production and command over labor that is identical to accumulation in the form of extended reproduction, but refers instead to the overcoming and absorption of capitals already formed. Competition demands the cheapening of commodities, and this can only be ultimately achieved through economies of scale and the immense and sophisticated new machinery available only to large blocs of capital; hence the larger capital generally beats, and often takes over, the smaller. As capital developed and pushed forward the level of the productive forces, in many cases a huge initial centralization of capital became necessary to even start up an operation which demanded massive and complex means of production.

Marx called the motion of capital eating up capital — as distinct from concentration pure and simple — *centralization*, and stressed its importance.

> . . . [A]ccumulation, the gradual increase of capital by reproduction as it passes from the circular to the spiral form, is clearly a very slow procedure compared with centralisation, which has only to change the quantitative groupings of the constituent parts of social capital.

The world would still be without railways if it had had to wait until accumulation had got a few individual capitals far enough to be adequate for the construction of a railway. Centralisation, on the contrary, accomplished this in the twinkling of an eye, by means of joint-stock companies. (*Capital*, Vol. 1, 627-628)

The greater productiveness of labor pushed on by capitalist accumulation further stimulated the world market, and this necessitated the expansion of credit. But credit itself soon developed into one of the most important weapons of competition (and methods of centralization); the capitalists most able to obtain it can gain a decisive advantage over their rivals: "...it soon becomes a new and terrible weapon in the battle of competition," Marx observed, "and is finally transformed into an enormous social mechanism for the centralisation of capitals." (*Capital*, Vol. 1, 626)

But while capital tends to become ever more massively concentrated in ever fewer hands, there are important counteracting tendencies working against some sort of "logical conclusion" into one single world capital; even the relatively cohesive national capitals of the advanced capitalist countries or the various blocs of capital within those countries contain antagonism and the constant motion to divide into two.

What's important to grasp here is that concentration goes on through competition, only to reproduce competition once again on a higher plane, in a spiral that tends toward higher levels of concentration and centralization — but again, on the basis of the sharpest and most rending sort of conflict. The accumulation of capital is not a clockwork affair. The expansion of credit, for instance, not only stimulates capital accumulation but also produces a new vulnerable point in the accumulation process; a chain of defaults (or conceivably even a single major one), brought on perhaps "by accident," can send a jolt ripping through the system that brings down the whole structure (a possibility testified to by financial panics that have set off serious crises throughout the history of capitalism). And the growth of some capitals, as shown, in turn implies (and comes about through) the destruction and ruin of others; however, the destruction of key sections of capital can both be necessary for the growth of others *and* at the same time endanger the accumulation process as a whole. The very process through which capital becomes more centralized and organized increases simultaneously the force of anarchy, and intensifies the contradiction between the two.

The Falling Rate of Profit

Marx noted in discussing centralization that while it "intensifies and accelerates the effects of accumulation, it simultaneously extends and speeds those revolutions in the technical composition of capital which raise its constant portion at the expense of its variable portion. . . ." (*Capital*, Vol. 1, 628) This points to another important dynamic in the accumulation process: the tendency for the rate of profit to fall.

What is meant by "constant" and "variable" capital? *Constant capital* refers to the machinery, raw material, buildings, etc. — the means of production generally — that the capitalist must purchase, while *variable capital* is that portion of capital paid out in wages. The ratio of the two is the *organic composition of capital*: or, c/v (constant capital/variable capital) = C (the organic composition).

While the value congealed in the constant capital is *transferred* (either all at once as in the case of some raw materials, or bit by bit as with machinery) to the commodities during the production process, constant capital itself creates no *new* value, and hence no surplus value. Since it transfers but doesn't add value, it is *constant* in the sense that the value contained in this form of capital does not increase as it is used. Labor power, on the other hand, does add value as it is used and the capital exchanged for it is therefore *variable*.

Though the surplus is produced by the variable capital, the accumulation of capital results in an ever greater mass of capital given over to means of production (constant capital); and a higher *percentage* of the surplus must be continually reinvested in constant capital, since with the growth of productivity the same amount of labor power can set in motion much greater masses of machinery and raw materials.

This has important consequences. In the earlier hypothetical case of two garment manufacturers, the first one's rate of profit was 25% (4,000 surplus [or s] divided by the sum of 12,000 constant capital [c] and 4,000 variable capital [v]). His rival, who mechanized, at first obtained a rate of profit of 60% (12,000s/16,000c + 4,000v). But this temporary advantage, remember, typically results in a new round of mechanization throughout the industry and an overall drop in the socially necessary labor time congealed in the commodity, and hence a drop in its value to $3 a shirt. Now the rival capitalist will sell his 8000 shirts for $24,000. Thus the rate of profit for the go-getter second capitalist — as for the industry as a whole — would soon drop as mechanization becomes general: $4,000s/16,000c + 4,000v$ = a 20% rate of profit.

Even if the new machinery results in the workers producing value equivalent to their wages in 3-3/4 hours instead of 4, so that the mass of surplus value produced in a single day increases absolutely (from 4,000 to 4,250), the rate of profit still falls relative to the earlier composition of the capital, from 25% to 22%.

The higher investment in constant capital may enable the capitalist to gain a competitive edge and perhaps drive out a competitor, or at least allow him to stave off extinction. A smaller amount of labor now sets in motion more means of production, i.e., labor power is more productive, and this is all to the good in his competitive struggle; but the corollary is that now more means of production are necessary in order to absorb the same amount of labor power (and produce a surplus) and this begins to exert a powerful pressure on capital, both individually and overall.

Greater masses of capital become necessary to start up new operations or to retool old ones whose technical composition has fallen behind. The sheer mass of values that must be reproduced through the sale of commodities increases; the capitalists must run ever faster to stay in the same place — nor can they merely stay in the same place. The rate of return on capital overall tends to drop while the amount that must be risked rises, and the whole accumulation process becomes more vulnerable to shocks and violent interruptions.

The tendency of the rate of profit to fall, however, is just that — a *tendency*, and not a one-way slide to extinction. Its role is more like that of a "goad" (in Marx's word), prodding the accumulation of capital ahead in its lurching, anarchic race, punctuated by crisis. In this overall process there are counteracting and contradictory tendencies as well which capital strives to bring into play, and which can in fact offset the tendency for the rate of profit to drop for certain times or in certain industries (or certain countries). But these very offsetting tendencies and their effects in the long run generate even more formidable barriers to the continued accumulation of capital.

For example, suppose that the capitalist can extract more surplus by forcing the worker to work harder with the same machinery, thereby lowering the length of time in which the worker produces the equivalent of his wages. But what here prevents competitors from merely following suit and cancelling out the effect? Or from deciding to mechanize and leapfrog over the first capitalist — which will set in motion once again the dynamic of a temporary advantage for one capitalist giving way to a general depreciation in value and a higher organic composition of capital across the board? This measure, then, can ultimately only reproduce the same factors giving rise to the tendency for the rate of profit to fall in the first place.

Marx points out in Volume 3 of *Capital* (Part III, "The Law of the Tendency of the Rate of Profit to Fall," 211-266) that with the huge masses of unemployed generated by the accumulation of capital, capital is able to start up new lines of production that can take advantage of this "cheap labor." These new lines of production begin with the variable capital as a considerable portion of the total capital and with the wages below average, and return an unusually high rate (and mass) of surplus value. But while this can counterbalance the decline in the general rate of profit, it also has the effect of drawing capital out of the more basic industries, which include those producing the actual means of production (thereby intensifying tendencies to stagnation). Further, these newer industries themselves soon fall prey to the same contradictions which lead to a high organic composition, and the net result is again to only reproduce the contradiction on a more extensive scale.

In addition, the fall in the rate of profit gives rise to a tremendous increase in attempts to "make a killing"; in frantic efforts to pull capital out of one industry and throw it pell-mell into an area where there may seem to be a temporarily lucrative possibility; and in speculation in precious metals, land, etc., instead of investment in industry or agriculture. Credit manipulations and swindles abound. Today the surplus value produced by giant steel companies, for instance, is often used not to expand or modernize steel production but to buy out or gobble up companies in other more profitable — at least for the moment — sectors of the economy (or parts of the world). All this of course intensifies the general chaos of capitalist accumulation and makes the entire process all the more fragile and tending to crisis.

A further countervailing tendency to the falling rate of profit — one assuming critical importance under imperialism — is the export not only of commodities, but of capital itself, especially to "underdeveloped" countries. Marx himself, though writing before the transition to imperialism, noted the importance of this and pointed out that capital exported to the colonies " . . . may yield higher rates of profit for the simple reason that the rate of profit is higher there due to backward development, and likewise the exploitation of labour, because of the use of slaves, coolies, etc." (*Capital*, Vol. 3, 238)

The fall in the rate of profit and the existence of masses of capital that can no longer be invested at a high enough rate of profit in the home country is a major impetus (though not the only one) to the export of capital all over the world by the imperialist countries. The full consequences of this can only really be dealt with in the next chapter, on imperialism. But it suffices to say for now that the effects of this measure in counteracting the fall in the rate of profit are themselves more than offset by the overall development of imperialism which — in its internationalization of the accumulation process as a whole, its drawing of billions of formerly isolated peoples into the world-historic process, and its generation of revolutionary wars (especially wars of national liberation against it in the colonies and world wars which strain it to its very limits) — is itself the "eve of the proletarian revolution."

In sum, Marx wrote that " . . . the rate of profit, being the goad of capitalist production (just as self-expansion of capital is its only purpose), its fall checks the formation of new independent capitals and thus appears as a threat to the development of the capitalist production process. It breeds over-production, speculation, crises, and surplus-capital alongside surplus-population." (*Capital*, Vol. 3, 241-242)

The tendency for the rate of profit to fall is not *the* "Achilles Heel" of capitalist accumulation, but is *one* important expression of how the anarchy of capitalist production both pushes forward capitalist accumulation *and* generates barriers to its further advance. The effects of the measures taken to counter this tendency, along with the other expressions of anarchy generated by the accumulation process (and the struggles of the masses of proletarians impelled by the accumulation of capital), increase the vulnerability of the entire process to severe crisis.

The Industrial Reserve Army and "Surplus Population"

As the accumulation of capital proceeds with a rising organic composition of capital, and the relative portion of the total capital spent on labor power declines, the demand for labor power diminishes relative to the growth of capital. With each improvement of machinery far fewer workers are needed than before to produce the same amount of products.

At the same time, the supply of labor power — that is, the amount of available workers — tends to increase absolutely. In the early days of capital this was accomplished through the ruin of handicraft workers and artisans, small farmers and peasants, and even unsuccessful capitalists who were involuntarily "drafted" into the proletariat. Today, with capital at the stage of imperialism and integrated in an overall way into a single world process, this finds international expression. Huge masses of peasants in the third world are driven off their land when the imperialists transform subsistence agriculture into mechanized, one-crop production for export. Artisans and other small producers are ruined by export of capital (and commodities). These masses are then crowded into unspeakable shanties where unemployment routinely runs 40% or 50%, or even more. This polarization proceeds to a less intense but still important scale in the imperialist countries, too, where millions and millions are kept on a shuttle between extremely low-paying jobs, unemployment lines, the streets and jail — a huge mass disproportionately made up of the oppressed nationalities within the imperialist countries and/or the immigrant workers driven there by imperialist domination of their homelands.

These great masses, described by the imperialists as "surplus population," are the industrial reserve army of the unemployed. The product of capital accumulation at a certain stage, the reserve army soon became an essential condition of its further development. Since capital develops in fits and starts, with one industry or region surging ahead while another stagnates, and since capitalism as a whole develops anarchically and through cycles — now rushing ahead only to race headlong into a crisis and slow to a crawl — it *needs* a surplus population available for exploitation in times of rapid expansion, and to be used as a pressure on employed workers, especially during times of crisis. The huge army of the unemployed is not just an unfortunate (and reformable) byproduct of capitalism, but is integral and necessary to its functioning. And the reproduction of capital reproduces the industrial reserve army as well, on an ever more extensive and international scale.

This so-called surplus population, of course, is "surplus" only in relation to the needs of capital. Even the "home citadels" of imperialism are filled with neighborhoods where housing is virtually uninhabitable, and for many is unavailable altogether, while unemployed and often homeless masses capable of constructive labor linger in front of boarded-up shells; in the nations dominated by imperialism, the contradiction is even more intense. What binds the hands of those workers is the fetter of capitalist relations, in which production can only go on if it realizes surplus value for capital, and surplus value at the highest possible rate at that, and in which their very unemployment serves to boost that rate.

Marx powerfully summed this up with the statement that the accumulation of capital at one pole means the accumulation of misery for the proletariat at the other. Today, especially given the relative stability and chance to "make it" that has been available to a significant minority of the working class in the imperialist countries, some say that Marx's indictment no longer holds true; on the contrary, it applies even more profoundly. The accumulation of capital now goes on globally, on a qualitatively greater scale than when Marx wrote *Capital*. The laws and trends he pointed to work themselves out all the more forcefully, with the *international* proletariat — including tens of millions in the imperialist citadels as well as hundreds of millions in the third world — at one pole, and world imperialism at the other. In fact, Marx's passage from *Capital* now strikes home even harder:

> ...within the capitalist system all methods for raising the social productiveness of labour are brought about at the cost of the individual labourer; all means for the development of production transform themselves into means of domination over, and exploitation of, the producers; they mutilate the labourer into a frag-

ment of a man, degrade him to the level of an appendage of a machine, destroy every remnant of charm in his work and turn it into a hated toil; they estrange from him the intellectual potentialities of the labour-process in the same proportion as science is incorporated in it as an independent power; they distort the conditions under which he works, subject him during the labour-process to a despotism the more hateful for its meanness; they transform his life-time into working-time and drag his wife and child beneath the heels of the juggernaut of capital. But all methods for the production of surplus-value are at the same time methods of accumulation; and every extension of accumulation becomes again a means for the development of those methods.

And his indictment remains undeniable:

> The law, finally, that always equilibrates the relative surplus-population, or industrial reserve army, to the extent and energy of accumulation, this law rivets the labourer to capital more firmly than the wedges of Vulcan did Prometheus to the rock. It establishes an accumulation of misery, corresponding with accumulation of capital. Accumulation of wealth at one pole is, therefore, at the same time accumulation of misery, agony of toil, slavery, ignorance, brutality, mental degradation, at the opposite pole, *i.e.*, on the side of the class that produces its own product in the form of capital. (*Capital,* Vol. 1, 645)

Development and Crisis

"The product controls the producer" — this applies of course to the proletariat, which finds itself enslaved and subjugated by the very wealth it produces. But it applies as well, though in a different way, to the capitalist. The laws of commodity production and of the accumulation of capital cannot be escaped or transcended within the framework of capitalist relations. The capitalist experiences them as compulsory commandments. What is the capitalist?, Marx asked in a slightly different context, and replied: nothing but capital personified.

Does this mean that the capitalist has no will, that any actions he takes to mitigate these contradictions can have no effect? No, that is not true, nor is it really the point here. As was touched on earlier in the section on centralization, the conscious initiatives of various capitalists both within the sphere of the accumulation process and even in areas separate from it (though ultimately linked to it) such as politics, science, and so forth, have a tremendous effect on that process — witness, for example, the effect of the opening up of America to Europe. And further, even in dealing with the contradictions presented by the development of accumulation, it is not as if there are no options open to the capitalists to try to deal with them.

But as was shown in the earlier discussion of the falling rate of profit, twist and turn as they might, the capitalists cannot escape the terms set by the unfolding of these contradictions and the laws of capitalist production. No single act, or series of acts for that matter, can stop the general trends towards centralization, a rising organic composition, and a fall in the rate of profit. Nor can the basically precarious nature of the accumulation process be changed, or fundamentally made secure. The steps that the capitalists take to offset these tendencies may or may not have the effect of postponing the inevitable collision — or they may even precipitate it — but in any case they ensure that when it comes it will be all the more severe and deep-going in its effects.

The accumulation process itself constantly produces barriers to its own continued reproduction. The need to realize surplus value gives rise to increasingly pell-mell expansion of production, extension of credit and speculation — a "steeplechase," in Engels' words, a mad anarchic race blindly leaping over ever-wider ditches. But commodities must be sold to realize surplus value, loans must ultimately be repaid, speculation cannot endlessly feed upon itself; in short, the dizzying pace of accumulation runs up against its limitations. The tremendous expansion that allows capital to create and dominate new markets outruns the ability of those markets to absorb commodities; the loans that allow for renewed expansion mount up, and default on a debt can rip through a financial system and collapse it. The very abundance that has been produced now sits there mocking society; it can no longer function as capital and therefore it cannot function at all.

> . . . [I]n capitalist society the means of production cannot begin to function unless they have first been converted into capital, into means for the exploitation of human labour-power. The necessity for the means of production and subsistence to take the character of capital stands like a ghost between them and the workers. It alone prevents the coming together of the material and personal levers of production; it alone forbids the means of production to

function and the workers to work and to live. Thus on the one hand the capitalist mode of production stands convicted of its own incapacity to continue the administration of these productive forces. On the other hand, these productive forces themselves press forward with increasing power towards the abolition of the contradiction, to their deliverance from their character as capital, *towards the actual recognition of their character as social productive forces.* (*Anti-Dühring*, 357)

And Marx, in Volume 3 of *Capital,* after enumerating the many expressions of the contradiction between anarchy and organization in the process of capitalist production and accumulation, and detailing the different actions taken by the capitalists to smooth over these antagonisms, finally concludes that:

> Capitalist production seeks continually to overcome these immanent barriers, but overcomes them only by means which again place these barriers in its way and on a more formidable scale.
> The *real barrier* of capitalist production is *capital itself.* It is that capital and its self-expansion appear as the starting and the closing point, the motive and the purpose of production; that production is only production for *capital* and not vice versa, the means of production are not mere means for a constant expansion of the living process of the *society* of producers. The limits within which the preservation and self-expansion of the value of capital resting on the expropriation and pauperisation of the great mass of producers can alone move — these limits come continually into conflict with the methods of production employed by capital for its purposes, which drive towards unlimited extension of production, towards production as an end in itself, towards unconditional development of the social productivity of labour. The means — unconditional development of the productive forces of society — comes continually into conflict with the limited purpose, the self-expansion of the existing capital. The capitalist mode of production is, for this reason, a historical means of developing the material forces of production and creating an appropriate world-market and is, at the same time, a continual conflict between this its historical task and its own corresponding relations of social production. (*Capital*, Vol. 3, 250)

Underconsumption?

In discussing overproduction and crisis, and the overriding tendency for capital to run up against its own immanent barriers, it is important to clarify again (and more deeply) that what is meant is overproduction of capital. This is opposed to the view first formulated by the classical bourgeois economist, Sismondi, and periodically resurrected by many claiming to be Marxist, which in place of the overproduction of capital, the real source of capitalist crisis, substitutes the underconsumption of the masses.

The problem, according to this line, is that the masses cannot buy the products that they have produced; the proposed solution, consequently, is a more equitable or rational distribution of wealth. This thinking leads away from the source of the problem. First, it's an example of circular reasoning. Problem: the masses are hungry and cannot buy food, though there is food galore rotting in warehouses. Why? Answer, from the underconsumptionists: because the masses have no money. The answer, in other words, is just a restatement of the question. Further, Marx points out — and it has held true since Marx, too — that overproduction crises are generally preceded by periods of unusually *high* wages, because capital is in a boom period and must take on more hands, thus reducing the wage-depressing effect of the reserve army of unemployed. So the underconsumptionist theory simply does not fit the facts.

But there is a deeper problem here too. This line seeks the cause of the problem not in the production process, but in distribution. If this indeed were the source of the problem, then it would be the easiest thing in the world to just reform the distribution process, raise wages, lower the capitalists' income, etc. In fact, one could even try to persuade the capitalists to undertake these measures for their own good, and there are no doubt rational men among them who would agree. Failing that, one could appeal over the heads of the *individual* capitalists to their state to carry out reforms — which in fact *is* the program of social-democracy and other reformist trends.

But overproduction is a phenomenon stemming from the production process of capitalism itself, with the tremendous expansive powers of the productive forces hammering against the confines of their character as capital. Capital is a stubborn, unreasoning thing — it exists only to expand itself. To realize this end, it will do all sorts of things that seem insane and are in fact bestial. Productive forces — and especially people — are only means to the end of capital's self-expansion. If the limitations of that self-expansion express themselves in overproduction and brutally destructive imperialist wars, if the rulers of this system necessarily act with the logic of madmen, it is a form of logic nevertheless. That its logic compels capital to act in such a way — over and over again — is borne out by history. It is inherent in its nature — its internal contradictions — which only revolution, and no reforms, can eliminate by eliminating the capitalist system itself.

Capitalist crises — whether in the form of overproduction crises or, especially under imperialism, in the more concentrated and devastating form of interimperialist wars — do not in and of themselves make capitalist accumulation impossible, and still less do they on their own spell the doom and collapse of capitalism. On the one hand, they are concentrated expressions of the contradictions of capitalism, nodal points at which these contradictions come to a head. At the same time, the massive destruction of capitals and the (partial, but in a sense basic) dissolution of the old framework for accumulation, serves to transform value relations. Productive forces are massively destroyed, inefficient capitals ground under and cleared out (with their assets often sold off for very little, which lowers the value of constant capital for the buyer), and a massive centralization of capital is effected which allows the opening up of new areas and fields for exploitation, the more efficient exploitation of the old and the construction of new circuits of accumulation. Thus, while they violently rupture the fabric of capitalist society and the framework of capital accumulation, crises also create the basis for a new spiral of accumulation — unless, that is, the contradiction is resolved through proletarian revolution.

In either event, these crises do not so much mark off cycles as they do spirals in the working out of the fundamental contradiction of capitalism. Through each one the system emerges more strategically vulnerable, and the contradiction becomes more mature and riper for resolution. This is expressed in the *Manifesto*:

> And how does the bourgeoisie get over these crises? On the one hand by enforced destruction of a mass of productive forces; on the other, by the conquest of new markets, and by the more thorough exploitation of the old ones. That is to say, by paving the way for more extensive and more destructive crises, and by diminishing the means whereby crises are prevented. (*Manifesto*, 114)

The *Manifesto* goes on to say that such crises "put on its trial, each time more threateningly, the existence of the entire bourgeois society." But while these eruptions put the whole of society on trial, it falls to the proletariat to deliver the verdict and execute the sentence.

The Fundamental Contradiction of the Capitalist Epoch

The basic change wrought by bourgeois society is the *socialization of production*; there lies its fundamental contribution to the advance of humanity. Engels notes how the rise of the bourgeoisie negated and leapt beyond the dwarfish crude tools characteristic of artisan and other individual production:

> To concentrate these scattered, limited means of production, to enlarge them, to turn them into the powerful levers of production of the present day was precisely the historic role of the capitalist mode of production and of its upholder, the bourgeoisie. In Part IV of *Capital* Marx gives a detailed account of how the bourgeoisie has historically accomplished this since the fifteenth century through the three phases of simple co-operation, manufacture and large-scale industry. But, as is shown there, the bourgeoisie could not transform these limited means of production into mighty productive forces without at the same time transforming them from individual means of production into *social* means of production only workable by *a collectivity of men*. The spinning wheel, the hand-loom and the blacksmith's hammer were replaced by the spinning machine, the power-loom and the steam-hammer, and the individual workshop by the factory commanding the co-operation of hundreds and thousands of workmen. Like the means of production, production itself changed from a series of individual operations into a series of social acts, and the products from individual into social products. The yarn, the cloth and the metal goods that now came out of the factory were the common products of many workers, through whose hands they had successively to pass before they were ready. No one person could say of them: "I made that, this is *my* product." (*Anti-Dühring*, 345-346)

These products were now in fact the creation of a single class, the proletariat. Further, socialization implies not only that a collectivity *within* a factory carries out production, but also that the most far-flung regions are welded together into a single productive circuit and — with the later transformation of capitalism into imperialism — that distant countries are integrated into a single international matrix.

But the more that socialized production drives out individual production and capitalist relations dominate society, the more those relations are transformed from a spur on development to a fetter. Not that the productive forces can no longer be developed in an absolute sense by capitalism — capitalism was, and still is, a dynamic mode of production that *must* transform productive forces and to a certain degree and in certain ways, the production relations. But the productive forces and relations increasingly develop in a warped and distorted way and only on the basis of massively destructive crises, wars of aggression against oppressed nations and peoples, and wars between the imperialist powers. Their development cannot be guided by the conscious efforts of the masses of producers — though this is now within humanity's grasp — but by the dictates of the law of value and the commands of capital accumulation, and they can only proceed through anarchy and wrenching.

The contradiction between the socialized productive forces and the capitalist form of appropriation is the fundamental contradiction of the bourgeois epoch, and of society today. All of current history, every event in human society, has its ultimate source and point of determination in the working out of that contradiction. This occurs through two forms of motion. On the one hand, capital's compulsive character both drives forward the transformation of the productive forces *and* gives rise to crises. "The contradiction between social production and capitalist appropriation," wrote Engels, "reproduces itself as *the antagonism between the organization of production in the individual factory and the anarchy of production in society as a whole.*" (*Anti-Dühring*, 352) And a key expression of this today, under imperialism, is the conflict between different national capitals — which while nationally rooted are only capable of accumulating internationally (more on this in Chapter 3).

The other form of motion consists of the contradiction between the bourgeoisie and the proletariat. The very anarchic workings of capital also call forth capital's "special and essential product" (*Manifesto*) on an ever-expanding scale: its gravediggers, the proletariat. The germ of the new struggling within the rotten husk of the old, the proletariat must carry forward, as Marx put it, "... the *abolition of class distinctions generally,* ... the abolition of all the relations of production on which they rest, . . . the abolition of all the social relations that correspond to these relations of production, . . . [and] the revolutionising of all the ideas that result from these social relations." ("The Class Struggles in France, 1848-1850," *MESW*, Vol. 1, 282)

Thus, on the one hand, there is the continual motion of the extension of capital leading only to greater and more destructive crises; and on the other, the growth and tempering of the proletariat and the development of the proletarian revolution. Engels summed this up, writing that: "It is the motive force of the social anarchy of production which increasingly transforms the great majority of men into proletarians, and it is the proletarian masses in their turn who will ultimately put an end to the anarchy of production." (*Anti-Dühring*, 352)

These two forms of motion — the contradiction between organization and anarchy, and between the bourgeoisie and proletariat (as expressed in class struggle) — themselves form a contradiction, in which there is struggle and identity. In outlining their relationship Bob Avakian wrote:

It is the anarchy of capitalist production which is, in fact, the driving or motive force of this process, even though the contradiction between the bourgeoisie and proletariat is an integral part of the contradiction between socialized production and private appropriation. While the exploitation of wage-labor is the form by and through which surplus value is created and appropriated, *it is the anarchic relations between capitalist producers, and not the mere existence of propertyless proletarians or the class contradiction as such*, that drives these producers to exploit the working class on an historically more intensive and extensive scale. This motive force of anarchy is an expression of the fact that the capitalist mode of production represents the full development of commodity production and the law of value. Were it not the case that these capitalist commodity producers are separated from each other and yet linked by the operation of the law of value they would not face the same compulsion to exploit the proletariat — the class contradiction between bourgeoisie and proletariat could be mitigated. It is the inner compulsion of capital to expand which accounts for the historically unprecedented dynamism of this mode of production, a process which continually transforms value relations and which leads to crisis.

In the era of imperialism the working out of the fundamental contradiction is a process in which there is constant interpenetration between the laws of accumulation and various political forces. More specifically, the working out of this process has taken place through spirals leading to conjunctures characterized by wars among the imperialists and intense revolutionary upheavals. However, *as long as the bourgeois mode of production is qualitatively dominant on a world scale,* the assertion of these laws of accumulation and particularly the motive force of anarchy will overall set the terms and framework of this process. (*RW*, No. 132, Nov. 27, 1981)

As long as it exists, capitalism can only produce and reproduce crisis on an ever more devastating and destructive scale; it is indeed *driven* to more broadly and deeply exploit the proletariat, and cannot ultimately mitigate the class contradictions. With the development of capitalism into imperialism — its highest and final stage — and the first attempts of the proletariat to overthrow the bourgeoisie and begin the revolutionary transformation of society, this fundamental contradiction took a leap in development.

3
IMPERIALISM

Capital, since its origin, has had a strong international character. Its rise both depended upon and intensely stimulated the world market; it not only impelled the forging of the first modern nations as discrete and critically important political and economic units, but shaped their interdependence as well. International political events, including revolutions and wars, in turn played a key role in the development of capital. Still, up to the time of Marx's death, the fundamental contradiction of capitalist society had principally unfolded and developed within individual capitalist nations taken separately.

By the late 1800s, however, this changed. Within the capitalist countries monopoly took root in and eventually dominated the key industries; banking and industrial capital began to merge into huge blocs of finance capital. The export of capital, especially to the colonies and less-developed countries, took place on an unprecedented scale, and an intense scramble by the various capitalist powers to grab up new colonies and spheres of influence followed in its wake.

All this found concentrated expression in two momentous political upheavals: a storm of national liberation struggles in the colonies and semi-colonies in the early 1900s, which included

China, Persia (Iran), the Philippines and others in its sweep; and the outbreak of World War 1, the first interimperialist war over the division of the whole world. These world-historic turns, and the challenges they posed to the revolutionary movement, made it undeniable that something very fundamental had changed about capital — but *what?*

Karl Kautsky, at the time the most recognized authority on Marxism in the world, held that all this signalled a new-found ability of capital to rationally order itself. True, the capitalist world was in the throes of a bloody, destructive global war — but Kautsky nevertheless maintained that within the huge monopolized blocs of capital there lay the possibility of "ultra-imperialism," a system which could supposedly enable capital to peacefully divide the world and escape such obviously self-destructive conflicts as world wars. Kautsky asserted that imperialism was above all a *policy*, and policies after all could be changed short of revolution. In Kautsky's view imperialism had not heightened the contradictions of capital but eased them — or at least made their easing *possible*, if the pressure of the working class combined with the enlightened self-interest of the rational capitalists could prevail. This formed the underpinnings of Kautsky's political stance in World War 1, when he opposed calls to turn the imperialist war into a civil war between classes as ridiculously premature, and fought against a break with those parties and leaders in the socialist movement which had supported their governments in the war. Kautsky instead called for the workers to pressure their respective governments for a "just peace." And his analysis and political line continues to assert itself today, when it finds expression both in the revisionist communist parties aligned with the USSR and the social-democratic parties and forces owing allegiance to the Western bourgeoisies.

It *is* true that by the 20th century capital seemed able to transcend the limitations of its earlier periods and the severity of its tendencies to crisis. Its field of activity was international in an unprecedented dimension. Production was not only highly organized on an enterprise level, but had been integrated on the level of entire industries and even whole regions of the world. At the same time, sections of the proletariat within the capitalist countries found themselves in a relatively stable position, and the socialist parties and unions had become powerful institutions in the parliaments and economic life of many of these nations.

But what all this signified was not the ending or easing of the fundamental contradiction of capitalism (in both its forms of motion), but rather a qualitative leap in the character of its aspects and *the plane on which it was unfolding*. The development and resolution of the contradiction between socialized production and private appropriation had become an internationally integrated process, and both its anarchy/organization and bourgeoisie/proletariat forms of motion found more intense expression as internationally determined processes. The terms of capitalist accumulation and the class struggle in any one country — or any set of countries, e.g., the imperialist powers of Europe — were "set" in the context of this international process, and could only be correctly understood in that light.

None of this, however, was immediately apparent, and the socialist movement was wracked with the most severe crisis in its history. At this crucial juncture, it fell to Lenin to confront and dissect imperialism from a truly Marxist standpoint. He showed that the source of the new phenomena characterizing imperialism lay in the contradictions of capital, and showed that the new phase of capitalism was indeed its highest and final stage. Viewed internationally — as capital *had* to be in a qualitatively new way, since its accumulation had become an international process in a qualitatively new and greater way — the new stage did not signify a lessening of its contradictions, but a sharpening. Revolution was *more*, not less, urgent and more possible as well — not, as Lenin explained, in an obvious straight-ahead, all-times-and-all-places fashion, but through the spiral-like heightening of contradictions and their concentrations at certain key junctures. As he wrote in the classic *Imperialism, the Highest Stage of Capitalism*:

> Imperialism emerged as the development and direct continuation of the fundamental characteristics of capitalism in general. But capitalism only became capitalist imperialism at a definite and very high stage of its development, when certain of its fundamental characteristics began to change into their opposites, when the features of the epoch of transition from capitalism to a higher social and economic system had taken shape and revealed themselves all along the line. (*Imperialism*, 104)

What were these features? How did they constitute an "epoch of transition" of the sort Lenin said? And what are the implications for the revolutionary struggle?

Basic Features of Imperialism

Monopoly

At the foundation of imperialism lies the emergence of monopoly capital in the advanced capitalist countries. Monopoly capitalism *is* imperialism; they are one and the same. During the late 19th century monopoly took root in and eventually gained dominance over one industry after another in these countries. Rough agreements between a handful of the biggest firms in a field were worked out over division of markets, prices, pace of technical innovation, etc., which allowed firms to fix prices above value and delay investment in new machinery, and hence to extract surplus profits (relative to non-monopoly capital).

This particular characteristic of imperialism is so conspicuous as to be almost self-evident. Take the U.S., where by 1900 monopolies controlled 66% of the iron and steel industry, 81% of the chemical industry, 85% of aluminum production, 95% of coal, etc.; or where a more current statistic reveals that today the top 200 corporations in the U.S. own almost two-thirds of the industrial assets. (This represents a significant increase from pre-World War 2 levels of concentration; at the beginning of the rise of monopolies following the Civil War the percentage was negligible.)

But why did monopoly develop? As discussed in Chapter 2, there is a tendency inherent in the accumulation of capital towards the increasing concentration of the means of production and command over labor power in the hands of a few capitalists, which, as Marx points out, widens the basis for large-scale production. By the late 19th century the tendencies to greater concentrations of capital, and hence larger-scale production, and to the centralization of capital (i.e., the absorption of one capital by another) developed to the point where monopolies could be — and soon had to be — formed in the main industries, and a qualitative leap in the organization of the social capital as a whole took place. [1]

Lenin sums up in *Imperialism* that:

> Economically, the main thing in [the transition to imperialism — *LW*] is the displacement of capitalist free competition by capitalist monopoly. Free competition is the fundamental characteristic of capitalism, and of commodity production generally; monopoly is the exact opposite of free competition, but we have seen the latter being transformed into monopoly before our eyes, creating large-scale industry and forcing out small industry, replacing large-scale by still larger-scale industry, and carrying concentration of production and capital to the point where out of it has grown and is growing monopoly: cartels, syndicates, and trusts, and merging with them, the capital of a dozen or so banks, which manipulate thousands of millions. (*Imperialism*, 104)

---

[1]Here a brief discussion of the "social capital" is necessary. The social capital refers to the aggregate of the individual capitals of a particular nation-state in which the capitalist mode of production is dominant. Marx writes in Vol. 2 of *Capital* that:

"Every individual capital forms, however, but an individualised fraction, a fraction endowed with individual life, as it were, of the aggregate social capital, just as every individual capitalist is but an individual element of the capitalist class. The movement of the social capital consists of the totality of the movements of its individualised fractional parts, the turnovers of the individual capitals." (*Capital*, Vol. 2,351-352) Marx goes on to analyze that the value-relations (for instance, the organic composition of capital, the value of labor power, the rate of profit, etc.) of the aggregate social capital of the nation form a framework within which the terms for the functioning of the various individual capitals are set (not smoothly and consciously, of course, but through contradiction and struggle). For example, the contradictory rates of profit in different enterprises and industries resolve themselves into a general rate of profit for the social capital as a whole around which, in turn, every individual capital tends to fluctuate. It is this general rate which *principally* determines the actual rate of return on an individual capital.

Further, just as individual capitals are components of the social capital, their movement also forms part of a larger, determining process; as Marx also notes: ". . .the circuits of the individual capitals intertwine, presuppose and necessitate one another, and form, precisely in this interlacing, the movement of the total social capital. Just as in the simple circulation of commodities the total metamorphosis of a commodity appeared as a link in the series of metamorphoses of the world of commodities, so now the metamorphosis of the individual capital appears as a link in the series of metamorphoses of the social capital." (*Capital*, Vol. 2, 353-354)

While imperialism qualitatively increases the tendency for capital to *overflow* its national framework, and in fact internationalizes the circuits of capital on a far higher plane than previously, capital nonetheless remains profoundly national. However internationalized its circuits become, capital is anchored in a particular nation; and the aggregate social capital principally refers to the aggregate social capital rooted in a particular national market, even as its operations take in capital invested all over the globe, and even as it interpenetrates with the social capital of other nations.

This very development, though, is contradictory, as Lenin notes:

> At the same time the monopolies, which have grown out of free competition, do not eliminate the latter, but exist over it and alongside of it, and thereby give rise to a number of very acute, intense antagonisms, frictions and conflicts. (*Imperialism*, 105)

Beginning in the 1870s there were a series of partial monopolies and unsuccessful (or only temporarily successful) attempts at monopoly in the advanced capitalist countries; but as the tendencies to concentration and centralization increasingly asserted themselves, by the end of the century monopoly had become general, and had laid the basis for imperialism. Monopoly carries with it (and partially results from) a further development of the productive forces; it does not generally take hold in the form of one or a few concerns dominating and/or owning many small workshops, but is bound up with an immense increase in the concentration of production. Huge, highly mechanized plants are typical, and a vast concentration of capital is necessary for even initial investment in most basic sectors of production.

But the concentration of capital, and of production on a new scale, erects a new barrier to continued capital accumulation: capital is now enormously overproduced relative to the national market alone. What Engels called the "expansive power of socialized production," and likened to the force of heated gas expanding in a container, geometrically multiplies, and the constraints of private appropriation, and in particular now the national market, make themselves felt all the more acutely. Hence the compelling pressure on capital to drive beyond its national framework. It has become superabundant, and must be exported in a qualitatively greater way than before to other countries in order to be most profitably employed (as well as for other reasons — more on this later).

Thus, the dominance of monopoly forms the basis for a qualitative leap in the socialization of production. No longer does the heart of the question of socialization lie in the organization of production on the plant level, but in the overall socialization and integration of the process on a *global* scale.

"Competition becomes transformed into monopoly," Lenin wrote. "The result is the immense progress in the socialization of production. In particular, the process of technical invention and improvement becomes socialized." And Lenin went on to stress that:

> This is something quite different from the old free competition between manufacturers, scattered and out of touch with one another, and producing for an unknown market. Concentration has reached the point at which it is possible to make an approximate estimate of all sources of raw materials (for example, the iron ore deposits) of a country and even, as we shall see, of several countries, or of the whole world. Not only are such estimates made, but these sources are captured by gigantic monopolist combines. An approximate estimate of the capacity of markets is also made, and the combines "divide" them up amongst themselves by agreement. Skilled labor is monopolized, the best engineers are engaged; the means of transport are captured: railways in America, shipping companies in Europe and America. (*Imperialism*, 24-25)

This entire phenomenon has gone even further since Lenin. What the capitalist economists call "the integrated global assembly line" is one example of the worldwide socialization. For instance, one Ford model in 1982, the Escort, got its doorlift assemblies from Mexico, its rearbrake assembly from Brazil, its shock absorber struts from Spain, the hub and bearing clutch from France, its manual transmission axle from Japan, the engine cylinder heads from Italy, the valve guide and bushing from West Germany, the wiring from Taiwan and the steering gear from Great Britain.

A more dramatic instance lies in the entire semiconductor and transistor industry which took off in the '60s. Midway in the process of manufacturing transistors or integrated circuits, many U.S. firms ship the unfinished components abroad for assembly and then ship assembled "chips" back to the U.S. for testing. The U.S. company Fairchild Semiconductors, for example, assembles components in plants in Indonesia, South Korea, Hong Kong and the Philippines, and then tests and warehouses them in Singapore — to be later used in computers that are almost the exclusive property of the advanced capitalist countries. Most of this semiconductor production goes on in what are known as export processing zones, or enclaves: sections of third world countries in which, on the one hand, the national labor laws, wage floors and taxes are suspended, and on the other, a tremendous amount of capital is concentrated in order to develop the infrastructure (i.e., the elec-

trical power, telecommunication, highways, ports, airports, etc.)
necessary for industrial production. Often this capital takes the
form of loans extended to the "host" country by international
financial institutions; the Export-Import Bank, for example, lent
money to the Philippines to build the Marong nuclear power
plant, which in turn is intended to service the Bataan export processing zone. The following passage from Lenin underlines both
the tremendous significance of this socialization of production on
a world scale *and* what gives it its distorted character:

> Capitalism in its imperialist stage leads right up to the most com-
> prehensive socialization of production; it, so to speak, drags the
> capitalists, against their will and consciousness, into some sort of a
> new social order, a transitional one from complete free competition
> to complete socialization.
> Production becomes social, but appropriation remains private.
> The social means of production remain the private property of a
> few. The general framework of formally recognized free competi-
> tion remains, but the yoke of a few monopolists on the rest of the
> population becomes a hundred times heavier, more burdensome
> and intolerable. (*Imperialism*, 25)

What's *possible*, on the basis of the socialization already
achieved, is a world in which production and distribution could
generally be — indeed, would have to be — organized and carried
out on a global scale with the view toward breaking down the in-
equalities, backwardness and misery still dominant in most of the
world, and overall advancing human society to a whole new
stage. But the fetters of imperialist relations reproduce disparities
and distortions in many spheres, including, markedly, what Bob
Avakian has called the "lopsidedness" in the world. Because of
the relations between the imperialist powers and the great majority of the world's nations, the global socialization of production
has gone along with, and in fact intensified, a situation in which
". . . in the vast bulk of the world 8% unemployment would be a
miracle — it's 30 or 40% all the time, let alone when there's a really
acute crisis. And outside of a few pockets, these places are extremely backward and the railroads don't even reach to most of
the areas, much less run on time, and the goods aren't moving
rapidly all over the country, and there is not an articulated
economy. . . ." (*Conquer the World?. . .*, 36)

In this leap in the socialization of production Kautsky saw the germ of control that he thought would allow the capitalists to endlessly manipulate their way out of crises. Nothing could be further from the truth, or closer to the heart of the contradiction. Monopoly and the organization of production on a world scale enables capital to better maneuver in the face of one set — or on one plane, if you will — of contradictions, only to project those contradictions onto a more all-encompassing and devastating plane; in Lenin's words, it "increases and intensifies the anarchy inherent in capitalist production *as a whole.*" (*Imperialism*, 28) Anarchy erupts in any number of ways, it springs from every pore: in the continued competition and struggle between monopoly and non-monopoly capital, in tendencies for blocs of capital to break into antagonistic rivals, and in the struggle between the monopoly giants themselves. The agreements between monopolies are in the nature of truces, and tend to give way to open and destructive warfare — both economic *and* military warfare between states.

Further, the need to find profitable avenues of investment of superprofits leads to risky investments, especially abroad; and in many investments, due to the increased mass of capital needed to start up or transform an industrial enterprise, much more is on the line from the very beginning. Also, with capital concentrated on such a massive scale and able to flow in and out of different and more profitable areas with great speed (more on this later), some sections of the economy in a country are rapidly built up while other less profitable ones (which may be just as vital to the functioning of the social capital as a whole) decay and stagnate — a disparity which is both an expression of anarchy and a factor further aggravating it.

Additionally, there is the fact that capitalist accumulation gives rise to the tendency of one capital to break into a number of competing capitals, and for blocs or alliances of capital to similarly break apart. This comes out, for instance, in the competition *within* huge conglomerates like ITT or GM between different divisions or production units over investment capital, allocation of surplus value and long-term investment strategy — or, to take the state-capitalist Soviet Union, in the struggle, say, between agricultural and heavy industrial sectors over *state-determined* investment policies, distribution of surplus, etc. This tendency asserts itself on a higher level in the conflicts *within* imperialist blocs between different nations, conflicts which can only be subordinated to (and partially and temporarily resolved on the basis of) more overriding contradictions with the *rival* bloc (or blocs). Indeed, the conflict between rival imperialist blocs over the division of the world — which can only be settled on the basis of political-military strength, with world war as the decisive measure of this — is the most critical and concentrated expression of the intensification of anarchy which imperialism entails.

The heightened way in which bourgeois production relations act as fetters on the now-internationalized productive forces makes the contradiction between the two all the more acute and the need to carry through the transition all the more urgent and undeniable; the tools now speak more forcefully and urgently, and in all the tongues of the planet, for a change in the production relations.

The Changed Role of the Banks

The monopolization of banking is also integral to imperialism. Today in the U.S., the 10 biggest banks hold $405 billion in assets, or 25% of the total bank assets, and just three of them — Bank of America, Citicorp and Chase Manhattan — together own over half of this. These figures don't include holding companies and other bank affilitates through which these top 10 effectively control another 50% of bank assets. [2]

---

[2] We should note here that the examples in this chapter are drawn mainly from the U.S. The development of imperialism in Western Europe and Japan generally parallels development in the U.S. (as a study of Lenin's *Imperialism*, which drew its examples mainly from Europe, reflects). Today, though these powers are integrated into a more or less cohesive bloc (if simultaneously rife with antagonism) under the hegemony of *U.S.* imperialism, they are nonetheless *imperialist* powers (and not victims of U.S. domination, as some claim). A concentrated illustration of this was seen in strikes that ripped through auto plants in Iran, in spring of 1982; the targets included not only General Motors, but also plants producing Mercedes Benz, Volvo and several Japanese cars.

The case of the Soviet Union — an imperialist power and head of a bloc rival to the U.S.' — presents a more complex picture. There imperialism developed on the foundation of what had been a centralized socialist economy, after the takeover by a new bourgeoisie in the mid-'50s (see Chapter 4). The *forms* of imperialist economic institutions differ from those in the West, but the essential content is identical. For instance, while the character and actual function differ in many particulars (and this is hardly surprising, given its origin in a formerly socialist economy and superstructure), the regional government ministries, production groups, state banking institutions, etc., in the USSR roughly correspond in their

The concentration of banking changes the bankers from numerous scattered middlemen into a handful of powerful monopolists. Lenin wrote:

> When carrying the current accounts of a few capitalists, a bank, as it were, transacts a purely technical and exclusively auxiliary operation. When, however, this operation grows to enormous dimensions we find that a handful of monopolists subordinate to their will all the operations, both commercial and industrial, of the whole of capitalist society; for they obtain the opportunity — by means of their banking connections, their current accounts and other financial operations — first, to *ascertain exactly* the financial position of the various capitalists, then to *control* them, to influence them by restricting or enlarging, facilitating or hindering credits, and finally *entirely determine* their fate, determine their income, deprive them of capital, or permit them to increase their capital rapidly and to enormous dimensions, etc. (*Imperialism*, 37)

The concentration of capital is immeasurably accelerated by monopoly in banking, as huge amounts of capital in the form of deposits, etc., are pooled (and huge loans floated or investments undertaken in consortium). This concentration is not only a matter of quantity, but more important of quality — that is, as Lenin points out above, the banks obtain *control* of vast amounts of capital. They develop and utilize experts and staffs relating to various industries and regions of the world, employ governmental ties and agents, and carry out operations all over the world.

The interweaving strands of capital and information that run through the banks made the industrial capitalist more dependent on bank capital. At the same time, industrial capital also got into bank capital. In the U.S. the Rockefeller capital, based largely in oil, began its own banks, as did other industrial capitalists like Mellon and DuPont, in order to continue expansion beyond what had become the constraints of a single industry.

---

role to corporations and banks in the imperialist countries of the West, and the concentrated power to shift investment around and determine overall economic strategies held by the top Soviet state officials is a form of finance capital (to be discussed shortly). Further, the Soviet Union also exports capital — an important characteristic of imperialism — in the form of loans, unequal trade agreements, arms sales, joint ventures, etc.; and it too faces the necessity for a new redivision of the world. See "The 'Tarnished Socialism' Thesis," in *The Communist*, Vol. 2, No. 2, RCP Publications, and "Social-Imperialism and Social-Democracy," in *The Communist*, Vol. 1, No. 1.

There is also the phenomenon that Lenin took note of:

> . . .[A] personal union, so to speak, is established between the banks and the biggest industrial and commercial enterprises, the merging of one with another through the acquisition of shares, through the appointment of bank directors. . . to the Boards of Directors of industrial and commercial enterprises, and vice versa. (*Imperialism*, 45)

Bank and industrial capital coalesced into huge blocs, and a higher form of capital emerged dominant with the transition to imperialism: finance capital.

Finance Capital

Finance capital straddles the divisions between different industries, firms and even countries; it is capital which is no longer confined to one or even several areas or sectors of the economy, but can be shifted in and out of many different enterprises and areas of the world to acquire and centralize the highest possible mass of surplus value. It developed out of and as part of the whole complex of contradictions that came together to produce imperialism when, owing to the increasing socialization of production, in order to advance accumulation it became necessary to pool and centralize many capitals. Only the emergence of these huge financial blocs from the intertwining of banking and industrial capital could do that. (One example of the sort of leap required was the then-unprecedented initial capitalization of U.S. Steel at $1 billion in 1900.) Further, the flexibility afforded to finance capital by its web of connections allowed it to carry out maneuvers and centralize capital in such a way as to forestall, even if only temporarily, certain barriers to continued accumulation of the aggregate social capital — as indicated, for instance, in its ability to transfer capital from enterprises of less profitability to huge new enterprises, areas of investment or regions of the world.

Capital at the level of the financial group functions differently than the classic entrepreneurial capital. It does not concern itself so much with organization and management at the enterprise level, as it does with *control* over a vast number of enterprises, the ability to exact "tribute" from them and more, to use them as chess pieces in its larger strategy. Finance capital does not eliminate competition but reproduces it in magnified form at the level of the competing financial blocs, which decide which enterprises, industries or even countries to finance in order to increase their financial control and weaken that of their adversaries. These blocs control and take their profits from a complex of highly interrelated industrial and banking institutions. They fight for control of a vast number of enterprises, without necessarily being committed to their success as such; in fact, a financial group may be just as interested in a particular company's demise if it serves the maximization of their overall gains.

The state is an extremely important arena in the struggle between contending blocs of finance capital. Here battles go on over government policy towards "ailing industries" or bankrupt countries, and over how monetary, financial and trade agreements are determined — not to mention geopolitical policy towards whole regions of the globe. John Kennedy's much-ballyhooed action as U.S. president of attacking the price policies of the major steel companies — an action which the Communist Party, USA hailed as "reawakening the great anti-monopoly tradition of America" — is in fact a good example of an internal conflict of finance capital handled through the medium of the state. Today questions like energy policy, or whether to bail out a Chrysler, hinge in part on the interests of which financial bloc are advanced and which weakened, and their relative strength (as well as the effects that the fate of various industries have on the underpinnings of the entire system, including — especially today — its ability to wage war).

As Lenin analyzed,

> Finance capital took over as the typical 'lord' of the world; it is particularly mobile and flexible, particularly interknit at home and internationally, and particularly impersonal and divorced from production proper; it lends itself to concentration with particular ease. . . . ("Preface to N. Bukharin's Pamphlet, *Imperialism and the World Economy*," *LCW*, Vol. 22, 105)

These characteristics derive from a number of things. While banks are not the same as finance capital, they often serve as critical institutions for a particular financial bloc (though at other times or in other cases they may themselves be battlegrounds for several different blocs), and a study of their methods of control of corporations reveals much. Banks often gain control through grabbing strategically significant holdings of corporate stock. The

Morgan Guaranty Trust Co. (linked to the Morgan financial group) is among the top five stockholders in 56 out of 122 companies that were studied in a 1978 U.S. Senate report. (These corporations studied, by the way, held one-fourth of the assets of *all* U.S. corporations, so the phenomena discussed typify the U.S. economy.) It is number one in 27 of them. But Morgan Guaranty is in deeper than that: it is also the number one stock-voter in Citibank, Manufacturers Hanover Bank, and Chemical and Banker Trust, as well as being the number one stockholder in Bank America Corp., the bank holding company with the largest assets in the U.S. It is revealing to note that today, due to the spreading out of shares among various stockholders (a "democratization" which actually increases the control of finance capital), holdings of 4% to 5% of stock can control a company, and that 1.5% can give the holding institution significant say-so in the firm.

Another method of control is "interlocking," touched on earlier, which is the connection of various corporations, financial institutions, etc., through directors who sit on two or more boards of directors. Almost 90 directors of the 130 companies studied in the above-cited report sat on six to ten corporate boards each. These individuals represent different blocs of finance capital and fight to influence the policies of the different corporations and banks in a way favorable (and subordinate) to the interests of their financial bloc.

The holdings by the main banks of billions of dollars in debts are also very important. Credit is extended not only to companies, but even more significantly, to many countries too. In the latter case, these loans are often conditional on the banks being granted authority to veto economic plans and enable them to greatly influence the pattern of national development, according to the interests of the financial group.

Standing out in all this is the *parasitical* character of finance capital; it skims the cream off of everything and, as Lenin put it, "... levies tribute upon the whole of society" at every step of the way. Its very ability to operate — and the essential feature of its parasitism — is in the first place the result of the shifting or export of huge sums of capital abroad and its feeding off the vast plunder drawn in from every corner of the globe.

Kautskyite trends sometimes curse this parasitism of finance capital as a blot on what they imply could be an otherwise healthy economy. This view is promoted both by the revisionist communist parties and the social-democrats who, despite their differences, at times join in chorus to bay against "the multinationals," or "the big banks," "Rockefeller," etc., as if capitalism itself could exist without finance capital at this stage of history. Politically, this generally goes along with a call to look towards a supposedly enlightened and non-monopoly section of the bourgeoisie to grant reforms, at least if properly pressured.

Parasitical as it is, finance capital is *necessary* to capitalism in its imperialist stage; it sets the terms on which other sections of capital can accumulate, and acts, in the short run, to overcome barriers to the continued accumulation of capital. While finance capital is in many respects antagonistic to other sections and types of capital and skims tribute from them, it also sits at the apex of the pyramid; it alone has the flexibility and ability to centralize capital that is necessary for capital's continued accumulation at this stage.

The proposal to nationalize the banks, big industries and so on as a way around this would at best only reproduce the content of finance capital in the form of bourgeois state ownership. Shifting a huge mass of capital into the hands of the state does not speak to which class controls the state (and hence the nationalized capital), and to what ends. (In fact, nationalization of particularly weak and stagnant industries goes on in some West European countries as a way to take the burden off an individual financial bloc and shift it around more "equitably," while keeping the industry functioning for the good of capital as a whole.)

Finance capital does not transcend the contradictions of capital; the vast control and concentration does not allow it to rationalize the system's workings. Just the opposite. The centralization of finance capital and its heightened flexibility can temporarily suspend certain barriers to accumulation — but again, only to place more formidable ones in its way overall and in the long run. Here, too, anarchy and the tendencies to severe crisis and breakdown are heightened.

For one thing, of course, these blocs of finance capital continually clash in and through the various institutions in which they confront each other, including the government. But beyond that, the very lifeblood of their continued existence, their parasitism, gives rise to heightened anarchy and increased factors for revolution. Look again, for instance, at the reliance of finance capital on debt and credit: while this enhances its control and makes possible continued accumulation, more fundamentally it increases the house-of-cards vulnerability of the whole global structure of capitalist accumulation. A chain reaction to one or several major defaults, a revolution fueled by a debt-related crisis or "austerity program" imposed by finance capital in an important country, a major bank failure in an advanced capitalist country — any of these could conceivably spark a devastating global crisis.

Export of Capital

Bound up with the predominance of monopoly and finance capital is a powerful tendency toward a superabundance of capital in the advanced countries. In part, this superabundance arises because agreements on carving up the market and setting prices remove some of the compulsion faced by the monopoly capitalists to continually reinvest in mechanization in their home countries (at least relatively and temporarily so); more important, however, the growth of finance capital concentrates ever larger masses of capital needing a profitable outlet. Meanwhile the tendency for the rate of profit to fall, and other crisis tendencies as well, add to the pressure in the form of increased overproduction of capital — overproduction, of course, relative to what can be *profitably* absorbed in any single national capital's circuit. The idea of a surplus, or superabundance, of capital in the imperialist countries does *not* mean that the home market is literally saturated with investment; rather it points to the geometrically increased *tendency* to superabundance that forces capital beyond the national bounds in a qualitatively greater way than before, so that the whole circuit may continue to reproduce itself.

Before the second half of the 19th century, increased export of commodities could help offset trends to overproduction. But as monopoly and finance capital assumed dominance and aggravated the contradictions, the expansion of trade as the main form of international commerce could no longer significantly mitigate these tendencies.

Imperialism meant a qualititative leap; in Lenin's words, "Typical of the old capitalism, when free competition had undivided sway, was the export of *goods*. Typical of the latest stage of capitalism, when monopolies rule, is the export of *capital."* (*Imperialism*, 72) Commodity export, of course, continued with imperialism, and the export of capital had gone on to a smaller extent earlier; but imperialism marked a *decisive* shift in the significance of capital export to the continued functioning of the system.

The export of capital to the noncapitalist areas of the world yields an extraordinary rate of return. Lenin explained:

> In these backward countries profits are usually high, for capital is scarce, the price of land is relatively low, wages are low, raw materials are cheap. The possibility of exporting capital is created by the fact that a number of backward countries have already been drawn into world capitalist intercourse; main railways have either been or are being built there, the elementary conditions for industrial development have been created, etc. (*Imperialism*, 73)

The volume and importance of capital export increased so that circuits of production, credit and trade developed into international webs. The capital invested in the backward parts of the world, and the surplus value extracted, entered into these overall international circuits of capital — which were and are controlled by finance capital in the advanced countries — and played a pivotal role in their maintenance and expansion.

These developments were concentrated in the urgent struggle for colonies carried out by the advanced countries in the late 1800s. In 1885, following several decades of struggle almost leading to war between the European powers and after a series of rebellions throughout Africa, that continent was literally carved up at the Berlin Conference like so many pieces of turf by gangsters — only to give rise to still more intense rivalry and scramble. In 1898 the U.S. went to war with Spain to grab up the Caribbean and parts of Latin America as *its* preserve, and later seized the Philippines as well (though it was not seized without a long and bloody war against the Filipino people); 1900 saw Japan, Germany, Britain, France and Russia send troops to China to crush an anti-imperialist uprising; and by 1904 Japan and Russia went to war over China and the Pacific.

The increased importance of the export of capital relates more deeply as well to the emergence of imperialism as a single world process. Before this, while both money and commodity trade were international — in the sense that capital in these forms flowed

across national borders and that there was an integral world
monetary system and a world market — only with imperialism
does the circuit of productive capital become international.

The development of imperialism since Lenin has borne out
his analysis on the role of capital export and in fact demonstrated
this on a much more pronounced scale. This is reflected, in the
first place, in the sheer volume and the growth of that volume
over the last 80-odd years. In 1914, for example, the overseas
capital of the combined imperialist powers (including direct investment, stocks, bonds, etc.) totaled $44 billion, of which $21.5
billion was in the third world; by 1973 these totals were, respectively, $541 billion and $251 billion.[3] And U.S. capital exports,
while always important, have mushroomed since World War 2
and form in large part the basis for the unprecedented expansion
of the post-war period. In 1929 the book value of U.S. foreign
direct investment — a category which excludes bank loans and
some other forms of capital export but is nevertheless an important index of capital export as a whole — totalled $7.5 billion; by
1950 this had grown only to $11.8 billion. But over the next ten
years direct foreign investment jumped to $32.7 billion, and by
1970 stood at $78.2 billion — a seven-fold increase in 20 years. By
1980 this had nearly tripled again, to $213.5 billion. (Much of this
latter increase, however, reflected the huge inflation of the '70s,
as the international economy began to contract and the importance of bank loans in relation to direct corporate investment
greatly increased — more on this shortly.)

But the sheer volume of capital export alone does not ade-
quately reflect its *qualitative* role. As touched on earlier, the
higher rate of return on exported capital helps retard the overall
tendency for the rate of profit of the aggregate national capital to
fall. In 1950, for example, U.S. foreign direct investment totalled
less than 5% of all U.S. corporate investment, but accounted for
7.3% of all after-tax profits; by 1970 foreign direct investment
stood at nearly 10% of all direct investment, but accounted for
26% of all corporate profits! And while the rate of profit on all
U.S. corporate investment (domestic and foreign) in that year
stood at just over 5%, the rate of return on foreign direct in-

----

[3]The 1973 figure excludes capital exported by the Soviet bloc.

vestment alone was over 14%, almost triple.[4,5]

This is important because the actual return on any given investment in a capitalist country is more determined by the average rate of profit for the capital of the whole nation than by its own particular organic composition. Marx explains in Volume 3 of *Capital* the process through which the rate of profit on various particular capitals fluctuates around the average rate of profit for capital as a whole. While each capital chases after the highest rate of profit, nevertheless behind its back its rate of profit is determined by the average rate throughout society. Thus the higher rate of return on the exported capital — a rate which results in significant part from the *superexploitation* of the proletariat in the colonial countries, who are paid wages far below the cost of their labor power — factors into the average rate of profit for the aggregate social capital of the "home" country and helps offset the

---

[4]The above figures are cited in the forthcoming *America in Decline: An Analysis of the Developments Toward War and Revolution, in the U.S. and World-wide, in the 1980s*, Banner Press, and come from *International Capital Movements During the Inter-War Period*, published by the UN Secretariat, Dept. of Economic Affairs; selected issues of the *Survey of Current Business*; data published by the Joint Economic Committee of the U.S. Congress; and "American Economic Interests in Foreign Countries," by Thomas E. Weisskopf, a paper published by the University of Michigan Center for Research on Economic Development.

[5]In their book *Global Reach*, Barnett and Müller reveal how the *real* rate of return of third world investment is hidden in official figures: "To get a true picture of the annual return on investment that a U.S.-based global corporation derives from its subsidiary in, say, a Latin American country, it is necessary to include in the calculation overpricing of imports and underpricing of exports as well as reported profits, royalties, and fees repatriated to the global headquarters. This total can then be divided into the declared net worth of the subsidiary. Vaitsos performed this exercise for fifteen wholly owned drug subsidiaries of U.S.- and European-based global corporations. He found the effective annual rate of return ranged from a low of 38.1 percent to a high of 962.1 percent with an average of 79.1 percent. Yet that year these firms' average declared profits submitted to the Colombian tax authorities was 6.7 percent. In the rubber industry the effective profit rate on the average was 43 percent; the declared profit rate, 16 percent. Vaitsos' investigations are corroborated by other studies which conclude that during the ...[1960s — LW] the *minimum* rate of return of U.S.-based manufacturing corporations in Latin America could not have been much below 40 percent.... Another and equally revealing approach has been taken by economists at the University of Lund, Sweden. In an analysis of 64 mining operations of U.S. companies in Peru between 1967 and 1969, they found that while the companies reported to the local government total profits of 60 million dollars, the declarations to the U.S. government on the identical operations showed profits of 102 million dollars." (*Global Reach*, Richard Barnett and Ronald Müller, Simon and Schuster, 1974, p. 160)

overall tendency for the rate of profit to fall.

Further, the capital exported to the colonial and dependent countries is often concentrated in raw materials and extractive industries — for example, oil in the Mideast, copper in Chile and Zambia, bauxite in Jamaica, tin in Bolivia, and on and on in what could be an almost endless roll call of countries whose resources are integrated into the circuits of imperialist capital. The super-exploitation of the workers also lowers the cost of the raw materials, and thus the proportion of capital invested in the category of constant capital relative to variable capital *throughout* all sectors of the imperialist economy falls, since the raw materials make up a significant part of the constant capital. In this way, too, the export of capital retards the tendency for the rate of profit of the social capital to fall, and *all* the capitalists in the imperialist country rely on this continued piracy.[6]

The opening of vast new areas of the world to capital export enhances the flexibility of capital; capital can now reorganize itself on an international basis. But this new ability is at the same time a *compulsion*, for it can *no longer* reorganize itself on a higher level within its national framework. The result then is not the endless mitigation, or resolution, of the contradictions inherent in capital, but especially as the entire world was divided up, their projection onto an international — and more far-reaching and potentially explosive — plane.

The plunder from the oppressed nations and regions of the world, then, is nothing short of *essential* to imperialism, and this greatly heightens the parasitical character of imperialist societies. The huge superprofits which flow from these areas into the coffers of finance capital are necessary to the continued functioning of *all* capital in the stage of imperialism, and are indispensable to the much vaunted and bragged about higher standard of living and stability in the imperialist countries. This parasitism finds expression in luxury industries, certain services, etc., whose entire

---

[6]In addition, the imperialists rely heavily on these countries for many strategic raw materials. The U.S. imports over 90% of its bauxite (the key alloy in aluminum), chromium (essential to jet fighters), cobalt (essential to jet engines), diamonds, graphite, manganese, mica, platinum, tantalum and strontium. In each case, the bulk of these imports come from third world countries — and in some cases, exclusively so. The military importance of these minerals, in turn, further compels the imperialists to secure and dominate these regions.

DIFFERENTIAL HOURLY WAGE RATES*
IN SELECTED INDUSTRIES,
OPPRESSED NATIONS VS. USA
(Based on a wage-rate study for 1966 and 1970)

| | Average Hourly Rate (in dollars) | |
	Oppressed Nations	USA
Consumer electronic products		
Hong Kong	0.27	3.13
Mexico	0.53	2.31
Taiwan	0.14	2.56
Office-machine Parts		
Hong Kong	0.30	2.92
Taiwan	0.38	3.67
Mexico	0.48	2.97
Semi-Conductors		
Korea	0.33	3.32
Singapore	0.29	3.36
Jamaica	0.30	2.23
Wearing Apparel		
Mexico	0.53	2.29
British Honduras	0.28	2.11
Costa Rica	0.34	2.28
Honduras	0.45	2.27
Trinidad	0.40	2.49

*Hourly wage rates for a given country and the USA are for comparable task and skill levels.

Source: G.K. Helleiner, "Manufactured Exports from Less-Developed Countries and the Multinational Firms," *Economic Journal*, March 1973, p. 21.

existence is predicated on plunder. Additionally, employment in the financial, commercial and state sectors balloons in order to facilitate the continued ability to enforce and carry out these international relations. Finally, and extremely critical, the huge military expenditures and entire industries devoted to the military also exist mainly and essentially to deal with both the resistance of the peoples of these countries and the challenges from their imperialist rivals; and in turn these military expenditures are only possible through feeding off the spoils that they ensure.[7]

In response to the militarization of the imperialist countries, some raise the demand to take the money away from military spending and channel it into better housing, health care, etc., for the masses — or, as it's often put, for "jobs not war." This actually promotes dangerous illusions and shares with Kautskyism the notion of an imperialist system, or bourgeois ruling class, capable of infinite maneuvering to "rearrange its priorities." As long as capitalism stays capitalist — that is, short of proletarian revolution — it has no option but to be militaristic, for it is ultimately military power which secures its preserves in the oppressed nations and enables it to contend with its rivals. Election year rhetoric to the contrary, guns vs. butter is simply not the choice; the gun is what ensures imperialism its ability to milk the superprofits from the oppressed nations of the world, combat its rivals. . .and spread a few crumbs.

Actually, as long as accumulation is on the upswing such military spending can stimulate the economy, and at least doesn't drain it. It is precisely the restructuring of capital achieved by the U.S. off of World War 2, and U.S. imperialism's consequent global domination — maintained with its military power — that enabled the U.S. bourgeoisie to both undertake infrastructure improvements like highway construction, public housing, etc., and

---

[7]As an example of the depth of militarism in imperialism: from 1945 to 1980, official military expenditures in the U.S. amounted to one trillion dollars; from 30% to 40% of scientists and engineers in the U.S. are employed directly or indirectly by the Department of Defense; and one out of ten workers in the manufacturing sector are producing goods for the military. As for the Soviet Union, U.S. government estimates place its military expenditures at 13-14% of its gross national product, a tremendous burden which can also be "made good" only by their use in a successful redivision of the world.

to extend concessions to the masses in the U.S., such as poverty programs, wage hikes, and increased "upward mobility," etc., especially from the '50s to the mid-'60s. To call, in whatever form, for a return to the "good old days" or to demand "jobs not war" *masks* the essential relations at the heart of imperialism that allow temporary booms and concessions, and that make possible the higher standard of living among the masses in the advanced countries. And such a slogan can only lead, whatever the intentions of those who raise it or are rallied behind it, to channeling the masses of the oppressed within the imperialist countries — who have a powerful basis to unite with revolutionary struggles raging in the oppressed nations and in the other imperialist citadels — away from that international unity and into ultimately fighting for a strengthened position for "their" bourgeoisies during imperialist war. The example of Kautsky himself, who went from notions of a reformable imperialism into justifying the lining up of the workers of the imperialist nations behind World War 1, shows the dangers of this sort of seemingly innocuous slogan ("jobs not war"), and more than that the line underlying it.

Imperialism: Not Just "Capitalism on a World Scale"

While imperialism is a *world process*, it is far more than "capitalism on a world scale." That is, imperialism is not the sum total of the many different capitalist countries, or the emergence of all countries into capitalist development, but is truly a new and higher stage of development of the process. Consider the leap in biological evolution from single-cell organisms to multi-cell organisms. The multi-cell organism is not just an agglomeration or federation of single cells, each of which carries on its processes in much the same way as before, but is a higher level of biological organization, with a division of labor between cells. The function and development of each individual cell is basically determined by the development of the contradictory processes of the organism overall (processes which are of a qualitatively different character than that of a single cell). Of course, individual cells and organs still contain particular contradictions, and the developments in one of course play a role in and have an influence on the overall development; still, they are subordinate to and integrated within something on a much higher level.

Imperialism represents a roughly analogous leap, and must not be mainly analyzed from the standpoint of its individual organs (i.e., for the purposes of analogy, the internal contradictions of particular nations) but principally from the dynamics of the whole organism.

Yes, capital is introduced into the oppressed nations, and capitalist social relations develop (in a distorted form); but this hardly signals the embarkation of these countries on a road of development just like, or even remotely similar to, the courses taken by the original capitalist countries. Nor does it mean that industrialization of these countries through capital export is "closing the gap" between the advanced capitalist countries and the so-called underdeveloped ones. In fact, the very term "underdevelopment" serves to mask the essence of the matter here, as it lends itself to the idea that the problem is purely one of a slight delay or lag in a timetable, i.e., that the relationship is quantitative alone. This is far from the truth. While there is tremendous quantitative inequality in development between the advanced and "backward" countries, (itself enforced in large part by imperialism) this flows from the *qualitative* character of the relationship.

Capital takes root in the oppressed nations, but it takes root as extensions of the finance capital of the imperialist countries. Within the oppressed nations capitalism does not develop as an integral cohesive system, with the different sectors of capital developing in a roughly proportional way, as it did in the original capitalist countries. To take one important aspect of this, Marx, in analyzing reproduction of capital within a capitalist economy, attaches great importance to the proportionality between the sector of the economy that produces consumer goods and that which produces means of production. This contradiction is very important to the development and dynamism of the capitalist economies (as well as an important source of fragility and crisis). While even in the capitalist countries this proportionality is only approximate and rough, and, anarchy-ridden, develops through jolts and dislocations, in the oppressed nations these sectors don't even achieve a *rough* proportionality.

What *does* happen in Pakistan, Nigeria or Indonesia, for example, is something quite different. There the phenomenon of *disarticulation* occurs — that is, distorted and one-sided development, in which the economies of the oppressed nations are consigned to a very particular role in an international division of labor conditioned by the needs of finance capital based in the imperialist nations. Regions of these oppressed nations often exist in relative isolation and disconnectedness from one another, with rapid development in one part and total stagnation in another; the development of transport and communication is to a large extent conditioned by the needs of commercial intercourse with the imperialist powers; and the different sectors stressed by Marx develop in a stunted, disconnected and incohesive way.[8]

Further, the surplus value that is sucked out of these areas flows back into the finance capital based in the imperialist countries, and it is reinvested according to the global needs of that capital, and not according to the needs of all-around development of the oppressed nation. It becomes part of the huge pool of surplus value controlled by finance capital that is shifted from place to place, sector to sector, country to country, continent to continent, in pursuit of the highest rate of profit.

Beyond the incredible volume of capital exported to the oppressed nations in the form of direct investment, and the surplus value removed on that basis, the role of lending and debt is extremely important — both as a form of capital export, and as a means of ensnaring these countries more deeply into the net of exploitative relations. Operating both through private banks and international institutions like the World Bank, finance capital lends money for various enterprises and development projects, etc.; in conjunction with this, through lending institutions like the International Monetary Fund, the domestic policies and financial structures of these countries are forceably brought into conformity with the needs of imperialist capital and expansion. The importance of all this is partially reflected in the total debt of the "underdeveloped countries" to imperialist institutions of the Western bloc alone — which in 1982 was close to $300 billion! Because of the size of the loans, and because of the whole international web of political and economic relations in which they occur

---

[*]To take one stark example, though efforts were made to join Senegal and The Gambia into a single political unit ("Senegambia") in 1981, these adjacent African nations are more closely connected to their respective imperialist patrons (France and Britain) than to each other; that is, it is easier to catch a plane or place a phone call from Senegal to France, than it is from Senegal to The Gambia, or even from one part of Senegal to another.

(and which they reinforce), the lending institutions are able to determine the actual uses to which loans are put — thus projects and contracts serving the interests and needs of finance capital alone are undertaken. Further, in many of these countries, especially in the last two decades, a cycle has arisen in which increasingly higher percentages of the borrowing country's gross national product, and even of the new loans it must take out, are paid out merely as *interest* on their debt.

The effect of this can be seen in the case of Mexico. As of 1979 its foreign debt was $33 billion; three years later it had leaped to an estimated $85 billion![9] Of every dollar *borrowed*, 81¢ must go right back to pay interest on what was previously borrowed! Whatever currency is earned through export must also be applied to debt payments. In human terms this means, to take just one manifestation, that over half of the winter vegetables on the tables of the U.S. are grown in Mexico, while over 40% of all Mexicans suffer malnutrition. And these figures are from before the 1982 peso crisis and the consequent austerity program demanded by imperialism.

When countries cannot pay their interest on time (an increasingly common phenomenon), the banks and international financial institutions demand and get an even higher degree of direct control of the currency arrangements, investment policies and government spending of these countries in return for "rescheduling" (i.e., postponing the due date of) the debt. What follows are slashing attacks on the masses' standard of living, devaluations and all-around attempts to intensify the superexploitation of the masses and recreate the basis for profitable accumulation.

The third world economies are reduced to "junkie economies" — totally dependent on fixes from finance capital to just keep staggering along, purchased with the lifeblood and futures of the masses of the country. Volumes have been filled (and should be studied) detailing the crimes of the "everyday" functioning of imperialism in the third world. Here we will focus on two examples which in their different ways bring out the content of imperialist domination.

---

[9]This huge increase illustrates not only the importance of such debt, but how *rapidly* the crisis is escalating.

The Cases of Zaire and Brazil

Zaire is a land rich in copper, cobalt, zinc, diamonds and other minerals, but its 23 million people live in some of the most wretched conditions in the world. Colonized by Belgium in the late 1800s, kept in a state of forced illiteracy and backwardness, with the masses dispossessed of their land and driven to work in mines that were little better than graves, Zaire — or the Belgian Congo — was a keg of dynamite which finally exploded in rebellion in 1958. By 1960 Belgium was forced to promise independence, as the forces of revolutionary nationalist leader Patrice Lumumba swept through the country. That summer the U.S. bloc, with Soviet cooperation, had UN troops sent to the Congo to suppress Lumumba and shift power to more pliant and pro-imperialist forces; in February of 1961, Lumumba was murdered by the CIA, and within several years the unabashed U.S. puppet Mobutu Sese Seko consolidated his grip on Zaire.

As Mobutu "stabilized" Zaire through building up the army (with U.S. and Israeli aid) and repressing dissent, imperialist capital again began to flow into the country. In the early '70s Bankers Trust lent Zaire $25 million, and as the price of Zaire's main export, copper, rose, more followed. A series of loans from banking syndicates from various imperialist powers — Citibank from the U.S., the French Societé Generale, the British Morgan Grenfel — were made, and the U.S. Export-Import Bank financed a 1000-mile power line from the Atlantic Ocean to the copper mines.

But in 1974-75 the most serious economic crisis of the post-World War 2 years (up to that time) ripped through the Western imperialist bloc. Copper collapsed to one-third its previous price. In June of 1975 Zaire stopped payment of the interest on its debts. While Zaire at the time only owed $400 million to foreign banks — a small sum by current standards — that still was enough to put its main lender, Citibank, in a highly vulnerable position. A default would have seriously threatened Citibank and could possibly have started a crisis of confidence in the whole international credit system, leading to its collapse.

Thus a cycle began in the mid-'70s in which Zaire's creditors continually agreed to stretch out its loans, only for Zaire to once more fail to meet its obligations when the notes fell due. But all this was taking place at a time when the rivalry between the U.S. and Soviet blocs had begun to seriously intensify and express itself in a series of bloody proxy wars. While the Zairean economy was collapsing in shambles, and the conditions for the masses were spiraling downwards — by 1980 food prices had gone up 540% in four years, real wages and salaries were 60% below their 1970 level, and much of the population was literally starving — the Soviet Union sponsored its own move into Zaire. They used an army of former residents of the mineral-rich Katanga (or Shaba) Province. Many of them had previously fought for the Belgian colonialists against Patrice Lumumba; later, in the mid-'70s they were hired by the Portuguese to suppress resistance to their rule in Angola. Now, trained by Cuban advisors, they marched out of Angola and pushed the Zairean army out of Katanga. Immediately Moroccan troops were flown into Katanga by the French Air Force and fought the exile army to a stalemate.

Meanwhile, the whole country descended further into chaos. All payments on Zaire's debt (continually growing as it was being stretched out by its Western creditors) again stopped; and this time the International Monetary Fund insisted on sending in its own man, a West German, Erwin Blumental, *to take direct control* of the Zaire Central Bank. Mobutu readily agreed. Shortly thereafter the Katangan secessionists again went on the offensive, and this time French and Belgian troops invaded to restore order.

As the crisis deepened, Mobutu's puppet strings to the West were pulled still tighter, while the imperialists' fortunes were even more deeply linked to maintaining a regime that was threatening to explode either politically, economically or both, and tear a gaping hole in the carefully woven fabric of the "Free World." In 1978 the Belgians came in to train the Zairean army; in the same year the West Germans took a lease on a sizeable chunk of territory for missile testing. By 1979 Zaire's total debt had risen to $3 billion and inflation was running at an annual rate of 200%.

Zaire — where the stability of the Western imperialist international credit system totters; where both blocs joined to crush a revolutionary nationalist movement of the early '60s while today military *conflict* between those blocs periodically erupts; and where the wealth of the country has flowed out in an unending stream over the last hundred and more years while the masses have been subject to grueling exploitation, enforced backwardness and squalor — Zaire is indeed a concentration of the character of imperialist sponsored "development."

Still, even the imperialists and their spokesmen will often admit that "there are problems" in Zaire (they can hardly deny it), while of course disclaiming responsibility. So let us turn to one of the countries which they consider a "showcase" — Brazil.

Brazil has a high rate of growth. It is the seventh largest automobile manufacturer and has the tenth largest economy overall in the U.S. bloc. All this has been dubbed the "Brazilian miracle" by its U.S. promoters.

In 1964 the Brazilian president, Joao Goulart, apparently heading for some petty reforms to placate the masses who were rising in rebellion, was overthrown by the military. The U.S. has long acknowledged its involvement in this overthrow, even down to the provision of the trucks by the Hannah Mining Co. for the troops that launched the coup. Of course, far more decisive than the trucks was both the role of the CIA in orchestrating the political campaign leading up to the coup and the close ties that had been forged between the U.S. and Brazilian militaries.[10]

With the coup the U.S. made sure that transformations necessary for renewed expansion of capital would be carried out decisively in Brazil. These changes were part of the Alliance for Progress orientation of the time (which was also applied far beyond Latin America), which entailed breaking up some of the backward and stagnant social relations in the oppressed nations that stood in the way of more extensive and intensive capital accumulation. After 1964, as the Brazilian military carried out repression and torture on a wide scale, and as wages were cut, a massive influx of loans and advisers began (and not from the U.S. alone, as others like West Germany and Italy also moved in). In 1968, the "miracle" had taken off. Brazil began production of cars, refrigerators and other consumer goods for the international market in a big way.

---

[10]A rather bald admission from the chairman of the House Foreign Affairs Committee at the time of the coup: "Every critic of foreign aid is confronted with the fact that the armed forces of Brazil threw out the Goulart government and that U.S. military aid was a major factor in giving these forces an indoctrination in the principles of democracy and a pro-U.S. orientation. Many of these officers were trained in the U.S. under the AID program." The representative was, of course, speaking in favor of more of the same.

But the more that development under the aegis of finance capital proceeded, the more extensively did distortion and disarticulation reproduce themselves. While auto boomed, production was virtually entirely foreign owned and a considerable portion of it geared for export. The technical requirements of many such "boom" sectors had to be met in large measure through imports — adding to the country's debt burden, while much of this technology has limited applicability outside these sectors. At the same time, the state oversaw costly infrastructural investments (also requiring foreign loans) to support these sectors. Brazil was integrated into these already existing imperialist dominated industries in an international division of labor.(One social consequence of this was the polarization of wages between workers in the "boom" sectors and those in other sectors.) *Business Week* magazine, in a blatant 1976 "special report" entitled "Reversal of Policy: Latin America Opens the Door to Foreign Investment Again," (sic!) noted in relation to Brazil that the real wages of the lowest 80% of the population "have been steadily dropping since 1964 — the year the generals took over — despite a tripling of the gross national product to $80 billion." That would seem to make the "miracle" one of trans-substantiation — not, in this case, water into wine, but the blood of the masses into the superprofits of imperialism.

Things were also happening in the rural areas with the "reforms" of the Alliance for Progress. Companies such as Volkswagen and Swift Meat Packing were given big tax write-offs when they purchased land. In one incident an Italian company was allowed to buy six million acres of land in the territory of the Xavantas Indians; 60 Indians were killed when they resisted eviction.

In fact, the gap between industry and agriculture widened sharply, with a large portion of the Brazilian people existing totally outside of the money economy. The expropriations that were carried out produced millions of landless peasants, many of whom were driven to the cities in a futile search for work. Some areas of the country, especially northeast Brazil where 35 million people live, were more or less written off, drained of resources, and allowed to rot.

Such were the boom years of 1968 to 1974. But Brazil, now integrated into the imperialist world economy in a big way, found itself especially hard hit by the international economic crisis of the Western bloc of the mid- and late-'70s. By 1980, 75% of Brazil's export earnings were going for foreign debt payoffs. 100% inflation wracked the economy. Rebellion and repression (including significant stirrings among the rapidly expanded Brazilian proletariat in the cities, and the Indians in the countryside) both intensified.[11]

But any collapse of the "Brazilian miracle" would have ramifications far beyond its borders. To note only *some* of the economic stakes involved, both Chase Manhattan Bank and Citibank (two pillars of the U.S. and Western imperialist banking system and finance capital) draw fully 10% of their income from Brazil! And the *political* shocks of a major crisis in Brazil would reverberate all the more powerfully; consider the effect when Iran, itself a former "miracle" and "island of stability in a sea of turmoil" (to quote Jimmy Carter), exploded in revolution in the wake of a crisis brought on by a similar development process.

Brazil is certainly a showcase, then — one that exhibits the distortions generated by the export of capital and domination by finance capital, and the criminal character of these relations. But both Brazil and Zaire also reflect how intertwined the world system of imperialism now is, how inextricably linked are the fates of the different countries, how essentially fragile and vulnerable to shock the imperialist system is.

All this shows the cycle of ever deeper imperialist involvement in these countries as long as they are enmeshed in the web of finance capital; but this ever deeper involvement and dependency also creates its opposite. For one thing, even with the disarticulation and distortion, capital here still creates its essential product . . . the proletariat, its gravediggers. "The export of capital," wrote Lenin, "affects and greatly accelerates the development of capitalism in those countries to which it is exported." It expands and deepens "the further development of capitalism throughout the world." (*Imperialism*, 76) The growth and tempering of the proletariat in the oppressed nations, especially since World War 2, is a profoundly significant development.

---

[11]In January, 1983, Brazil announced its inability to repay principal due on its extensive foreign debt — by then estimated at over $90 billion.

Further, the measures taken by the imperialists to intensify their superexploitation of the oppressed nations themselves turn into their opposites, as indicated in the discussion of Brazil. In the area of credit and debt, for example, a draft document (*Basic Principles*) prepared by the the Revolutionary Communist Party of Chile and the Revolutionary Communist Party, USA, notes that:

> [T]his is a double-edged sword the imperialists are holding: after a certain point the bankruptcy or near bankruptcy of many of these countries becomes a threat to the whole financial structure of the imperialists themselves, and beyond that the increased suffering of broad sections of the masses is bound to and does give rise to increased and more powerful rebellion. And yet the imperialists can in no way let go of this sword. (*Basic Principles,* 10, para. 50)

Rivalry and Redivision: Imperialism Means War

The export of capital goes on within a framework conditioned by the economic, political and military power of the contending imperialists and the struggle between them. But this framework is *limited*, and the imperialists encounter obstacles and barriers to continued extended reproduction. It is limited by the revolutionary struggles of the masses of the oppressed nations and the continued class antagonisms in the imperialists' home base, and it is limited as well (as is shown in the examples of Brazil and Zaire) by the inability of capital to indefinitely stave off tendencies to overproduction and the boomerang effects of the very measures they take to escape it. Beyond that, the imperialists run up against the power and prerogatives — and *compulsions* — of their rivals as obstacles to their own continued accumulation.

Which capitals will be exported where, and on what terms? How will monetary and credit arrangements be determined? Which regimes in what regions will be built up to play certain economic and political roles, how exactly will they be integrated into the imperialist division of labor, and in the service of which imperialist power? These issues are critical to the different national capitals of the imperialist countries, and they can ultimately be decided only through force. The terms of capital export in a world that is more or less totally divided — and the world was first divided among the imperialists by the beginning of this century — are set by the relative political and military power of the different capitalist states and arrived at through *struggle* between them.

This interimperialist rivalry inevitably tends toward war. It is true, of course, that the imperialists are not *continually* warring on one another; they do draw up treaties, hold conferences, and otherwise "peacefully" divide the world (though with force always the final arbiter). But the antagonism underlying every imperialist carving of the world inevitably asserts itself. Lenin, refuting Kautsky's argument that a peaceful and permanent division of the world between the imperialist powers was possible, exposed the basis for "peaceful" division:

> Let us assume that *all* the imperialist countries conclude an alliance for the "peaceful" division of . . . Asia, . . . this alliance would be an alliance of "internationally united finance capital." There are actual examples of alliances of this kind in the history of the twentieth century, for instance, the attitude of the powers to China. We ask, is it "conceivable," assuming that the capitalist system remains intact — and this is precisely the assumption that Kautsky does make — that such alliances would be more than temporary, that they would eliminate friction, conflicts and struggle in every possible form?
>
> It is sufficient to state this question clearly to make it impossible for any reply to be given other than in the negative; for any other basis under capitalism for the division of spheres of influence, of interests, of colonies, etc., than a calculation of the *strength* of the participants in the division, their general economic, financial, military strength, etc., is *in*conceivable. And the strength of these participants in the division does not change to an equal degree, for the *even* development of different undertakings, trusts, branches of industry, or countries is impossible under capitalism. Half a century ago Germany was a miserable, insignificant country, as far as her capitalist strength was concerned, compared with the strength of England at that time; Japan was the same compared with Russia. Is it "conceivable" that in ten or twenty years' time the relative strength of the imperialist powers will have remained *un*changed? Absolutely inconceivable. (*Imperialism*, 143-144)

Lenin went on to characterize imperialist alliances and agreements as:

> . . .*in*evitably nothing more than a "truce" in periods between wars. Peaceful alliances prepare the ground for wars, and in their turn grow out of wars; the one conditions the other, giving rise to

alternating forms of peaceful and non-peaceful struggle out of *one and the same* basis of imperialist connections and relations within world economics and world politics. (*Imperialism*, 144-145)

This tendency to war is not reducible to a matter of one imperialist power or bloc growing faster than another, or wanting to flex its muscles or get its due. The imperialists are driven to war by a complex of factors — including the viability of their capital circuits, the stability of their military and political positions (including their grip on the masses in their home bases), as well as the changes in their *relative* strengths (and weaknesses). War can be just as necessary to the more established power as to the new "up-and-coming" one; each is driven to overcome the barriers to expansion and to redivide the world at the expense of the other. In sum, many factors work to upset the relative equilibrium between imperialist powers forged at certain points (including after interimperialist wars), and to give these periods of peace the character of temporary truces.

The Fundamental Contradiction Under Imperialism

In the stage of imperialism, war is the only means to break through the obstacles to continued capitalist accumulation and expansion, and to set a new framework for accumulation; in this, war is integral to the workings of the whole system in a way beyond its earlier (and important) role during the reign of industrial capital, and before that, merchant capital.

While there still exists the motion toward economic crisis characteristic of competitive capitalism, these crises no longer play the same purgative role as before. On the one hand, through the more centralized character of finance capital (including the heightened role of the state) and due to the export of capital especially to the oppressed nations, capital can to a certain extent ameliorate these crises for certain periods of time; on the other hand, this really only has the effect of transferring the contradictions to a higher level and making the eventual explosion all the more destructive. Further, when these economic crises do occur on a devastating scale, they do not serve as before to more or less thoroughly clear the decks for a new expansion; thus the stagnation of the Great Depression never really broke, and only World War 2 and its outcome made possible the necessary restructuring.

Thus far interimperialist war, and specifically the new relations established through this all-out violent confrontation between imperialists, has objectively functioned as the mechanism which has both ruptured the old framework of accumulation and set the terms for a new one. Again, this is *not* in some sort of Kautskyite sense that views war as one option, perhaps among several, that the imperialists choose in order to stimulate the economy (though it sometimes, especially in the early stages, has that effect), but in its objective role in forcibly clearing the decks of inefficient capitals, restructuring value relations and centralizing capital to a higher degree, and giving the victorious power the temporary strength and flexibility to begin a new round of world accumulation. On the other hand, neither is war some sort of mechanically determined economic act. What has happened historically is that the different imperialist powers increasingly confront a situation in which not only is their share of the world no longer sufficient to maintain and expand the reproduction of capital, but their rivals also face similar severe pressure, and *each* is driven both to expand and to defend what they already have. At a certain stage the needs of the imperialist power in conjunction with its position vis-à-vis its rival make war imperative, and the imperialists try to undertake such a war — which today will almost undoubtedly include large-scale exchange of nuclear weapons with all their attendant horror — on what they calculate as the most favorable possible terms for their victory. It's important here to note that the Kautskyite portrait that endows the imperialists with more or less absolute free will in deciding to go to war (often ascribing war to the war-like nature of this or that imperialist politician or power, or to their blunders, or, again, to some sort of scheme to "boost profits") implies a flip side picture of a reasonable bourgeois representative who can be appealed to to stop such a destructive thing in his own class interest. This covers over the fact that while the imperialists indeed have a will, they exercise it — *all* of them — within the very narrow parameters set by the workings of the system they sit atop, and in particular they must do whatever is required to enable the capital that they represent to continue — or renew — its cycle of expansion.

(One important current expression of the Kautskyite denial of the compulsion driving the imperialists is the widespread view that while all may not be right with the Soviet Union, and while it may pursue policies that could only be called great-power chauvinist, it is after all *not* imperialist, and does not *have* to either weld together a bloc or go to war with its rival. This, too, denies the compulsory laws at the bottom of the drive to war.)

To grasp more clearly the dynamics driving imperialism into interimperialist war, let's look at World War 2. This was not a scheme to increase production . . . still less was it a battle on the part of the Allies to "defend democracy" (or of the Axis to "barbarize" the world); rather this war grew out of the inability of all the imperialist powers to carry out accumulation on a profitable scale within the confines of the world's division at the time. Each needed to go to war, and each embarked on it with its own clearly defined and imperialist objectives (even if those objectives changed in part under the force of circumstances and development); and the result was six years of war and the murder of 50 million people before a winner emerged and capital could decisively restructure itself — this time under the extraordinarily centralized control of the U.S. — and set a framework for another round of extended accumulation. This is shown, for example, by internal memos and articles of the Council on Foreign Relations (a U.S. imperialist foreign policy "think tank") in the late '30s; these frankly addressed the inability of the U.S. to continue to operate within its former spheres of influence, and outlined the need for the U.S. to integrate the Pacific and most of the then-British Empire into its domain (as well as posing suggestions on how to portray the war for public consumption).[12]

The crucial way that interimperialist war — as well as political and military struggle generally, not to mention revolution — affects the accumulation of capital points to the important intensification of the role of politics and nation-states under imperialism, and the much more fluid interpenetration between politics and economics. The state becomes much more central to

---

[12] See "Shaping a New World: The Council on Foreign Relations Blueprint for World Hegemony, 1939-1945," Shoupe and Minter, in *Trilateralism*, ed., Holly Sklar, South End Press, 1980.

the accumulation process; it not only intervenes to aid the further centralization of capital, but also mounts a huge bureaucracy, army, etc., to enforce imperialism's parasitical rule in the colonies and contend with its rivals.

All this is bound up with the heightened internationalization of capital, and its need and ability to straddle national borders. But this doesn't mean that capital has transcended the nation — or still less, become "disloyal" to it — as one tenacious opportunist line holds. Capital clutches the national flag more firmly than ever.

For one thing, capital is not an ideal; it exists in the material world, and its worldwide manipulations serve a circuit that continues to be rooted in the imperialist nation. It needs its base of operations. Thus attention is paid to maintaining vital industries in the home base in a certain condition even at great expense or loss. Capital must contend internationally with *national* strength; political and/or economic erosion in the home base carries a great risk. It's hardly as if "they don't care about the people at home" — no, they pay great attention to trying to tie "the people at home" to the national flag in one way or another so as to gain popular support for actions in the international arena, including the threat and actual use of military force. And the essential political-military conflicts among the imperialists have not taken the form of different blocs of finance capital mounting their own private armies, buying and stationing (or using) missiles and nuclear warheads, etc.; rather this is done by the imperialist states (and alliances of these states), through war and military force which clearly have a decisive influence on the existence and reproduction of these blocs of finance capital.

All this in no way negates the *economic* basis underlying imperialism, but it makes clear that this should not be narrowly construed. During the brutal and truly genocidal U.S. war against Vietnam, for example, some forces on the left began to claim that the real cause of U.S. aggression was its desire to control suspected oilfields off the coast of Vietnam. While intended to expose U.S. imperialist motives in this war, this explanation ended up being narrow, economist and reformist, in that it ultimately reduced the war — an extremely important watershed event in world history — to the interests of the "oil companies." In fact, what was at stake for U.S. imperialism in Indochina, and this was revealed openly by the *Pentagon Papers,* was its fear that the example of Vietnam would spread to other countries, inspiring liberation struggles with redoubled intensity throughout the third world (which in fact it did) and would generally shake U.S. political hegemony in the world. The U.S. aims in Vietnam flowed out of the entire empire and system that it had set up coming off of World War 2, based on its superior political and military strength; and the impact and shocks of the Vietnamese people's struggle extended way beyond Vietnam, beyond even the third world. It influenced and interpenetrated with the renewal of revolutionary struggle within the U.S. and other imperialist powers, the beginning of the crumbling of the U.S. monetary agreements with Europe in the late '60s, the increased opportunity for the Soviet Union to push out and more aggressively pursue its imperialist interests, and the beginning phase of crisis and stagnation within the Western bloc. In fact, Vietnam was pivotal in heightening the contradictions throughout the world.

The Fundamental Contradiction

Imperialism, as we have emphasized, is a system in transition to something higher; but the very anarchy that drives forward the socialization of the productive forces on a world scale (if in a distorted form) also reproduces barriers to continued accumulation. And the growing complexity and convolution of capital, arising from the machinations it must undertake to continue its reproduction, make the entire structure that much more vulnerable.

At bottom, imperialism cannot escape the contradictions inherent in the basic form of the commodity. The huge superstructure of credit, state intervention, financial manipulation, political rivalry, military conflict, etc., rests on the foundation of the production and exchange of commodities produced by socialized labor but appropriated privately. And these commodities must be *sold* in order for the value and surplus value which they contain to be realized. Here, then, is a simple but potentially explosive contradiction. For while a commodity must be sold in order for its value to be realized, there is no guarantee it will be sold. If the time between the production and sale of a commodity becomes too great, if, in the words of Marx, "the split between the sale and the purchase becomes too pronounced, the intimate connection between them, their oneness, asserts itself by producing — a crisis." And Marx went on to say that:

> The antithesis, use-value and value; the contradictions that private labour is bound to manifest itself as direct social labour, that a particularised concrete kind of labour has to pass for abstract human labour; the contradiction between the personification of objects and the representation of persons by things; all these antitheses and contradictions, which are immanent in commodities, assert themselves, and develop their modes of motion, in the antithetical phases of the metamorphosis of a commodity. These modes therefore imply the possibility, and no more than the possibility, of crises. The conversion of this mere possibility into a reality is the result of a long series of relations.... (*Capital*, Vol. 1, 114)

That "long series of relations" has developed in a spiral-like form that led from competitive capitalism into imperialism, in which the globally socialized productive forces strain against the capitalist shell — with its added weight of parasitism — that contains them. The crises implied in the germ of a single commodity now assert themselves with incredible power and destructive force. But the anarchic drive which has lent capital its unprecedented dynamism has in essence done nothing but cast dragon teeth into the soil of every corner of the planet, from which spring the gravediggers of capital itself. Engels' powerful statement — that "it is the motive force of the social anarchy of production which increasingly transforms the great majority of men into proletarians, and it is the proletarian masses in their turn who will ultimately put an end to the anarchy of production" (*Anti-Dühring*, 352) — expresses itself under imperialism especially on a world scale in an epoch of war and revolution. And while revolutionary upsurges ebb and flow, at no time since the leap to imperialism has the world been quiet.

The elimination of bourgeois social relations by proletarian revolution and the forging of a qualitatively higher form of society — communism — on a world scale is a process still in its infancy, but through the tortuous and zig-zag development of wars and revolutions of the last 80-100 years, the fundamental contradiction of the bourgeois epoch has moved closer to resolution. The productive forces have become more massive and socialized through each round, and the expressions of anarchy more severe and wrenching; the proletariat, even as it has proceeded through spirals of revolutionary advances and bitter setbacks, has through it all tempered itself, constantly gained new legions from all over the world and discovered and absorbed important principles and lessons concerning the task of the revolutionary transformation of society.

What are the dynamics involved in the working out of the fundamental contradiction of bourgeois society? What are the components of the whole process that revolutionaries are trying to advance, and therefore must understand? During its polemics with Soviet revisionism in the early '60s, the Chinese Communist Party pointed to four main contradictions that had emerged with imperialism. These include the contradiction between the imperialist powers and the nations they oppress; the contradictions among the imperialist powers themselves; the contradiction between the bourgeoisie and proletariat within the imperialist countries; and the contradiction between imperialism and socialist countries (when they exist). Other contradictions, of course, also exist and at times play exceedingly important roles; but the unfolding and interpenetration of these four contradictions forms the main content of the development of the fundamental contradiction of the bourgeois epoch. At any time, one or another of these contradictions may be principal, that is, one of these contradictions will overall influence the development of the others more than it in turn is influenced by them, and this contradiction will then most determine (and is the main, if partial, expression of) the working out of the fundamental contradiction at any given stage. This relation, however, is fluid; contradictions interact and shift in their relations, they transform one another even as they run up against certain relative limits in their own unfolding, and nodal points occur when the formerly principal contradiction reaches a certain point of resolution (or mitigation) and is superseded by a new principal contradiction.

We have already touched on how the contradiction between anarchy and organization finds concentrated expression in imperialism in the rivalry and wars between imperialists; but there is another form of motion involved in the fundamental contradiction as well — the revolutionary class struggle — and the transition to imperialism has profound effects on that too. The contradictions between imperialism and the oppressed nations, and between the proletariat and the bourgeoisie within the imperialist countries, become intertwined and their changed character and relation with one another are critically important to grasp.[13]

With imperialism, capital is exported on a large scale to the backward countries, and that very export integrates the entire society into the matrix of international capital, stimulates the development of the proletariat, and draws the masses in those countries into *world* history. Their struggles and resistance now take place on the stage of a single international process, and assume a tremendously important role in this process. Further, many of these countries (despite the export of capital) continue in the main to contain feudal (or semi-feudal) relations and — though this is contradictory — imperialism often allies with and props up elements of the feudal ruling classes in concert with a stratum of bureaucrat-capitalists (who have amassed fortunes by virtue of their government positions and their service to imperialism, e.g., the Marcos family, the Somozas, Mobutu, etc.) to suppress the masses and secure the country for imperialist exploitation. At other times, the imperialists may actually go against the interests of the feudal lords (for instance, in many of the "reform" programs of the '60s and early '70s in the third world) when they stand in the way of transformations necessary for the expansion of capital.

But in any case national capitalist development is blocked, the peasantry is suppressed and denied land, and the reforms and transformations of relations characteristic of the bourgeois-democratic revolution are held back or violently aborted. Thus imperialism not only creates detachments of the international proletariat in these countries, but in its suppression of the aspiring native bourgeoisies (and the intelligentsias generally attached to them) and its exacerbation of the already crushing burdens on the peasantries, it creates revolutionary tinderboxes in the form of national liberation struggles in the oppressed regions of the world. In these countries the struggle is as yet generally at the bourgeois-democratic stage, but in new historical and world conditions; imperialist domination brings imperialism itself squarely into the sights of this struggle. National liberation struggles which aim at the expropriation of foreign capital and the total ouster of im-

---

[13]The contradiction between imperialist and socialist countries will be treated in the next chapter as part of the discussion of the dictatorship of the proletariat.

perialism (as well as those sections of domestic capital and the landowning classes that serve as props and agents for imperialism); at the breaking up of feudal relations generally and the distribution of land to the tiller; and at the general razing of backward institutions, ideas and so on associated with, implanted or propped up by imperialism — these struggles have, since the turn of the century, struck increasingly powerful blows at world imperialism.

And again, as stated earlier, the development of these countries, uneven and distorted as it may be under imperialist domination, still leads to a growth and concentration of the proletariat. This, combined with the experience and tempering of the proletariat internationally in the years following the emergence of imperialism, has laid the basis for the proletariat to lead a united front of various oppressed classes and strata in these struggles for national liberation and to carry the mass struggle forward to a second, socialist stage. (And in fact, unless the proletariat does assume leadership in this way, it is highly unlikely that even the stage of national liberation can be basically consolidated and carried through — these countries cannot be developed on a capitalist basis without becoming inextricably entangled in the pervasive imperialist relations that govern the world market, once again on a subordinate basis.)[14] Thus the oppressed nations of the world can be transformed through revolution from the crucial preserves of capital to revolutionary base areas of the international proletariat and oppressed peoples.

These struggles, therefore, even when and if not initially led by the proletariat, hold critical importance for the international proletariat. Lenin particularly struggled against the chauvinist trend in the working class movement in the advanced countries that either failed to support or straight-up opposed these struggles, and repeatedly emphasized that:

> The revolutionary movement in the advanced countries would in fact be nothing but a sheer fraud if, in their struggle against capital, the workers of Europe and America were not closely and completely united with the hundreds upon hundreds of millions of "col-

---

[14]This is discussed, for instance, in *On New Democracy*, by Mao; see also "On the People's Democratic Dictatorship," *MSW*, Vol. 4, 411-425.

onial'' slaves, who are oppressed by that capital. (''The Second Congress of the Communist International,'' *LCW*, Vol. 31, 271)

Lenin's point is all the more pressing in light of the profound
ways in which the leap to imperialism alters the character of the
struggle within the imperialist countries themselves. Within
these citadels are highly-developed transportation and communication systems, as well as far better health care, cultural and
educational services than exist in the third world. Also, within the
more parasitical sections of the imperialist economy — finance,
government, advertising, etc. — opportunities open up for people
to advance, and the booty from the oppressed regions provides
the basis for a relatively big petty bourgeoisie to carve a niche.
Further, to the extent that they can muster it, the imperialists
want ''peace'' in the home front to carry out their international
plunder, and thus are willing (when they can) to grant concessions
in wages, etc., to a significant section of the working class (combined, of course, with the club and gun, especially for the lower,
less privileged sections of the proletariat). All this amounts to an
objective bribe, and forms the basis both for a significant minority
of the proletariat to become a sort of labor aristocracy (which
tends strongly to think and act as a social base for its own bourgeoisie *against* the masses internationally), and for even broader
sections to become temporarily (if also significantly) bourgeoisified in their outlook and actions in periods of relative stability and
prosperity. The core of this labor aristocracy generally resides in
the highly skilled (and rather individualized) trades. These
workers, numbering in the millions in a country like the U.S.,
receive a significant cut of the blood-soaked crumbs of imperialist
plunder. Further, the influence of this section combined with the
transformation of the unions into chauvinist bourgeois political
machines, as well as the ability of the imperialists to also temporarily pass crumbs along to workers in basic industry — all this
has given rise to a significant bourgeois ''pole'' within the working class of the advanced countries.[15] While sections of this social

---

[15]A grotesque but not atypical example of the wretched outlook promoted by the
union officials, in this case at the local levels, was found in the Jan. 7, 1982 *New
York Times*. We quote: ''[The] financial secretary of Local 599 of the U.A.W. in
Flint, Mich., an important leader of the rank and file, said he was opposed to con-
cessions unless they were accompanied by concessions from the auto companies.
'My way of thinking is, if I'm going to give you something, then I expect something

base — especially of the more temporarily bourgeoisified workers — will no doubt be won over to revolution (and more perhaps to the not-unimportant stance of "friendly neutrality"), during times of severe crisis and profound political and social upheaval this pole will continue to be an important factor for the bourgeoisie.

But imperialism's bribery of one section inevitably generates its opposite, creating a profound polarization and the conditions for a split within the working class; if the basis for national chauvinism increases, the basis (and necessity) for a thoroughly revolutionary internationalist section of the working class arises in direct opposition.

This expresses itself in many different ways: take, for instance, the often profound influence of immigrant workers on the consciousness and struggle of the workers (as well as other sections of society) in European imperialist countries. These workers have been driven there to serve as cheap labor by the oppressive conditions in their homelands, but they become an important part of the proletariat in the imperialist countries, and often bring with them — and spread the spirit and lessons of — experience in armed revolutionary struggle against imperialism. Or think of the advanced role played within and vis-à-vis the U.S. working class by Vietnam veterans, especially in the early and mid-'70s, many of whom saw first hand what imperialism meant to the peoples of the world, rebelled against it — and were ready and eager to spread that rebellion. This revolutionary potential can also be seen in the influence within the U.S. working class of Black workers and other minority nationalities, and the struggles of the oppressed nationality peoples as a whole, as well as the increasing (and overall revolutionary) impact of immigrants within the U.S. working class.

Lenin, in a very important article, "Imperialism and the Split in Socialism," pointed out that "the trusts, the financial oligarchy, high prices, etc., while *permitting* the bribery of handfuls of the

---

in return, right?' he said.

'If I give you a dollar and instead of closing a plant in Flint, you close a plant in Brazil,' he said, 'well, maybe you've given me something to think about. If I give you a dollar and you give more to the stockholders and I'm not able to buy bread and butter, then to heck with it.' "

top strata, are increasingly oppressing, crushing, ruining and tor-
turing the *mass* of the proletariat and the semi-proletariat." He
continued:

> On the one hand, there is the tendency of the bourgeoisie and the
> opportunists to convert a handful of very rich and privileged na-
> tions into "eternal" parasites on the body of the rest of mankind, to
> "rest on the laurels" of the exploitation of Negroes, Indians, etc.,
> keeping them in subjection with the aid of the excellent technique
> of extermination provided by modern militarism. On the other
> hand, there is the tendency of the *masses*, who are more oppressed
> than ever and who bear the whole brunt of imperialist wars, to cast
> off this yoke and to overthrow the bourgeoisie. It is in the struggle
> between these two tendencies that the history of the working-class
> movement will now inevitably develop. (*MEM*, 377)

While today the imperialists have been temporarily able to bribe
wider sections of the proletariat than in Lenin's day, there nevertheless still exists a *real* proletariat within the imperialist countries, and Lenin's insistence on the pivotal importance of this split
and the need to fight for the tendency of proletarian internationalism is more relevant than ever.

The two trends of the split focused on by Lenin are, of course,
proletarian internationalism vs. Kautskyism. Fundamentally
Kautskyism (even if today it is often not directly associated with
the name of Kautsky) finds its social base in the labor aristocracy
and the more bourgeoisified sections of the working class within
the imperialist countries.[16] And today, again as emphasized
throughout this chapter, the ensemble of views first put together
by Kautsky finds expression in the most diverse forces — revisionist communist parties, social-democrats, other reformers of
various stripes — all of which attempt to base themselves on and
appeal to that social base; and the influence of Kautskyism in-

---

[16]It should be noted, though, that Kautskyism takes on a particular cast within the
oppressed nations. Lenin, for instance, criticized Kautsky for at one point attempting to reduce imperialism to *only* the annexation of the backward agrarian nations
by the advanced industrial capitalist ones. "This definition," Lenin wrote, "is ut-
terly worthless because it one-sidedly, i.e., arbitrarily, singles out only the national
question (although the latter is extremely important in itself as well as in its relation
to imperialism). . . ." (*Imperialism*, 108). Here too what is denied is the overall and
systematic heightening of *all* the contradictions of capital, their interrelation and
the inability of finance capital to indefinitely transcend its contradictions through
some sort of sheer plunder.

evitably extends as well into the ranks of honest revolutionaries.

To sum up the essential point: Kautskyism attempts to evade and gloss over the contradictions of imperialism, and to ascribe to the imperialists near-total freedom in transcending them, as opposed to Lenin's grasp that imperialism is precisely the *heightening* of all the contradictions of capital; Kautskyism trains the proletariat to look at every question from the standpoint of how it affects its situation vis-à-vis its own bourgeoisie (which in event of war ultimately and inevitably leads to capitulation and betrayal of the international proletariat) rather than in the Marxist-Leninist view of proceeding as Lenin put it, "not from the point of view of 'my' country...but from the point of view of *my share* in the preparation, in the propaganda, and in the acceleration of the world proletarian revolution." (*Renegade*, 80)

Lenin's call to "go down *lower* and *deeper*" into the real proletariat, and the necessity, as Bob Avakian has stressed, to be firmly rooted in "a social base for proletarian internationalism," continue to be the correct strategic orientation of the proletariat in the advanced countries. The internationalist tendency which must be developed, and this not only in the imperialist countries, is nothing less than "working wholeheartedly for the development of the revolutionary movement and the revolutionary struggle in *one's own* country, and supporting (by propaganda, sympathy, and material aid) *this struggle*, this, *and only this*, line, in *every* country without exception." ("The Tasks of the Proletariat in Our Revolution," *LCW*, Vol. 24, 75)

The basis and necessity to make proletarian internationalism the foundation and starting point, and to evaluate every struggle in every country from the yardstick of how it advances the worldwide struggle for proletarian revolution and the elimination of class society, is made even more essential by the material way in which imperialism qualitatively strengthens the ties between the different struggles throughout the world.

"Proletarian internationalism is not something that the workers in one country 'extend' to the workers in other lands," Bob Avakian wrote in light of this. "It is the outlook of the international proletariat and represents the starting point for its struggle, on a world scale and within the different countries." ("For Decades to Come — On a World Scale," A report by Bob Avakian adopted by the Central Committee of the RCP, USA, excerpts of which appeared in *RW*, No. 98, March 27, 1981)

It was Lenin's acute understanding of the links between the international matrix and the situation in any one country that enabled him to see — when virtually no one else did — the tremendous opportunity (and urgent necessity) to carry through the Russian Revolution of 1917 to socialism. The necessity confronting the Russian bourgeoisie after the February Revolution to continue to fight in World War 1, in which it was already enmeshed and which had in the first place "brought on" the revolution, would make new crises inevitable and the stabilization of bourgeois rule difficult. At the same time, given the explosive mood of the masses in other countries, a revolutionary attempt in Russia — to which many were already looking for leadership after February — could have an igniting effect internationally; conversely, a failure to act by the Russian proletariat could throw cold water on the inflammable material. That understanding, of course, didn't solve the whole question of *how* then to proceed to make socialist revolution; but Lenin's sweeping and internationally-founded analysis *did* make clear that revolution was on the agenda, depending on the activities of the revolutionaries.[17]

Historic Conjunctures

The experience of October, 1917, in fact, points to another important aspect of imperialism: the emergence of historic conjunctures when the entire system of imperialism is stretched thin and vulnerable to shock and rupture — and to revolutionary advances of an unprecedented nature. Such conjunctures formed up around both World Wars 1 and 2, in which — as Stalin said of World War 1 — all the contradictions were gathered into a single

---

[17]In February, 1917, while sections of the Russian bourgeoisie linked to the British and French were moving to depose the Tsar for his conduct of the war, the proletariat burst through the fissure thereby created, decisively overthrowing the monarchy and setting up *soviets* (councils of workers, soldiers and peasants) as their own organs of power. These organs of power were embryonic, however, and existed alongside the bourgeois state, an exceptional situation which Lenin analyzed could not last long. Through the intense period of February to October, the Bolsheviks, beginning as a decided minority, were able to keep their bearings through incredible twists and turns, and won a decisive enough section of the masses to proletarian revolution to launch a successful armed insurrection by October.

knot and thrown "on to the scales, thereby accelerating and facilitating the revolutionary battles of the proletariat." (*The Foundations of Leninism*, FLP, 1975, p. 6) At these times, the imperialist powers have to throw most everything into the battle, in an all-out effort to win the war and emerge on top; but this very all-out effort pivots on an extremely vulnerable Achilles Heel, which is the imperialists' need to politically mobilize the masses to carry out the war.

This is not to say that war or the preparations for war cannot have a temporarily tonic effect on the imperialists — but any such effects depend for their prolongation on continued advances and victories in the war, and in any case hold the real potential of turning into their opposite in a profound sense. When Kautsky advanced the excuse for capitulation that "never is government so strong, never are parties so weak, as at the outbreak of a war," Lenin answered by pointing to the *essence* of the situation:

> A political crisis exists; no government is sure of the morrow, not one is secure against the danger of financial collapse, loss of territory, expulsion from its country. . . . All governments are sleeping on a volcano; all are *themselves* calling for the masses to display initiative and heroism. ("The Collapse of the Second International," *LCW*, Vol. 21, 214)

Lenin showed that the strength of governments at the start of a war was temporary, and that in fact never were governments so in need of the support of the masses as in war; and he went on to point out that not only would the various governments increasingly have to subject the masses to terrible deprivation and brutality, but to do this they must also drag those masses into political life. While this is done to serve the bourgeoisie's purposes, in doing so the bourgeoisie summons, as Bob Avakian put it, the genie from the bottle, ". . . and once this 'genie,' the masses of people, and most especially the working class, is roused up, *everything* can be thrown up for grabs — including just who is going to stuff who into what bottle." ("1980—A Year, A Decade of Historic Importance," RCP Publications, Chicago, 1980, p. 4).

While such historic conjunctures, representing the heightening and concentration of world contradictions, can dramatically change the situation in advanced countries, they also open up even greater scope for revolutionary struggle in those oppressed regions where, generally speaking, at least for the last forty years or so, the opportunities for revolutionary struggle have been greater all along. This was true in a beginning way in World War 1, and in a qualitatively greater way in World War 2 and its aftermath (especially with, but not limited to, the Chinese Revolution).

The potential impact of such a world-historic conjuncture was emphasized by Lenin:

> It *is not so often* that history places this form of struggle on the order of the day, but then its significance is felt for decades to come. *Days* on which *such* method of struggle can and must be employed are equal to *scores of years* of other historical epochs. ("The Collapse of the Second International," *LCW*, Vol. 21, 254)

Revolutions, of course, are not limited to historic conjunctures; throughout the development of imperialism important revolutionary opportunities have opened up in all periods, "without warning," and have advanced the struggle of the international proletariat and demanded its support — with the war in Vietnam being only the starkest example in recent times. Whatever the situation, and whatever the country, the task of the class-conscious proletariat remains fundamentally to heighten the revolutionary consciousness of the masses, imbue them with an internationalist perspective, and prepare to seize and push ahead every opportunity for advance that presents itself.

"Imperialism," as Lenin concluded, "is the era of proletarian revolution."

4

THE STATE

"Some things were just meant to be — they've always been that way, and they always will." Everyone who's ever asked "why?" — why is there war, or classes, or injustice, or whatever — has at one time or another run up against that sort of answer. And you get it especially frequently when you ask why some people must be empowered to rule over others.

But things *haven't* "always been that way"; there is the example, for one, of the Iroquois tribe of North America. By the mid-17th century, when the invasion by Europeans began in earnest, there were 20,000 Iroquois. They controlled a rather large territory, and carried out the arbitration of complex questions, the settlement of disputes, a division of labor, production and distribution, large-scale military expeditions, defense of the tribal lands against Europeans, selection of leaders, etc. Yet they did all this without a state apparatus — without, that is, that institution which seems to stand above society as a whole while claiming to represent the social will, and which is able to enforce its dictates against any individual member of society through its exclusive monopoly on the use of force (in the form of its army, police forces, courts, prisons, etc.). In addition, the Iroquois also lacked two other "can't-do-without-'em" institutions deemed essential for society: the patriarchal family and private property.

Because of all this the study of Iroquois society can shed light on the origin of those institutions, and for that reason Engels focused on it in his extremely important work, *The Origin of the Family, Private Property and the State*. Engels' interest was hardly scholastic; for if certain oppressive institutions arose only out of certain specific material contradictions, then it's entirely possible that they may in turn vanish or be superseded when conditions change and those contradictions are resolved. Engels wanted to uncover the origins of those institutions in order to grasp better what was needed for their elimination, and to hasten that process.

The basic social unit of the Iroquois was the gens, a sizable related group of people tracing descent from a common ancestor. The Iroquois gens was matrilineal, i.e., membership was reckoned through descent from the mother, and the common ancestor was thought to be female. The matrilineal extended "family" (kinship system would be a more scientific term, since the word "family" itself is identified with and only arose on the basis of later developments — more on this later) was linked to other important differences in the status of women between Iroquois and other societies.

For one thing, while the leaders, called sachems, were male, they were chosen by women. And if the sachem did not perform his duties to their liking, the women of the clan could remove him. Women also owned the longhouse,[1] the garden plots (even though they were cleared by men) and the tools used to cultivate the land. Women maintained order in the longhouse and, of course, all property was inherited through the mother's line. The husband, while maintaining membership in his original gens upon marriage, moved into the wife's lodging.

Returning to the sachem and his powers for a minute, it's important to note that he had neither means of coercion nor a special police force at his disposal; when the tribe deemed it necessary to bear arms (either to settle disputes with other tribes, or to defend against the European settlers), all males were liable to join in the armed parties (whose formation was subject to veto by the women of the tribe).

---

[1]These longhouses were long rectangular houses with several compartments, housing several different families.

What was the basis for this? Fundamentally it arose not from some "special nature" of the Iroquois, but out of the level of development of the productive forces in Iroquois society, and the relations of production that went with them. The Iroquois obtained most of their food from horticulture (gardening), which was entirely the responsibility of the women, while the men were engaged in the supplementary activity of hunting and trapping. The high status of the women rested on the importance of the labor they carried out. While this division of labor may have arisen spontaneously on the basis of women's biological role in childbearing and breastfeeding, it obviously at that point did not entail their subjugation to the men.

As for private property, there was none, at least in any significant sense of the term. While individuals owned tools and weapons, the land and hunting territory belonged to the gens as a whole, and not to any individual. Yet this people flourished, even for a time in the face of what can only be called a genocidal onslaught by a technologically more advanced society — all without the benefit of private property, division into classes, a state apparatus or patriarchal nuclear family. Indeed, as Engels showed (based on the work of other anthropologists), evidence suggested that the Iroquois pattern was far from unique in early society and may well have been something of a typical case. How then, and why, *did* the state, private property and the family arise?

Here Engels turned to the development of ancient Greece from gentile (i.e., gens-based) to class society.[2] There the gens — at least when it entered written history — existed on the basis of *father right*. This was due to the basic difference between the Iroquois and the Greek tribes in the level of the productive forces. In Greece, herding and animal husbandry had been developed. Arising spontaneously on the old division of labor between men and women, the herds belonged to the men; these herds, however, were not mere tools, but constituted a *surplus* which could be exchanged. They were wealth, a totally new source of economic

---

[2]Engels discussed the Roman, Celt, German and other peoples, as well as the Iroquois and Greeks. While the development of all peoples has obviously not been uniform, the contrast between the Iroquois and the Greeks can show the material basis for the transition from stateless society to "civilization," and some of the contradictions involved in that transition.

power beyond what earlier society could produce (and preserve) through either the hunt or the household industry carried out by women. Later, the domestication of cattle, along with the development of metal forging, led to field cultivation by ox-drawn plows.

In matrilineal society, however, the herds and other wealth of the man would not be inherited by his children on his death, but would revert instead to his original gens.[3] Engels explains that:

> Thus, in proportion as wealth increased, it on the one hand made the man's position in the family more important than the woman's, and on the other hand created an impulse to use this strengthened position in order to overthrow, in favor of his children, the traditional order of inheritance. This, however, was impossible so long as descent was reckoned according to mother right. Mother right, therefore, had to be overthrown, and overthrown it was. This was by no means so difficult as it looks to us today.... A simple decision sufficed that in the future the offspring of the male members should remain within the gens, but that of the female should be excluded by being transferred to the gens of their father. The reckoning of descent in the female line and the law of maternal inheritance were thereby overthrown, and the male line of descent and the law of paternal inheritance were substituted for them. (*Origin*, 63-64)

How this was done is not yet known; *that* it was done is virtually as certain as the moment in history when one primate species began to walk upright.[4] Engels continues:

> The overthrow of mother right was the *world historical defeat of the female sex*. The man took command in the home also, the woman was degraded and reduced to servitude; she became the slave of his lust and a mere instrument for the production of children. (*Origin*, 65)

This, significant as it was, was not the only great change that developed in the wake of the improvements in the productive

---

[3]This is because husbands in gentile society did not *possess* wives (or wives husbands, for that matter); each partner retained membership in the gens in which they were born. Thus the children belonged to the mother's gens, while the husband still belonged to *his* mother's gens; hence his property did not revert to his children.

[4]Engels in his preface shows how this overthrow forms the subject of a number of myths, including the Greek tragedy *The Oresteia* . . . in which two children murder their mother to avenge their father, and two sections of the gods struggle over whether they should be punished or upheld. Their vindication symbolized the triumph of patriarchy.

forces and the increasingly complex division of labor. *Slavery* for the first time became advantageous. In Iroquois society slavery was unheard of — prisoners were either set free, killed or adopted into the tribe. But once a surplus became possible, the more labor power, the larger the potential surplus; cattle in particular multiplied faster than the family and more people were needed to tend them. Thus prisoners were taken and enslaved, owned by the men of the gens. At the same time, women and children also came under the father's domination, and soon his literal owner- ship. In fact, the Latin root word of family is *familius*, meaning slave; the word assumed its modern meaning through being used to refer to the entire unit of women, children and slaves which a man owned, and over which he had power of life and death.

Inheritance allowed accumulation of wealth within parti- cular families, and the contradiction between the family and gens sharpened. *Exchange* between the owners of private property developed, and along with it piracy and raids on land and sea, for the first time on a systematic basis. The new productive forces, and the revolution in the production (and social) relations that came in their wake, had outrun the institutions of primitive com- munism. Slaves, after all — especially as they became a significant force, and later a majority — had to be kept in check; wealth had to be protected on an ongoing basis from raids and piracy; a framework to regulate exchange was needed.

But the gentile form of society could do none of this. Engels notes that:

"...in short [in ancient Greece on the verge of civilization — *LW*] riches [were] praised and respected as the highest good and the old gentile order misused to justify the violent seizure of riches. Only one thing was wanting: an institution which not only secured the newly acquired riches of individuals against the communistic tradi- tions of the gentile order, which not only sanctified the private pro- perty formerly so little valued and declared this sanctification to be the highest purpose of all human society; but an institution which also set the seal of general social recognition on each subsequently developing new method of acquiring property and thus amassing wealth at continually increasing speed; an institution which perpetuated not only this growing cleavage of society into classes, but also the right of the possessing class to exploit the non- possessing, and the rule of the former over the latter. And this in- stitution came. The *state* was invented. (*Origin*, 127)

The first constitution of Athens empowered a central administration to pass laws and regulate activities over all the territory of the various Athenian tribes and gentes; this uniform code of conduct was made necessary by increased exchange, and by the consequent travel by members of one gens to areas of other gentes to which they did not belong and were thus not accountable. This step, in which ties of blood were in large part superseded by considerations of territory, severely weakened the authority of the gens vis-à-vis the state. The Athenian constitution further divided all people according to classes — nobles, tillers of the land and artisans (slaves were considered sub-human and had no rights at all) — and systematized different duties and prerogatives in each case. Again, this was both a recognition of new economic relations that had outstripped the gentile form, as well as a new classification more important than blood ties. Further, a professional police force distinct from the armed people as a whole had to be formed under the central authority to keep the slaves in check, to regulate relations between the other classes and to protect merchants from marauders. Laws concerning money, debt, credit, usury — all phenomena that arose with commodity exchange — were drawn up and enforced.

The growth of commodity exchange and subsequent division of society into antagonistic classes, then, led to the invention of the state; from the beginning it served as an organ to suppress the exploited and mediate conflicts among the exploiters. And, together with the division into classes and slavery, there came the subjugation of women and the rise of the family.

How fitting and revealing it is that ancient Athens, a state in which more than 80% of the people were slaves, is portrayed as the "cradle of democracy"; and that ancient Rome, so celebrated for its uniform legal codes, developed those codes as a means to subjugate the barbarians they conquered, many of whom were as yet unblessed by the institutions of slavery, the oppression of women and state power. Indeed, as they so tirelessly proclaim, the modern Western bourgeoisies really are the continuators of the "Greco-Roman heritage."

Bourgeois Democracy and Capitalist Democracy

The state, then, arose from the division of society into classes; its purpose is not to reconcile those divisions — for the antagonism between exploiters and exploited, slave and master is *ir*reconcilable — but to serve as an organ of domination of one class over another.

This, however, is continually denied by the bourgeoisie and its apologists, as well as by others whose outlook and position in society obscures their understanding of this decisive question. In the U.S.,[5] *pluralism* is the dominant ideology on the state. This view portrays the state as an essentially neutral mechanism which mediates the competing claims of various "interest groups," including classes, "minority and ethnic groups," and other "communities," "constituencies," etc. (e.g., peace groups, environmentalists, and so on). While the state in other times and places may constitute the rule of the elite over the many, this view maintains that modern democracy has changed all that, for now the have-nots can speak out, organize and make their demands felt, especially at the polls.

Straight off, however, this line of reasoning ignores (actually, covers over) the heart of any and every state apparatus — its monopoly on military power to enforce the dictates of the class it represents. As Mao put it, "political power grows out of the barrel of a gun." The use of secret police and troops against the Black liberation and other movements in the U.S. in the '60s glaringly points up the real essence and role of state power in even the "freest" of bourgeois democracies; on a lesser scale, the routine calling out of cops and sometimes troops to protect scabs and attack strikers in militant economic strikes bears out the same point. The hammer of state power comes down on any struggle that threatens to go beyond certain limits, and these limits are narrow indeed. This, and not scholastically styled fairy tales about

---

[5]Since the U.S. bills itself as the land of democracy and head of the "free world," it can justly be taken as the prime example of bourgeois democracy.

the "reconciliation of differing interests," conditions bourgeois democracy.

Two additional points, however, arise in relation to this.

First, the bourgeoisie is not limited to sheer force, but utilizes both club and carrot. Concessions are selectively granted in order to cool o⸺ ⸺ain struggles and split the masses, to propel them into co⸺ ⸺hemselves over what are essentially crumb⸺ ⸺ke the threat of force all the more e⸺ ⸺ he realistic — if you g⸺ ⸺ if you play ⸺ bette⸺ influ⸺ ang⸺ dir⸺

⸺

deception. This, ⸺ didates, the campaigns, the v⸺ basic and fundamental (even in terms o⸺ among the bourgeoisie — more on that later), but ⸺ rigidly set the terms of political debate. They mark out the parameters of the "acceptable positions" on major political questions and defuse mass anger and upheaval in the passive act of voting, politically pinning the masses to the tail of one or another bourgeois jackass (and bourgeois politics in general). Marx's apt characterization of bourgeois elections — as the masses deciding every few years which member of the ruling class is to crush and deceive them — hasn't aged a bit in the hundred years since he made it.

Second, the imperialists maintain the relative elasticity of these tactics *only* on the basis of the most *extreme* repression in the third world. Their ability to make concessions to the workers in their home countries following World War 2 gained them political and ideological hegemony over the majority of these workers, which often rendered unnecessary more open suppression. (Of course, the reformist policies followed by the communists in those countries in the years prior to and during World War 2 — a cornerstone of which was a refusal to oppose the colonial and neo-colonial policies of their own bourgeoisies — were no small factor in the *extent* of this hegemony and the bourgeoisie's relative ease

in gaining it.) The platform of democracy in the imperialist countries (worm-eaten as it is) rests on fascist terror in the oppressed
nations: the real guarantors of bourgeois democracy in the U.S.
are not the constitutional scholar and Supreme Court justice, but
the Brazilian torturer, the South African cop, and the Israeli pilot;
the *true* defenders of the democratic tradition are not on the por-
traits in the halls of the Western capitols, but are Marcos, Mobutu,
and the dozens of generals from Turkey to Taiwan, from South
Korea to South America, all put and maintained in power and
backed up by the military force of the U.S. and its imperialist
partners.

Executive Committee of the Ruling Class

At the same time that the state suppresses the masses, it
secondarily serves the bourgeoisie as an arena in which to thrash
out its own conflicts and contradictions. There are in fact real differences and contradictory interests *within* the bourgeoisie, inherent in its nature as a mass of *competing* capitals, and an important function of the bourgeois state is to act as a sort of "executive
committee" of the bourgeoisie in resolving those contradictions.
These internecine conflicts have become more intense, and the
arena of the state all the more concentrated a battlefield, with the
rise of imperialism and the much more decisive role and wider
functions of the state in relation to the accumulation process itself
(both economically in its various interventions and policies, and
more important *politically*, in the effect of its policies vis-à-vis the
oppressed nations, its rivals, etc., on accumulation).

Here is where democracy really applies: amongst the bourgeoisie itself. Lenin's remark that a democratic republic is the
"best possible shell" for capitalism — a maxim rarely if ever repeated and in any case systematically distorted by today's revisionists who hypocritically claim Lenin's mantle — relates not
only to its capacity for deception of the masses, but also to the flexibility it affords the bourgeoisie in resolving its intraclass conflicts. Again, this democracy within the bourgeoisie is not reducible to elections — nor are they the most essential form through
which this is played out — but works itself out via struggles in a
whole complex of institutions (e.g., Congressional hearings, leaks
to the press and other forms of creating public opinion, legal in-

dictments, etc.). Nor is *this* democracy absolute either, as the assassinations of various bourgeois political figures in the U.S. in recent years illustrate.

The relative character of bourgeois democracy stands out in fascism, in which the bourgeoisie dispenses with virtually all bourgeois-democratic rights and rules through open terror. Fascism, it is important to grasp, is fundamentally a more extreme form of the same basic content of bourgeois rule; it is a particular form of superstructure, adopted in some extreme crises, that is nonetheless erected on and designed to protect the same system of exploitation and oppression.

For this reason, even at times when the bourgeoisie may appear to be moving towards fascism, the class-conscious proletariat should *not* reduce itself to fighting for a "milder, more democratic" form of oppression. While it is important to fight all reactionary measures of the bourgeoisie, the orientation of the proletariat and its party must be to find the ways to utilize the often sharpened contradictions such a move by the bourgeoisie reflects so as to intensify the struggle for revolution. Further, reactionary pogroms, jail and murder are hardly unique to periods of fascism; the proletarian party must expect and prepare to function in conditions of total illegality *at any time*, maintaining its ability to politically expose the bourgeoisie, unite with the struggle of the masses, and divert that struggle into revolutionary channels — no matter how difficult the conditions.

Fascism does *not* represent the ascendancy of the "most reactionary, most chauvinist section of finance capital," as the international communist movement held in the 1930s.[6] The old international communist movement never repudiated this line, and it retains influence today not only among revisionists but revolutionary forces as well. That view naturally led to a strategy of seeking out a supposedly less reactionary, more democratic wing of the bourgeoisie to ally with (and in fact shelter under) in a fight to restore (or protect) bourgeois democracy — a strategy that can only end up keeping the proletariat subordinate to and at the mercy of the bourgeoisie.

---

[6]For the most concentrated presentation of this position, see *United Front Against War and Fascism*, by Georgi Dmitrov.

Again, even in its most democratic form, bourgeois democracy (as Lenin summed up) "always remains, and under capitalism cannot but remain, restricted, truncated, false and hypocritical, a paradise for the rich and a snare and a deception for the exploited, for the poor." (*Renegade*, 20) It's not only, however, that the bourgeoisie is extremely hypocritical about its professed democratic ideals — these ideals themselves are not eternal goals to be striven for. They are anchored in bourgeois production relations and bound by the narrow horizons of life within those relations.

The Democratic Ideal

The bourgeois democratic revolutions promised, as Engels put it, the realm of reason, in which ". . . superstition, injustice, privilege and oppression were to be superseded by eternal truth, eternal justice, equality based on nature and the inalienable rights of man."

The reality was different. He continued:

> We know today that this realm of reason was nothing more than the idealised realm of the bourgeoisie; that eternal justice found its realization in bourgeois justice; that equality reduced itself to bourgeois equality before the law; that bourgeois property was proclaimed as one of the most essential rights of man; and that the government of reason, Rousseau's Social Contract, came into being, and could only come into being, as a bourgeois democratic republic. (*Anti-Dühring*, 20)

This had — and has — everything to do with the production relations which the bourgeois revolution arose to enforce and defend. The eternal self-evident truths of individual freedom and equality have their roots in commodity production and the marketplace.

The commodity owner brings his commodity to the market of his own volition. It is *his*, and he aims to strike the best possible deal for it. He perceives his exchanges with other commodity owners as more or less random. Through these apparently random encounters, however, he is involuntarily bound by the choices of other commodity producers (do they desire his product?) and the vagaries of the market as a whole. Further, beneath his seeming freedom lies an inexorable compulsion: he must sell or die. The free choices of the individual commodity owner are in reality no more voluntary than the choice before the industrial capitalist as to whether to reinvest the surplus he has extracted from his workers (which, as shown in Chapter 2, is not an option but a commandment).

If a gas molecule were conscious, it would perhaps view its random activity as self-willed and purposeful; it would not necessarily understand that this activity, studied in light of the overall mass of which it is a part, conforms to more or less definite laws. As long as things were stable it would celebrate its freedom. But if at some point the heat of this mass of gas should drop so that the gas assumes a solid state and molecular movement slows down drastically, or should rise to the degree that the molecules are split, our anthropomorphic molecule would rail against either repression or anarchy. Similarly the bourgeois democrat conceives of an ideal marketplace in which he would be free from the compulsory and anarchic workings of the underlying laws of capital; and then, consciously or not, he translates this into his political ideals as the sanctity of individual rights and free choice.[7]

The dream here — speaking not of the unsentimental finance capitalist but of the small producer or petty-bourgeois intellectual who *believes* in the dream — is often recognized as unattainable; in reality he settles for the assurance that he will be left alone should he raise his voice to gripe. And it has in fact been possible in the imperialist countries (especially in the Western bloc) for certain strata in the last period to realize this modest aspiration (though this has all along been quite relative, and even this leash tends to tighten up in periods of severe crisis and/or approaching interimperialist war . . . as today's is).

But why is the individual's right to be left alone to do (or at least think) whatever they want the highest possible aspiration for a person (or society)? The ideal that poses freedom as the absence of *any* compulsion is a false and unrealizable fantasy; authentic

---

[7]The bourgeoisie's demand for freedom had another dimension as well during its fight against feudalism. The bourgeoisie needed freedom for itself from the restrictive tariffs of the feudal estates and the monopolies of the guilds upon certain branches of production, and it also needed freedom for the peasantry and others. As touched on earlier, the obligation of the peasantry to the landlord, and of guild workers, especially apprentices, to the guilds, stood in the way of the massing of a proletariat; capital needs laborers who are free, in a double sense: free to sell their labor power as a commodity, and "free" too from any ownership of means of production — so that they are *forced* to exercise this first freedom.

freedom lies precisely in *comprehending* the often hidden laws that drive society forward, and in using that understanding to transform society, and material reality generally. This kind of freedom can only be gained and exercised by entering *into struggle*, not retreating from it, and only collective struggle at that. In these two diametrically opposed conceptions of freedom are concentrated two fundamentally different world outlooks, the bourgeois and proletarian, and two different dreams — going forward to classless society and communism, or vainly trying to turn history back to an idyllic yesterday of petty commodity producers that really never existed.

Equality

The political ideal of equality between individuals is also rooted in bourgeois production relations. The demand for equality, while heretical in feudal society which held that God himself assigned each person their station in life, suited the rebellious bourgeoisie and corresponded to the equality of commodity owners entering the market place. Here hereditary rank and privilege must count for nothing and every commodity must be judged (and exchanged) "on its own merit" — i.e., the amount of socially necessary labor congealed in it. All are equal before the law...of value. And so this political demand of the bourgeoisie was at first openly (and always essentially) limited to equality between commodity owners (originally "men of property" alone were allowed to vote in the bourgeois democracies).

But even as that demand has become general it continues both to flow from and to conceal the real class relations of society. The heart of the question is, what sort of equality is possible between exploiters and exploited?

To take the most everyday sort of example, what does equality before the law mean when it has been documented by various insurance agencies that 80% of the arson committed in the U.S. — which takes hundreds of lives each year! — is ordered by landlords, yet very few of these landlords ever serve anything but the lightest sort of slap-on-the-wrist type sentence? Compare this to the far from atypical case of the revolutionary writer and activist George Jackson, who as a Black working-class youth of 17 was sentenced to what turned out to be 12 years for a $70 gas station holdup (and who was later murdered in jail by the authorities). And this doesn't even touch on the fact that in class society members of the bourgeoisie hardly suffer a need to rob "equal" to that of unemployed proletarians. Formal equality — i.e., the idea that both the IBM executive and the unemployed youth enjoy the equal right to spend hundreds of thousands of dollars on the best lawyers and to use all the business and political connections at their disposal should they be brought to trial — masks a real and concrete inequality, and oppression. The solution is not some sort of absolutely equal justice (unrealizable anyway), but a society with neither classes, nor the compulsion to steal.

At the same time as it has professed (and to a degree instituted) equality, capitalism has arisen on the foundations of profound *in*equality between nations, and between men and women. During the early period of the formation of bourgeois nation-states, the first ones to develop subjugated the weaker or less developed areas and nations, and then took advantage of forced backwardness and denial of rights to use the toilers of those nations as cheap labor; such, for example, is the root both of England's oppression of Ireland, which began in real earnest in the 1600s, and of the oppression of the Black people in the U.S., who after the Civil War were forged into a nation in the Black Belt South, but on a suppressed and unequal basis (and who have been oppressed ever since, first as sharecroppers in the semi-feudal South, and later in a caste-like position within the working class). With the transition to imperialism and the carving up of the whole world, the inequality and oppression of nations was transformed into a global question at the heart of the continued existence of the system.

While the dynamics are different, the bourgeoisie has also locked women into an oppressed, subordinated position. The subjugation of women is bound up with the division of labor which became stamped with the seal of oppression with the rise of *classes*, and can only be really unravelled as part of ripping up the whole fabric of class society. The economic relations of capitalism form an especially powerful material basis to reinforce that oppression and inequality. The subordinate position of women within the family, and in society generally, guarantees the labor essential to holding the family unit together and raising new generations, and beyond that provides a lightning rod for the suppressed anger of men. Further, her oppressed position allows the capitalist to pay her much less when she is drawn into the workforce — which has in fact to a degree taken place, but under the even more warped and distorted forms of women's oppression characteristic of imperialism.

The oppression and inequality of the oppressed nationalities and of women enables the bourgeoisie both to extract extra profits *and* to foster and reinforce divisions and bourgeois ideology in the working class and among the masses generally. As to the first point, the discrimination against women and oppressed nationality workers (including immigrants from nations oppressed by imperialism) is tied into what bourgeois economists call a "two-tier economy" common within the imperialist countries. While in the U.S., for example, the lower tier of poorly-paid and superexploited workers contains many white male proletarians, it is still disproportionately made up of oppressed nationalities and women. This division corresponds to the split in the proletariat analyzed by Lenin. The higher profits available in this lower tier have been a crucial element of the maintenance and expansion of the imperialist economies.

Beyond that, though, within the superstructures of the imperialist countries there exist pervasive structures of male and white (or European) supremacy — based on real, if ultimately petty, privileges accruing to males and white (or native born) people, including within the working class (and related to the split in the proletariat) — that reinforce among the better-off workers a chauvinist identification with "their own" rulers and a feeling of having a stake to defend in the current system. These institutions thus serve as essential pillars of bourgeois ideological and political hegemony, pillars which the bourgeoisie will go to every length to defend — whatever their professed ideals.

The proletariat has every interest and *necessity* to eliminate such inequality under its rule. Unless it systematically attacks and uproots social inequality in both the economic base and the superstructure — and as part of that wages a concerted fight against national chauvinist and male chauvinist thinking, customs, etc. — proletarian unity would inevitably be corroded and reduced to a hollow phrase. Beyond that, if the necessary struggle is not waged to assure equality for the formerly oppressed nations (both inside and outside the imperialist countries), then capitalist relations will be reproduced between different nations and provide the soil for reaction and for new bourgeoisies to take root. The same thing holds for the inequality of women.

At the same time, the elimination of social inequality only *begins* to address the matter of wiping out the oppression of nations and of women. The goal before the proletariat is to move beyond equality *and* inequality (after all, social equality can only have meaning as a concept as long as its opposite, social inequality, continues to exist) and to the abolition of all classes and all class distinctions.

Majority Rule?

Part of the way in which the ideal of equality of individuals is used to cover over the real *class relations* of society relates back to the question of elections. According to the bourgeoisie, all citizens are equal in the voting booth, and it is from there that the bourgeois state (in its democratic form, at least) derives its "legitimacy." Not class dictatorship, they say, but majority rule of the whole people. In fact, as we shall see later, it is only with the dictatorship of the proletariat that the majority of society *really* begins to rule. But here again, let's look closer at the entire question of "majority rule" in the first place.

To begin with, the political ideal of majority rule echoes nothing so much as Adam Smith's invisible hand. Smith, one of the early leading bourgeois political economists, said that the individual actions of every commodity owner in the marketplace only seemed anarchic and were in fact guided by an "invisible hand" which resolved these different (and competing) interests to the benefit of all concerned. Translated into politics, we are told that the will of the majority, if only somehow left unimpeded, will ultimately lead to the greatest good for the greatest number. Smith's invisible hand, of course, was the law of value, and the only thing the unhampered workings of *that* ever produced was (and is) the accumulation of capital at one pole and misery at the other. Similarly, the "marketplace of ideas" does not produce truth, but only the continuing ideological and political subordination of the proletariat to the bourgeoisie.

The limitations of majority rule become glaringly apparent as soon as you seriously examine any major political question. Take the war in Vietnam, for instance — at the beginning a majority of the American people supported the U.S. war effort, or were at least willing to go along with it. And even if you added in the Vietnamese population to the "vote tally," neither the outcome — nor the method — would be any better. Did that make it correct or just? Or did it mean then that the Vietnamese people should have laid down their arms, or that opponents of the war in the U.S. should have ceased going against that majority and doing everything possible to expose and oppose that war?

The fact is that on any major and complex political question the bourgeoisie will be able to rally majorities at the beginning; that's part of the advantage of having bourgeois state power. As long as the bourgeoisie rules, the broadest masses will not be trained to see things *critically* — which is not at all the same thing as the everyday skin-deep cynicism of bourgeois society, but denotes the ability to scientifically grasp the real motive contradictions beneath events and political questions — and it will be relatively easy at certain points for the bourgeoisie to manufacture and manipulate majorities. On the other hand, state power does *not* give the bourgeoisie a total lock on the masses; there are times when the contradictions inherent in bourgeois relations open up fissures in society through which (to paraphrase Lenin) the long-suppressed rage of the masses erupts.

When the masses *do* rise up and consciously take revolutionary initiative, the bourgeoisie does not rely on "majority rule" but on force of arms (as well as every other means at their disposal). When it gets down to the nitty-gritty of seizing and/or holding on to state power, "majority rule" and "equality" don't even enter into it. Even though in a minority, and even facing the arms of an aroused proletariat, the exploiters fight tooth and claw to regain their position and utilize all their many advantages in that battle. As Lenin summed up in the midst of the civil war which followed the insurrection in October:

> There can be no equality between the exploiters — who for many generations have stood out because of their education, conditions of wealthy life, and habits — and the exploited, the majority of whom even in the most advanced and most democratic bourgeois republics are downtrodden, backward, ignorant, intimidated and disunited. For a long time after the revolution the exploiters inevitably continue to enjoy a number of great practical advantages:

they still have money (since it is impossible to abolish money all at once); some movable property — often fairly considerable; they still have various connections, habits of organization and management, knowledge of all the "secrets" (customs, methods, means and possibilities) of management, superior education, close connections with the higher technical personnel (who live and think like the bourgeoisie), incomparably greater experience in the art of war (this is very important), and so on, and so forth.

If the exploiters are defeated in one country only — and this, of course, is typical, since a simultaneous revolution in a number of countries is a rare exception, they *still* remain *stronger* than the exploited, for the international connections of the exploiters are enormous. That a section of the exploited from the least advanced section of the . . . masses, may, and indeed do, follow the exploiters has been proved hitherto by *all* revolutions, including the Commune . . .

In these circumstances, to assume that in a revolution which is at all profound and serious the issue is decided simply by the relation between the majority and the minority is the acme of stupidity, the silliest prejudice of a common or garden liberal, an attempt to *deceive* the *masses* by concealing from them a well-established historical truth. This historical truth is that in every profound revolution, a *prolonged, stubborn and desperate* resistance of the exploiters, who for a number of years retain important practical advantages over the exploited, is the *rule.* (*Renegade,* 34-35)

The "Ready-Made Machinery" . . .
and Why It Must Be Smashed!

The above passage comes from *The Proletarian Revolution and The Renegade Kautsky,* a polemical reply to Kautsky's attack on the dictatorship of the proletariat in general, and the Russian Revolution in particular. Going along with his "ultra-imperialism" line, Kautsky also popularized the notion of "peaceful transition to socialism" — that is, the idea that the proletariat could institute socialism through electing a majority in the bourgeois parliaments and congresses. Today this line is often propagated by the revisionist parties aligned with the Soviet Union, as well as by the social-democratic parties that are literally descended from Kautsky. The CPUSA, for instance, envisions (at least for public consumption) a scenario featuring a constitutional amendment to nationalize all the major means of production, backed by a majority so overwhelming that the bourgeoisie may not move against it.

This fantasy denies the real lesson pointed to by Lenin — and paid for by the masses in blood — that the issue of state power invariably is settled by *force*. In a revolution as unprecedentedly thoroughgoing as the proletarian revolution must be, this is all the more true. What distinguishes the proletarian revolution from every other is that the proletariat is not attempting to replace one system of exploitation by another, but to abolish exploitation altogether.[8]

This in turn leads to even more underlying reasons why, in Marx's words, "the working class cannot simply lay hold of the ready-made State machinery, and wield it for its own purposes." (*The Civil War in France*, FLP, 1977, p. 66) The state machinery of the bourgeoisie was built up over centuries *by* the bourgeoisie to serve and protect its interests; its very structure and institutions *reflect* its role and its origin as an organ of bourgeois suppression.

The *New Programme* of the Revolutionary Communist Party, USA underlines the point that the proletariat must not only "smash and dismantle the old forms of rule and political institutions" but "create in their place new ones which actually represent, rely on and involve the masses in ruling and remolding society in their interests and according to the principles of proletarian internationalism." It then points out that:

> This certainly cannot be done just by appointing Party members, and/or elected representatives of the workers and other oppressed masses, to take charge of the old institutions or of ones different in name but structured along the same lines as the old ones. If workers are selected as judges in the courts, for example, but the courts have the same position above the masses and follow the same rules and procedures as before, then these worker-judges will quickly turn into oppressors of the people and the courts will yet again serve as instruments of bourgeois dictatorship over the masses. The same principle applies to the bureaucracies, police and armed forces, etc. (*New Programme and New Constitution*, 48)

---

[8]This makes the CPUSA's citing of the Emancipation Proclamation as "precedent" for their plan both wrong-headed and perhaps unwittingly self-exposing: it is inaccurate because the Civil War (which in fact accomplished the abolition of slavery) was certainly violent (and in its last decisive battles fought in large measure by the slaves themselves), and self-exposing in that chattel slavery was replaced by wage slavery (and semi-feudal bondage).

Or take the army. As the *New Programme* further points out:

> The purpose of the bourgeois armed forces — to carry out reactionary war against the interests of the vast majority of people of the whole world, including the U.S. — are reflected both in their strategies of fighting and their internal organization, with a dictatorial hierarchy resting on the absolute authority of superior officers and most fundamentally on the intimidation of the rank and file soldiers and their ignorance of the real purpose of the wars they are called on to fight as well as of the plans and policies guiding particular campaigns and battles. (*New Programme*, 49)

In truth, unless the bourgeois army is *smashed*, defeated and dismembered by the armed proletariat (and the real army that it forges in the course of the revolution) then the core of reaction will remain and rebuild to smash the proletariat — no matter who has won what election, or what the popular will is. The heart of the matter is that the bourgeois state, whatever its personnel, can do nothing but reproduce bourgeois political domination; it *cannot* serve the tasks of the proletariat.

This, again, was the famous conclusion drawn by Marx in his analysis of the Paris Commune. The "peaceful transition" proponents, whatever their petty amendments of the moment (and whatever their "hidden agendas"), deny this principle, distort reality...and betray the masses.

Chile, Poland and the Road Forward

Two recent and bitter experiences drive this home: Chile and Poland. In Chile, a coalition led by Salvador Allende and including the revisionist Communist Party of Chile came to power through an election in 1970, an event hailed by none other than Fidel Castro as an example of the efficacy of the peaceful transition strategy.[9]

---

[9]Actually, in this case, peaceful transition was a cover for a more complex move carried out internationally by the Soviet Union, relying on its revisionist parties, which involves gaining a foothold as a minority within governments in the U.S. sphere of influence. This strategy of "historic compromise" remains in force today (although increasingly complemented by "armed revisionism," in which the Soviet Union in other more contested areas supports military coups by army officers friendly to it) and is exposed and analyzed at length by Jorge Palacios in his book, *Chile: An Attempt at "Historic Compromise"* (Banner Press, Chicago, 1979). Here however we focus on Chile to the extent that the rhetoric and reasoning of peaceful transition were employed there, and what this in turn reveals about that rhetoric and rationale.

The U.S., working through the CIA with bourgeois and certain petty-bourgeois sections of Chilean society, launched a three-year campaign designed to "destabilize" Allende's rule, and ultimately to topple his government. Throughout this time the CP of Chile assured the masses that the army would "remain neutral" in the "best Chilean tradition" and the CP went so far as to oppose armed land seizures by the peasants and to literally disarm the workers, who had stocked guns in the factories, just days and hours before the coup! Even as the military moved and Allende was murdered, the CP pleaded for "calm." Here is a case where the "peaceful road to socialism" is littered with the corpses of roughly 30,000 peasants, workers, students and intellectuals; the blood that stains that road is *equally* the responsibility of imperialist terror . . . and revisionist treachery.

The case of Poland proves much the same thing from the opposite side (and with the two superpowers in something of a role-reversal). After all, if it's bourgeois democracy you want, no country in the world was as democratic as Poland between August 1980 and December 1981. Can anyone imagine the capitalists in the U.S. sitting still for a minute for even a fifth of the demands — or a tenth of the actions — of the Polish proletariat (which they so loudly supported — as long as it was "over there")? But the leadership of that struggle, including sections with very close ties to the U.S., had its own version of peaceful transition and historic compromise, if not in exactly those words. They attempted to channel the struggle into certain cosmetic "structural reforms" which would have given pro-Western elements in Poland a foothold in the Polish state apparatus, but would hardly have fundamentally altered the *class* relations between the workers and their rulers. Here, too, the workers were assured by the leaders that the army would never "dare" fire on fellow Poles. But no bourgeoisie could indefinitely tolerate the sort of challenge posed by the Polish workers, and even as the conventional methods of rule became paralyzed in the face of the upsurge, the army finally moved to crush it.

Both experiences underscore, among other important lessons, that the proletariat can *only* achieve power through armed insurrection, through a violent revolution against the bourgeois state; and that any line to the contrary is not at all harmless, but an attempt to divert the proletariat from this crucial understanding and from preparations for revolution, and to reduce it to a pawn for one or another bourgeoisie, or bourgeois clique.

But the question immediately arises: after smashing the state machine of the bourgeoisie, with what is the proletariat to replace it?

The Dictatorship of the Proletariat

Even as its army moves forward to decisively defeat and suppress the bourgeoisie, the proletariat must begin constructing a new society upon the ashes of the old. To do this it forges a state apparatus unlike any in history: the *dictatorship of the proletariat*. With this new type of state the workers (and masses of oppressed generally) for the first time seize the levers of their own destiny. Further, the proletarian state doesn't mask its class character (or its dual aspects of dictatorship over the exploiters and democracy for the masses) but openly proclaims it.

But this, while extremely significant, is still not the *essence* of its unique character. The crucial point is that this proletarian dictatorship exists not to perpetuate indefinitely the rule of one class, but to eliminate all classes and all states; it is a means to the end of wiping out all class distinctions, all machinery of oppression, and the state itself; it is a bridge to communist society. All its various characteristics, plans, accomplishments and struggles have to be measured and analyzed in that light.

Marx emphasized this early on:

> This socialism is the *declaration of the permanence of the revolution*, the *class dictatorship* of the proletariat as the necessary transit point to the *abolition of class distinctions generally*, to the abolition of all the relations of production on which they rest, to the abolition of all the social relations that correspond to these relations of production, to the revolutionising of all the ideas that result from these social relations. ("The Class Struggles in France," *MESW*, Vol. 1, 282)

The dictatorship of the proletariat, then, is above all else *transitional* to a higher form of society, classless and hence stateless. As Bob Avakian has pointed out, to lose sight of this and treat proletarian dictatorship as an absolute leads to capitalist restoration.

Marx's later important work, *Critique of the Gotha Programme*, indicated the distinguishing characteristics of communist society, and outlined the material and social prerequisites for its attainment:

> In a higher phase of communist society, after the enslaving subordination of the individual to the division of labour, and with it also the antithesis between mental and physical labour, has vanished; after labour has become not only a means of life but itself life's prime want; after the productive forces have also increased with the all-round development of the individual, and all the springs of co-operative wealth flow more abundantly — only then can the narrow horizon of bourgeois right be crossed in its entirety and society inscribe on its banners: From each according to his ability, to each according to his needs! (*Critique of the Gotha Programme*, FLP, 1972, p. 17)[10]

In communist society, each of its members will function as both planner and worker, and labor will be transformed from numbing drudgery into the medium through which "all mankind voluntarily and consciously changes itself and the world." ("On Practice," *MSR*, 81) Humanity will have overcome the blind and irrational compulsion of commodity relations, its anarchy and its whip of hunger, and the struggle among society's members to advance their mastery over nature and their own social relations will no longer be bound in the constrictive orbit of class antagonism.

But while *class* contradiction and the methods of class struggle — including the mechanism of the state — will have been transcended under communism, *social* contradictions themselves will not. Contradictions between productive forces and production relations, between the production relations (economic base)

---

[10]*Bourgeois right* originally referred to the equal right of each member of socialist society to be paid according to their work. While a great advance over capitalist society (as it basically, if relatively, eliminates exploitation), this equal right retains an aspect of commodity relations to it, in that it is still fundamentally an expression of the labor theory of value. Further, since individuals possess different capabilities and different needs, this formal equality masks real inequality, and thus, as Marx pointed out, right in this case was still *bourgeois* right. Since that time, bourgeois right has acquired a broader meaning among Marxist-Leninists, standing for all the relations of socialist society that contain seeds of the old capitalist commodity relations, and *which must be eliminated for the achievement of communism.*

and the ideological and political superstructure, between the old and new, between correct and incorrect ideas, and even between leadership and led will continue, and the struggle arising from them will be the motive force in society's further development. But again this will be on a level of social development and on a scale that justifies Marx's classing of all history prior to communist society as *pre*history.

Communism will of necessity be global. For one thing, the productive forces of modern society are global and can ultimately only be rationally utilized on that level. Further, the class struggle is international, and so long as the bourgeoisie retains control in any country (or even continues in one form or another to exist as a class), that country will serve as a potential base area for attacks on proletarian rule. Thus the achievement of communism is bound up with eliminating class distinctions *internationally* and breaking down national boundaries and nations altogether, replacing them with higher forms of human society.

The destruction of bourgeois rule, in even a single country, marks a tremendous leap for the proletariat toward achieving this goal. But this struggle doesn't develop evenly. Proletarian revolution hasn't broken out all over the world simultaneously, and even where victorious it has not been able to abolish all bourgeois relations overnight — or even over decades. If the revolution endows the proletariat with tremendous new freedom, it also presents it with a whole new necessity.

To begin with, taking the fact that the proletariat has up till now seized power in one or several countries at a time (a pattern which will no doubt hold true for some time to come), we find what has proven to be an extremely difficult contradiction: between seizing power in a specific country (or countries), and wielding that power as a force first and foremost for the *international* proletarian revolution. On one hand, with successful revolution the proletariat gains what in a certain sense amounts to a *base area* from which to provide political, material and military support for its international struggle. The newborn Soviet state in 1918, to take a dramatic example, prepared to mount a three-million-strong army to aid the German proletariat if the revolutionary situation there developed into a full-scale contest for power — a step which would have risked the proletariat's own grip on power in Russia for what was perceived to be a greater good for the international movement. (The German revolution did not mature to the point where such aid would have really played a key role, however.) Even beyond straight-up military aid, potentially important though that may be, there is political support and inspiration from the proletarian state; Mao once pointed out in discussing the Chinese Revolution that the "salvoes of the October Revolution brought us Marxism-Leninism," and thereby laid the basis for a leap in the century-long struggle of the Chinese people against imperialist domination. The main orientation of the proletariat in power in any given country, then, must be toward pushing forward the greatest possible gains in the world revolution.

However, within that there are times in which overall the revolutionary struggle on a world scale goes into relative ebb, and the proletarian state may have to focus more than usual on consolidating what has been won (the better to advance later); this may entail, in the face of imperialist encirclement and subversion, compromises with imperialist powers and utilizing contradictions within their camp. This contradiction has found sharpest expression precisely at those times when the world is heading toward a major conjuncture; then the pressure on the socialist state (or states) tends to immeasurably increase, while the seeds of new opportunities for worldwide advance may have only just begun to germinate. How, then, the international proletariat weighs the relationship between using — and risking — state power where it has it, in order to advance the struggle where it doesn't, and how it makes use of its base areas to advance the world proletarian revolution without lightly or needlessly sacrificing them, becomes crucial in determining whether the proletarian state stays red and, moreover, whether the world revolution advances.[11]

---

[11]Here a word on Trotskyism (and its progenitor, Leon Trotsky) is necessary. Trotsky joined with the Bolsheviks several months before the October Revolution. Later, when the international upsurge that took place around World War 1 and the October Revolution had ebbed, Trotsky held that it would be impossible for the Russian proletariat to establish a socialist system in one country. Rather than grapple with the contradictions actually facing the international proletariat, Trotsky retreated, albeit behind a "left" mask of calling for revolution throughout Europe all at once. In the absence of conditions for such an advance, Trotsky soon ended up apologizing for capitulation — with a programme for the Soviet Union of draconian military discipline against both peasants and workers, and reliance on foreign capital to develop the country. He was exposed and defeated by Stalin, who went on to lead the Soviet state in socialist construction and transformation.

Interpenetrating all this is the lopsided development of the world due to imperialism. Thus far revolution has taken place in the more backward areas of the world (even Russia was the most backward of the imperialist countries) and this has meant tremendous problems in the form of political, military, economic and ideological pressures from without. And while revolution in a citadel of imperialism would tremendously alter the terms of this contradiction, the contradiction itself — that is, the concentration of productive forces and the phenomenon, or legacy, of parasitism in the imperialist, or formerly imperialist, nations as against the distorted and stunted development of the oppressed nations — will likely be with us for some time to come. This underscores the fact that even production within a socialist country takes place within an overriding international context and that the proletariat in these countries — and this applies especially to the proletariat in power in a former imperialist citadel — must carry out production to serve the world revolution (and not principally to build up the particular socialist country).

All this sets the context for the sharp contradictions that are relatively *internal* to socialist society. Here, too, there is tremendous new freedom as well as new necessity. In this light it's important to recall Marx and Engels' point that the proletariat "cannot just lay hold of" the old bourgeois machine and make it work for new proletarian ends. The proletarian state must be qualitatively different from any state (whether initially revolutionary or not) which went before because its historic task is so different. Bourgeois revolutions (whose goals have all been to replace feudal with bourgeois exploitation) drew in the masses only insofar as they were needed to break the power of the old rulers; after the revolution the bourgeoisie invariably moved to clamp the lid back down. Napoleon's ascendancy to emperor after the French Revolution, and the white terror unleashed in the U.S. South after Reconstruction, in part illustrate this general phenomenon.

The proletariat, however, has as its final goal a society marked by the conscious participation and struggle of all its members, and draws its main strength from the *masses* and their conscious activism. It is true and very important that by socializing ownership of the means of production the proletariat gains a powerful new material base — but even maintaining and pushing forward this material base depends on the consciousness of the masses. The proletariat can neither meet its immediate tasks nor advance to the final goal without a state apparatus that draws the broadest sections of the masses into political life, helps to raise their consciousness and works to sustain and broaden their activity through the ebbs and flows of struggle (in particular, as those ebbs and flows take place in the most decisive — and more complex — context of the international struggle). Therein lie the particular challenges that face the proletariat "organized as ruling class" — and therein as well its tremendous advantages.

Lenin viewed the proletarian dictatorship as a powerful lever to move millions of hitherto passive and dormant masses into active political life, and he counted on this in struggling for the party to undertake the October Revolution. Arguing against those who held that the proletariat was too weak to carry through an insurrection and consolidate power, Lenin replied:

> *We have not yet seen*, however, the strength of resistance of the proletarians and poor peasants, for this strength will become fully apparent only when power is in the hands of the proletariat, when tens of millions of people who have been crushed by want and capitalist slavery see from experience and *feel* that state power has passed into the hands of the oppressed classes, that the state is helping the poor to fight the landowners and capitalists, is *breaking* their resistance. *Only* then shall we see what untapped forces of resistance to the capitalists are latent among the people; only then will what Engels called "latent socialism" manifest itself. Only then for every *ten thousand* overt and concealed enemies of working-class rule, manifesting themselves actively or by passive resistance, there will arise *a million* new fighters who had been politically dormant, writhing in the torments of poverty and despair, having ceased to believe that they were human, that they had the right to live, that they too could be served by the entire might of the modern centralised state, that contingents of the proletarian militia could, with the fullest confidence, also call upon *them* to take a direct, immediate, daily part in state administration. ("Can the Bolsheviks Retain State Power?," *LCW*, Vol. 26, 126)

And later, in the midst of the invasion by 14 different imperialist armies (at one time or another) during the grueling civil war, Lenin summed up that "the most important conclusion to be drawn from the two years of developing the Soviet Republic" was that "only workers' participation in the general administration of the state has enabled us to hold out amidst such incredible difficulties...." ("Two Years of Soviet Rule," *LCW*, Vol. 30, 28-29)

The dictatorship of the proletariat is dictatorship *over* the bourgeoisie; and for the first time real democracy becomes possible for the proletariat and the great masses of people. But this is democracy of an entirely different dimension than *bourgeois* democracy — as can be seen in Mao's comment in criticizing the revisionist version of proletarian democracy found in a Soviet textbook:

> . . . we find a discussion of the rights labor enjoys but no discussion of labor's right to run the state, the various enterprises, education and culture. Actually, this is labor's greatest right under socialism, the most fundamental right, without which there is no right to work, to an education, to vacation, etc.
>
> The paramount issue for socialist democracy is: Does labor have the right to subdue the various antagonistic forces and their influences? For example, who controls things like the newspapers, journals, broadcast stations, the cinema? Who criticizes? (Mao Tsetung, *A Critique of Soviet Economics*, Monthly Review, 1977, p. 61)

The proletarian dictatorship will, for example, throw open to the masses the vast means of communication currently dominated by the bourgeoisie and its ideologues. While this will be under the overall leadership and guidance of the proletarian party, and while the bourgeoisie will *not* be granted this freedom, the masses will not be suppressed in putting forward and struggling over ideas, even ones held to be backward and mistaken. Even in the case of counter-revolutionary attempts to hide behind this right, it is, again, the masses who must and will be relied upon to struggle against, expose and suppress such people, and to distinguish through such struggle what are backward and mistaken ideas among the masses and what are real attempts at counter-revolution.

The proletariat, then, will have to forge new forms which really do draw millions into the struggle against the bourgeoisie (and the different form the bourgeoisie begins to assume under socialism — more on this later) and the interlinked battle to transform all of society and reshape the world. The state organs, the courts, the army — all must reflect both the necessity for the proletariat to carry forward the struggle against the bourgeoisie in all its dimensions, and its freedom in doing that to unleash and rely on the conscious activism of the masses.

Anarchism vs. a Genuine Transition
to Communism

But it is *not*, contrary to anarchism, possible to abolish the state overnight and replace it with some sort of network of self-sufficient communes or autonomously-run factories and/or cooperatives. In the anarchist model of the world, these decentralized units would informally make their own decisions and if attacked would defend themselves through arming the entire people as one, thus allowing for the immediate abolition of state organs and the army.

From the very beginning this view tends to "forget" that the proletarian revolution is a worldwide process, and that the proletariat has the responsibility anywhere it seizes power both to strengthen its apparatus as a base and springboard for other revolutions, and — especially during ebbs — to wage determined struggle to preserve and further transform the base areas it has won. Because of the uneven development of the proletarian revolution, all socialist states thus far have had to field a *professional* army, necessarily standing apart to a significant degree from the masses, and charged with much of the responsibility for repelling invasion. Even where the masses are broadly organized into militias under a correct line, and where measures are taken and fought for to keep proletarian politics in command of the army and militias, there is no getting around this objective need for an army, and this itself is a major expression of the fact that the state cannot be immediately abolished.

Further, there is a material basis necessary for the full transition to communism, which — while indefinite in a sense — at the least must include the basis to eliminate, as Marx put it, humanity's "enslaving subordination to the division of labor." This division of labor today has a real material basis in that the skills of technicians, scientists, administrators and so on are both necessary and they are impossible to master overnight; this inevitably gives rise to a tendency for those who have those skills and knowledge to hoard them like capital, to bargain against the proletariat in power and to try as far as possible to resist the restriction of the division of labor. Thus the proletariat needs a mechanism — and call it what you will, but in essence it will be a state — to "bribe" these strata to work, to win over those who can be won over and to enforce the transformations in the division of labor that *can* be carried out at any given time, against the resistance that large sections of these strata are bound to put up.

The same general contradiction holds true for other strata intermediate between the proletariat and the bourgeoisie, especially the peasantry,[12] which forms the vast majority of the population in many third world countries and a significant portion in all of them. While a broad and deep basis of unity exists between the proletariat and the peasantry, there is also a powerful spontaneous tendency in the countryside towards bourgeois relations. This tendency finds roots in the still primitive character of the productive forces (generally used by individuals), the continued class differentiation (between richer and poorer peasants, and between agricultural technicians, administrators, party officials, etc. — at least those who strive to hold on to their relatively privileged position — and the masses), and finally in bourgeois forms of ownership. Even collective ownership which is not yet state ownership retains a strong bourgeois aspect if the collective attempts to improve its position in relation to other collectives or the state. The tendency to bourgeois relations also feeds on the narrow and individualist outlook handed down through centuries — which to a significant degree is reinforced by the powerful survivals of bourgeois right and the backward material conditions generally that remain for some time in socialist society, especially in the countryside.

These contradictions alone sharply point up the limitations in the anarchist schema. But something even more fundamentally wrong is involved in the very way in which the anarchists conceive of the final goal.

Essentially, anarchism equates communist society to some sort of "pure" democracy on the town meeting model, and then extends this to the production relations. To take the latter aspect first, to make workers' control of "their own" factories the highest goal ignores the necessarily internationally integrated

---

[12]A further earmark of Trotskyism is its insistence that the proletariat cannot forge a durable alliance with the peasantry. Here again, while the task of leading the peasantry from individual production has proven to be full of contradiction and struggle, it has also been shown to be both possible and necessary if the revolution is to go forward, and especially if the revolution in the oppressed nations is to play its full role.

character of production in this era and cuts against the need for society as a whole to appropriate and master it on an international level. If there is to be some sort of network that integrates these factories, then how are the contradictions between the individual factories and the overall plan to be resolved? Without, that is, using some form of administration in society to which lesser, smaller units are subordinate — and in a society still divided into classes this can only mean a form of *state*.

Leaving revolution at the level of the workers in a single factory more or less acting as the proprietors is not only profoundly reformist — after all, there are even cases in capitalist society where the workers raise the money to take over and run a failing plant — but even if somehow implemented could only lead back to capitalism. Bob Avakian, in an interview focusing on anarchism, pointed out that:

> You will have the marks of the division of labor, the unevenness between the workers. And you will still have leftovers of commodity production and so on. These things will exert their influence, whether you want to think so or not. The result will be that within the individual factories and between them you will get capitalist competition, stratification, and you will have bourgeois relations immediately — and I mean almost literally immediately — re-emerging and these factories will be run along a bourgeois basis. And in fact a bourgeois state will be reconstituted to enforce the interests of those bourgeois forces who float to the surface, so to speak, or who step on the others to get to the top. Because along with things in the material sphere, ideologically the people will still be bearing the birthmarks of the old society. (*There's Nothing More Revolutionary Than Marxism-Leninism, Mao Tsetung Thought*, RCP Pubs., 1982, p. 8)

Politically, in its emphasis on "pure democracy" at the basic level, anarchism is very close to economism — and, especially in the imperialist countries, to chauvinism too. Anarchism sounds a retreat from the struggle of the proletariat to master "affairs of state," take up the cardinal political questions facing all of society, and exercise dictatorship in every sphere. This retreat may take place under a radical cover, but it's nonetheless capitulation to the hegemony of the bourgeoisie.

And anarchism is chauvinist in that it glosses over or ignores the problems of the oppressive production relations between different nations, a tendency which can only end up in (or rather, persist in and deepen) the domination of the oppressing nations. It's no longer a novelty for states to proclaim themselves communist or socialist, and to institute certain internal reforms — even, for example, the workers' self-management teams in "socialist Sweden" — while carrying out and sharing in the spoils from the most brutal exploitation of the oppressed nations. This oppression is a fundamental component of the platform for such reforms and marks the content of these states as imperialist and bourgeois, whatever their label.

What finally shines through in anarchism, however, is the outlook of the petty proprietor, whose highest goal is the power to determine the immediate conditions of his own life; a viewpoint which is ultimately opposed to that of a class which is collective and international in character and which must strive to transform the world on that basis.

Revisionism: Defense of the Backward and Counter-revolution

On the other hand, all this points to some of the real contradictions that face the proletariat in carrying out its dictatorship and carrying through its revolutionary mission. And the necessity posed by these contradictions has historically been exploited by revisionism, which has been, and certainly still is, the main ideological and political danger to the revolutionary movement on this question.

It is true, for example, that an army is necessary, and that the proletarian army will be qualitatively different from bourgeois ones; at the same time, such an army is nevertheless a double-edged sword which can cut back *against* the proletariat in certain conditions. Should a revisionist clique gain control of the army, it has a powerful base for a move against the proletarian dictatorship. Those within the army who, for instance, treat the maintenance of its "professional standards" as their highest goal can easily end up resisting the revolutionary upheaval and turmoil within socialist society — turmoil which inevitably touches on and stirs up the army — and find themselves opposed to the struggle necessary to advance society further towards communism at any given juncture (which includes not only struggles internal to socialist countries, but also the demands of the world revolution, which at times may even necessitate the temporary sacrifice of power in one or another socialist country or certainly the risk of this).

In fact, in China the Defense Ministers Peng Teh-huai (in 1959) and Lin Biao (in 1971) led two of the attempts to overthrow the revolutionary proletariat and "restore order," and the military was generally an important base for other bourgeois headquarters and their reactionary revolts, including the coup of 1976 that began the restoration of capitalism. Still, the proletariat could not simply dissolve the army as a long-term strategy. Even had the revolutionaries been able after the 1976 coup to mount an effective rebellion against what had by then largely become a tool of the (new) bourgeoisie and smash it (as might well have been necessary), they would not have been able to indefinitely evade the contradictions which make an army necessary in the first place, and would have had to reconstitute one.

The same holds true with many other institutions and characteristics of the proletarian dictatorship, which are at one and the same time important advances but advances and weapons which can be turned into their opposites. Central planning, under proletarian leadership, can marshall the resources and labor of the entire country in the interests of the world revolution and the advance of socialist relations; under revisionist domination, it can reproduce the still remaining bourgeois relations on a vast scale and be used to suppress the initiative — and opposition — of the masses. And so on, in every sphere of society. The fact is that the basic crushing of overt bourgeois resistance through revolutionary insurrection and civil war, the setting up of proletarian power, and the initial transformations in the economic base do *not* settle the issue. As Mao pointed out:

> The class struggle is by no means over. The class struggle between the proletariat and the bourgeoisie, the class struggle between the different political forces, and the class struggle in the ideological field between the proletariat and the bourgeoisie will continue to be long and tortuous and at times will even become very acute. The proletariat seeks to transform the world according to its own world outlook, and so does the bourgeoisie. In this respect, the question of which will win out, socialism or capitalism, is still not really settled. ("On the Correct Handling of Contradictions Among the People," *MSR*, 463-464)

Lenin, too, stressed the contradictory nature of socialism and characterized the transition between capitalism and communism as a period "[which] cannot but combine the features and properties of both these forms of social economy." He continued:

> This transition period cannot but be a period of struggle between moribund capitalism and nascent communism — or, in other words, between capitalism which has been defeated but not destroyed and communism which has been born but which is still very feeble. (*Economics and Politics in the Era of the Dictatorship of the Proletariat*, FLP, 1975, p. 1)

This struggle runs through the entire period of the transition to communism, and it takes its most concentrated and crucial form as class struggle between the proletariat and the bourgeoisie, including the *new* bourgeoisie(s) generated within socialist society. To understand its dynamics it is necessary to examine more deeply the contradictions characteristic of socialist society.

Contradictions of Socialist Society

It is crucial again to keep in mind that even within socialist societies, the terms of the class struggle are set by the international situation. For instance, how the proletariat carries out the overall approach of unity and struggle with the various intermediate strata, how many concessions it must make to them — and how many concessions it *can* make, too — is determined by its strength worldwide. And the way in which the various contradictions of imperialism worldwide develop and interpenetrate lends different reserves at different times to the proletariat or the bourgeoisie within the socialist country (and may at the same time place special demands on those fighting for a proletarian line and policy within the socialist country). It is within that context that the internal contradictions of socialist society unfold and develop.[13]

As discussed in Chapter 2, the foundation of every society lies in its economic base, i.e., the production relations upon which the politics, culture, institutions, ideology, etc., arise as a superstruc-

---

[13]For a detailed examination of how this relation developed in China, see Bob Avakian, *The Loss in China and The Revolutionary Legacy of Mao Tsetung*, RCP Publications, Chicago, 1978.

ture. The economic base in turn is conditioned by the level of development of the productive forces. Generally speaking, the productive forces develop within the economic base and soon outstrip it, and — in Marx's phrase — "from forms of development of the productive forces these relations turn into their fetters." ("Preface to *A Contribution to the Critique of Political Economy*," *MESW*, Vol. 1, 504) The productive forces both demand change in the economic relations for their further development, and at the same time set the horizons (understood in a relative sense) for that change.

The first key step of the proletarian dictatorship in transforming the economic base is its appropriation of the commanding levers and lifelines of the economy, the control of production, finance and trade. With power consolidated, the proletariat moves more or less quickly to socialize ownership (according to the conditions and especially the level of development of the country). In the sphere of distribution, the proletarian state institutes payment according to one's work (and not according to capital owned), and from the very beginning the workers themselves undertake to a large extent the actual running of the factories and other workplaces.[14]

These measures constitute a basic rupture with bourgeois production relations, and provide the proletariat with a powerful material base from which to go forward; but unless they are followed up and deepened, capitalist elements will again grow back and predominate, even if in collective form.

Why is this so? Because, as Marx pointed out:

> What we have to deal with here is a communist society, not as it has *developed* on its own foundations, but, on the contrary, just as it *emerges* from capitalist society; which is thus in every respect, economically, morally and intellectually, still stamped with the birthmarks of the old society from whose womb it emerges. ("Critique of the Gotha Programme," *MESW*, Vol. 3, 17)

These birthmarks — which include the remaining commodity production and commodity relations; inequality between mental and manual labor, city and country and industry and agriculture;

---

[14]The economic relations of society are divided into the ownership system, the relations between people carrying out production, and distribution. See Chapter 2.

and even payment for work (which is ultimately an expression of the labor theory of value) — are characterized as *bourgeois right* and contain *the seeds of capitalist relations*, which are fostered in the event a revisionist line takes command.

Let's look at the important contradiction between mental and manual labor. In no socialist society thus far (and in no foreseeable socialist society that might emerge in the near future) has it been possible for everyone to obtain in a period of a few years the training and education necessary to break down the distinctions between technicians, engineers, planners, administrators, etc., on the one hand, and manual workers on the other. These differences *per se* do not connote exploitation. Yet the higher pay for such skilled work (which corresponds to payment according to work, and is generally necessary to obtain the cooperation of such strata) and the spontaneous tendencies for the mental workers to control the productive process make up *soil* from which exploitative relations can arise within a socialist shell. This is particularly important as it applies to cadre with overall responsibility for economic units.

Bob Avakian has written that:

> If the leading cadres do not take part in productive labor together with the masses; if at the same time they increase their income relative to that of the masses, through expanded wage differentials, bonuses proportional to wages, etc.; if they put profit in command [as the criterion for deciding what to produce and how to do it — LW]; and if they monopolize management and planning while the masses of manual workers are effectively barred from these things rather than being politically activated to take part in them and supervise the leading cadres; then in essence how much different is the relationship between the leading cadres and the working masses from that between the workers and the capitalists in capitalist society? (*Immortal*, 302)

And he then points to the more critical sphere of the overall control of different realms of production:

> And with regard to the high officials who exercise leadership in the ministries, in finance and trade, etc., if they follow the same revisionist line, divorce themselves from the masses and productive labor and effectively monopolize control over these spheres, how much different are they than executives of big corporations and banks in the capitalist countries? (*Immortal*, 302-305)

There is, of course, a difference, in that the proletariat holds state power and the economy (and society) have an overall socialist charater — unless or until there is a qualitative change in society as a whole, a seizure of power by the bourgeoisie. This crucial and fundamental point will be addressed in more depth shortly. However, continuing to focus on some of the contradictions within the economic base of socialism, it's important to grasp both the implications of the mental/manual division *and* the fact that this is hardly the only source of struggle within the economic base. The relationships between city and countryside, and between industry and agriculture, can also be transformed either forward or backward.

Both the unequal development between city and country, as well as the character of the socialist forms of ownership in the countryside, are important in this respect. In socialist China, in the main, ownership in agriculture did not go beyond collective ownership by the peasants of a locality. The collective sold its goods (or the great bulk of them) to the state, and the state in turn provided equipment, fertilizer, etc., to the collective. Here, ultimately due to the level of the productive forces, value relations had to be taken into account — it's not possible for this exchange to go on on the basis of need alone — and thus it had some character of *commodity* exchange even if basically determined by a state plan. If not correctly handled this could have generated antagonism between the workers and peasants and aggravated the gap between the two (either through making terms too unfavorable to the peasantry and trying to industrialize "off their backs," or alternately allowing the peasants, or better-off sections of them, to extort from the state and the masses). Further, the uneven development *between* different agricultural units will, if left to spontaneity, lead to the better-off ones monopolizing machinery, fertilizer, etc., and thus to a big gap — with capitalist-style competition and polarization — developing between them. [15]

In light of the above, the difference between the socialist principle of "to each according to their work" and the communist one of "to each according to their need" should be looked at again.

---

[15] The blatantly revisionist line and policies that turn over great stretches of collective land and resources to individual farming on a profit basis ("as an incentive") also obviously foster and reproduce bourgeois relations.

While the socialist distribution principle is an historic advance over capitalism — *basically* (though not absolutely), preventing anyone from living off the labor of another — it yet contains *seeds* of bourgeois relations. Not only do skilled workers receive more for their work than unskilled, but even among workers receiving the same pay there are different conditions (e.g., a single worker vs. a worker supporting a large family) which can make for polarization. And so long as collective ownership — rather than ownership by the whole people — exists, especially in agriculture, there will still be *significant* differences in pay between workers and peasants, and between peasants (or workers in collective enterprises) of different units. Finally, the idea of promoting "to each according to their work" as *the* great principle of socialism can feed a self-interested, "what's-in-it-for-me?" attitude — an attitude unavoidable among some sections for a time and exerting a pull in society in general, but which has to be struggled against and eventually fully overcome to reach communism.

Thus the simple development of the productive forces under state ownership cannot resolve the contradictions before the proletariat in leading the transition to communism. Made an end in itself, development of the productive forces can in fact do nothing but widen divisions and reproduce the old bourgeois birthmarks on an extended scale, providing a powerful material and social basis for those forces wanting to restore capitalism, even if the capitalism they want to restore has a socialist label on it and certain outer forms established under socialism (for example, state and collective ownership). The ownership system, and the socialist economic base as a whole, is not after all a machine with a button to press, guaranteed to grind out socialism; it is a very fluid and contradictory ensemble of social *relations* which can be transformed into its opposite if not constantly and continually revolutionized by the proletariat toward communism.

Commodity exchange and the law of value also continue to exist in socialist society and can reproduce bourgeois relations if not correctly handled by the proletariat. In socialist societies thus far (and, again, for the foreseeable future) consumer goods have in the main taken the form of commodities (i.e., they are exchanged for money). Further, relations between the state and the various economic units under its ownership, and between these units themselves, generally take the form of contracts that must be fulfilled and exchanges that must reflect to a significant degree the law of value; thus even the means of production have aspects of commodities to them. All this exists in contradiction to the degree that the proletariat is able in its masses to exert conscious control over the whole process of planning, production, exchange, and so on; and which aspect of that contradiction is expanded is a vitally important question in persevering in socialist transformation. Whether the proletariat consciously takes into account these remaining expressions of commodity production and exchange and the law of value, utilizing them while restricting them to the greatest degree possible — *or* whether spontaneity and, even more, forces that seek capitalist restoration, run rampant, eventually transforming the different sectors of the economy into pieces of capital anarchically competing with one another — is yet another important contradiction.

Further, the superstructure has a tremendous impact on the economic base. While this principally expresses itself in the overriding importance of ideological and political line in socialist society (more on this shortly), there is also the influence of such areas of the superstructure as education, art and culture, journalism, etc., on the economic base and their ability to transform it either forward towards communism, or backward to capitalist restoration.

Take education. Bourgeois education, as the *Manifesto* so aptly characterizes it, "is, for the enormous majority, a mere training to act as a machine." (52) Can such a system — with its tracking, its competition for grades, its view toward knowledge as personal property to be jealously hoarded and used as capital, its separation of theory and practice as well as its generally idealist and metaphysical method and its demand for the unquestioning obedience to authority — can this, or even elements of it, fail to harm the socialist base? And this doesn't even begin to take into account the highly political ways — *bourgeois* political — in which history, literature, social sciences, physical sciences, etc., are taught. Without, then, the fiercest struggle against the old and the most wide-ranging and deep-going creation of the new, the educational system will produce batches of technicians, officials, scientists, teachers — and *workers* — with the same bourgeois outlook as before, people trained to reflexively try to enforce, or go along with, the same capitalist-type hierarchical relations in production and indeed throughout society.

Or look at art and culture. The bulk of art in bourgeois society satisfies the needs and helps promote the outlook of the bourgeoisie and the backward in society. Further, the bourgeoisie suppresses advanced expressions in this sphere. Here the proletariat's tasks are again vitally important, as well as complex and far-reaching; it not only must criticize the old and sweep really reactionary filth off the stage, but even more must lead in creating new and higher works of art that really concentrate the forward motion of history, the interests and outlook of the international proletariat and the struggle in every sphere for communism.

Classes Under Socialism

The various contradictions in the economic base (and between the base and superstructure) and their ramifications were examined in depth in a significant work published in 1974 by the Revolutionary Union (forerunner of the Revolutionary Communist Party, USA), *How Capitalism Has Been Restored in the Soviet Union and What This Means for the World Struggle*. There it is pointed out that if the masses are not *politically* led to actively and consciously take up the planning and carrying through of the production process, *"then some other way must be found* to induce, and ultimately to *force*, the masses into production of a surplus."* Continuing:

> It is impossible for some classless group of "bureaucrats" to rule society in the name of the proletariat, because in order to maintain such rule these "bureaucrats" must organize the production and distribution of goods and services. If bureaucratic methods of doing this prevail and come to *politically characterize* the planning process under socialism; and if a group of bureaucrats, divorced from and not relying upon the masses, makes the decisions on how to carry out this process; then inevitably this will be done along capitalist lines.
>
> In the final analysis, the revisionists can only fall back on the law of value as the "lever" which organizes production. They must reduce the workers to propertyless proletarians, competing in the sale of their single commodity — their labor power — to live. They must appeal to the narrow self-interest of the worker in this competition, backing this up with the power of the state, as a force standing above and oppressing the workers, a weapon in the hands of the owners of the means of production. They must do this because they must find some way to organize production which they cannot do consciously in a planned way by themselves. *They have no choice but to become a new bourgeoisie.* (55-56)

"They have no choice but to become a new bourgeoisie." In other words, bourgeois relations — or even, rather, the seeds of bourgeois relations — within the economic base generate a bourgeois class which (to paraphrase Marx in *Capital*) personifies those relations. Further, these bourgeois forces find their soil not only in the economic base but in the superstructure as well (speaking in particular of the way in which bourgeois institutions, habits of doing things, ideas, etc., in government, education, art, etc., etc., react back on the economic base and influence it in a negative direction). This was summed up by Chang Chun-chiao in an important work, "On Exercising All-Round Dictatorship Over the Bourgeoisie":[16]

> . . . we must see that both ownership by the whole people and collective ownership involve the question of leadership, that is, the question of which class holds the ownership in fact and not just in name.
>
> . . . It is perfectly correct for people to give full weight to the decisive role of the system of ownership in the relations of production. But it is incorrect to give no weight to whether the issue of ownership has been resolved merely in form or in actual fact, to the reaction upon the system of ownership exerted by the two other aspects of the relations of production — the relations among people and the form of distribution — and to the reaction upon the economic base exerted by the superstructure; these two aspects and the superstructure may play a decisive role under given conditions. Politics is the concentrated expression of economics. Whether the ideological and political line is correct or incorrect, and which class holds the leadership, decides which class owns those factories in actual fact. (in Raymond Lotta, ed., *And Mao Makes Five*, Banner Press, 1978, pp. 213-214)

The struggle over political and ideological line is for that reason so intense and critical all through socialist society. If those leaders who pursue a revisionist line and fight for the capitalist road, and who in essence represent the bourgeois production

---

[16]Chang Chun-chiao was a major leader of the proletarian headquarters grouped around Mao within the Communist Party of China from the Cultural Revolution onwards, and this 1975 article came at an important stage of Mao's last great battle against the revisionist clique led by Zhou Enlai and Deng Xiaoping. Chang was arrested in the 1976 anti-socialist coup, and along with Chiang Ching — another important leader of the Cultural Revolution, who made particularly important contributions in the field of revolutionizing culture — set a stirring example of proletarian defiance at the counter-revolutionary trial in Peking in 1980-81.

relations which have been vanquished but not yet eliminated, are victorious, then they can transform relations between themselves and the masses under their leadership into ones of exploitation and oppression. Bourgeois relations thus arise within the collective form, and the representatives of those relations form the *new* bourgeoisie (as distinct from the dispossessed exploiters of the old society who, though making up a significant social base for capitalist restoration, are not the *main* threat — after they have been deprived of ownership of the means of production, as well as political rights). These new bourgeois elements seek out allies, form factions and headquarters, and wage a concerted fight for their line in every sphere — and ultimately for political power overall.

Mao's Historic Contributions

And this is exactly what led to a bourgeois coup from within the party in the Soviet Union in 1956. While clinging to the socialist label (and certain institutions like central planning, state ownership, etc.), the new Soviet bourgeoisie signalled its ascendancy with a major attack by Nikita Khrushchev on Stalin (and by extension on the practice of socialist construction and the international communist movement overall, which Stalin led for nearly 30 years, from the time of Lenin's death in 1924). Khrushchev also launched a major theoretical broadside which declared the concept of the dictatorship of the proletariat (among a number of other important Leninist principles) outdated and no longer applicable. This reversal confused and disoriented the majority of the international movement, and even among those determined to stay on the revolutionary road it was crucial to analyze the significance of Khrushchev's coup and his theoretical offensive.

This analysis was led by Mao Tsetung, who in a series of polemics with the Soviet party, as well as in other writings and talks, not only scientifically summed up the positive and negative experience of the Soviet Union under Stalin, but even more importantly, qualitatively developed Marxist theory on the transition to communism and the proletarian dictatorship.[17] Mao and

---

[17]See the collections, *Polemic On the General Line of the International Communist Movement* (Red Star Press, London, 1976), *Whence the Differences?* (n.p., n.d.), *And Mao Makes Five* (Banner Press, Chicago, 1978). While the polemics against the Soviets were not directly accredited to Mao, he gave basic guidance to them and directly wrote some.

the Chinese Communist Party summed up that Stalin was overall a great revolutionary who led in the unprecedented and difficult years of the construction of the first socialist state. He led the basic transformation of private ownership in the Soviet Union (including the really enormous task of socializing agriculture) and the new society's defense against incredible pressure from within and from without, concentrated in (but not limited to) the grueling attack by the main force of the German army in World War 2.

But Stalin also made serious errors, some of which were basically unavoidable in undertaking such an entirely unprecedented task as building socialism, and some of which were linked to important mistakes in ideological and political line. Stalin's theories concerning class struggle in socialist society and socialist construction in particular fed the strength of the new bourgeois forces.

Stalin by the mid-30s held that with the socialization of agriculture and the basic elimination of private ownership, antagonistic classes no longer existed under socialism; the source of all social contradictions, he reasoned, must then lie in the activities either of the remnants of the old exploiters, or of agents of one or another imperialist power. While these forces did wage struggle against the socialist state, they did not pose as great or immediate a threat to the proletariat and its state as the bourgeois forces generated within socialist society by the contradictory character of socialist relations and the socialist superstructure. But Stalin, not grasping this, tended therefore to treat *all* opposition and contradiction (including opposition from those who were mistaken, or who assumed an antagonistic position at a given point but were not necessarily die-hard counter-revolutionaries, or some who were even genuine revolutionaries) as counter-revolution, and hence seriously widened the target of the class struggle and carried it out too repressively. Still more important, however, the *real* bourgeoisie — which, as Mao was later to elucidate, had its headquarters in the top reaches of the communist party — got off the hook and even flourished.

This error was linked in turn to Stalin's espousal of what amounted to a form of the "theory of the productive forces." Stalin believed that once ownership had in the main been socialized, the key task in advancing to communism then lay in developing the productive forces under socialist ownership. As touched on earlier, however, development of the productive forces as an end in itself will reproduce bourgeois production and social relations, due to the soil of bourgeois right.

Here Stalin's tendencies to mechanical materialism asserted themselves and led to his negation or serious misunderstanding and misestimation of the important roles of the other aspects of the economic base (specifically, the relations between people and the relations of distribution) and of the superstructure. He did not grasp the ways in which the socialist economic base could be undermined unless revolution was carried out in the superstructure (or how the socialist ownership system could be undermined by largely unfettered bourgeois right in the other aspects of the base) and hence basically wrote off the importance of the struggle to transform these crucial spheres. This laid the basis for Stalin's increasing tendency beginning in the mid-'30s to rely on material incentives and the authority and machinery of the bureaucracy, instead of raising the consciousness of and politically mobilizing the masses.

The correct understanding of these key questions was only really first forged by Mao. While Stalin's errors were serious, they were not entirely his alone; neither Marx, Engels nor Lenin had foreseen the character (and crucial importance) of continued class struggle throughout a long socialist transition period (though all, on the other hand, did see socialism as a society more in flux and transition and full of contradiction than Stalin did).

But Stalin's problematical formulations were carried qualitatively further by Khrushchev and transformed into a straight-out bourgeois line. It was in opposition to this that Mao made his great contributions on the class struggle under socialism: continuing the revolution under the dictatorship of the proletariat as the central task of socialism, and pinpointing the bourgeoisie in the party as the main target of that struggle.

Mao forged this understanding not only in opposition to Khrushchev, but in the heat of the class struggle over the direction of Chinese society. That struggle came to a head in 1966, in the Great Proletarian Cultural Revolution.

The Great Proletarian Cultural Revolution

The Cultural Revolution was wholly unprecedented; for the first time the masses in a *socialist* country rose up and seized back sections of power that had been usurped by a new bourgeoisie with its headquarters high in the party. Here we need to backtrack momentarily and address again this question of "the bourgeoisie in the party." Mao had summed up in regards to the Soviet Union that "the rise to power of revisionism means the rise to power of the bourgeoisie"; conversely, the main target of the class struggle under socialism had to be the revisionists in high party leadership.

Why? Again this gets back to the character of political leadership under socialism and the pivotal role of line. In socialist society, power over the means of production and over distribution is concentrated as the power of political leadership; whether production serves the revolution (or the profits and comforts of those already in a privileged position), whether economic relations are transformed toward communism (or old bourgeois relations are fed and defended) and whether the superstructure is transformed to serve the socialist economic base and socialist transformation overall (or instead maintained as various strongholds of untouchable bourgeois authorities) is determined by what political line wins out, both overall and in each sphere.

Precisely because of the extremely close links between political and economic power in socialist society, the core of the bourgeoisie is identical to its most powerful political representatives: those people at the highest reaches of the party who persist in pursuing a revisionist political line (and inevitably form headquarters, factions, etc., to fight for it). They are the main target of the class struggle under socialism. And because the direction of society itself, as well as the terms of the struggle between proletariat and bourgeoisie, hinge on political line, the key link in the class struggle in socialist society lies in mobilizing the masses to grasp the cardinal questions of political line, and on that basis to struggle against the bourgeois headquarters, to identify and criticize its line, and to more deeply and powerfully transform society.

This is both what happened in — and in large measure what was learned from — the Cultural Revolution. While it was a landmark struggle on which volumes can and have been written (and should be studied), and while an exhaustive account (or even a more or less complete summary) is impossible here, a few key points about it do need to be made:

First, the Cultural Revolution was a *real* struggle in which nothing less than proletarian state power was at stake. Especially beginning in the late '50s, different views on which direction China had to go (in regards both to China itself and to its role in the world and its relation to world revolution) had coalesced around different headquarters. The central target of the Cultural Revolution — the forces grouped around Liu Shaoqi and Deng Xiaoping[18] — supported tying China to the Soviet Union and more or less copying the Soviet policies of profit in command, one-man management, material incentives, etc. Had they succeeded, China would have quickly degenerated into a neo-colonial vassal of the Soviet Union — an incalculable loss (especially considering what China *did* contribute on the basis of the Cultural Revolution!) to the international proletarian cause. And Liu and Deng did have real power, at points even majorities in the leading party and state apparatuses, the army, better-off sections of the people, etc.

Second, the method that was forged to deal with the revisionists was — in line with the need to rely politically on the masses — *revolution from below*, under the leadership of the proletarian headquarters in the party. *This* was truly unprecedented in the experience of socialist society; as Mao remarked in 1967:

> In the past we waged struggles in rural areas, in factories, in the cultural field, and we carried out the socialist education movement. But all this failed to solve the problem because we did not find a form, a method, to arouse the broad masses to expose our dark aspect openly, in an all-round way and from below. (in *9th Party Congress Report*, FLP, 1969, p. 27)

The masses flooded into every sphere of society, investigating, debating, criticizing and where necessary (and possible) setting up new organs of power. "The masses must liberate themselves," the original call to the Cultural Revolution insisted; and this they acted on, in turmoil and upheaval of the sort which Marx once said (in reference to capitalist society) could make the developments of a single day in revolutionary periods more significant than twenty years of peaceful times.

---

[18]When Deng reemerged in the mid-'70s, he was at that time tied to the U.S.

Finally, the upshot of it all was not only the defeat of a power-ful revisionist headquarters (and five years later the defeat of a new headquarters led by Lin Biao), but important transforma-tions throughout society — the most important of which was in the understanding and consciousness of the masses (in China and worldwide) of the contradictions and struggle involved in the transition to communism. In regards to this last point, Bob Avakian has written that:

> If any other method [besides relying on the masses — *LW*]is used, Mao summed up, then if revisionists seize leading positions and are able to put the official "stamp of approval" on a counter-revolutionary line — in the guise of Marxism — the masses will be in a passive position politically, and, in the name of adhering to the line of the party and loyalty to its leadership, they will be led back to the hell of capitalism. In short, the dictatorship of the proletariat must not be treated metaphysically — in a static and absolute way — or it will be lost . . .
> . . . That is why the real object of the Cultural Revolution . . . [was] not just to overthrow those capitalist-roaders who have, at that time, entrenched themselves in the party of the proletariat; rather, it must be to remold the world outlook of the masses of people, so that they take up the stand, viewpoint and method of the pro-letariat, Marxism-Leninism, and thus are increasingly armed to recognize, isolate and strike down revisionists whenever they raise their heads, while at the same time strengthening their mastery of society (and nature) and their ability to win over and remold the ma-jority of intellectuals, cadres, etc. (*Immortal*, 291-292)

It's true, of course, that this wasn't accomplished in any sort of uniform or across the board way, and that the bourgeoisie con-stantly counter-attacked and maintained dominance (or at least a good deal of power) in many crucial spheres and regions of the country. Mao himself pointed this out throughout the years sum-ming up and further advancing off of the Cultural Revolution, and he constantly reiterated the need for many such revolutions all through the transition to communism.

The bourgeoisie's continuing control of various units of pro-duction, and spheres of the superstructure, may make socialism seem like a checkerboard society, with some squares occupied by the proletariat and some by the bourgeoisie. And there's an ele-ment of truth to that — but only an element. For as long as society is overall ruled by the proletariat — as long, that is, as the pro-letariat holds the commanding heights of the superstructure (especially the state and the party), and production and class struggle go on in such a way as to overall contribute to the international proletariat's advance to communism — then society is socialist. But this is not static, or a cause for complacency; the bourgeoisie and proletariat are locked in struggle on all this, marshalling their forces in periodic all-out battles to determine whether society stays on the socialist road, or goes over to the capitalist road. If the proletariat does not prevail, the bourgeoisie does, and eliminates proletarian power *in every sphere*.

This struggle goes on as part of the overall worldwide struggle between proletariat and bourgeoisie, and proceeds with all the sharp breaks, upheaval and turning points typical of it. And the development of the fundamental contradiction on a world scale gives rise within the socialist countries to critical junctures (occurring as part of, and reacting back on, such junctures worldwide) that compel the proletariat and bourgeoisie into all-out trials of strength on the overall nature and direction of the society. This happened in China, for instance, with the struggle over the Great Leap Forward in 1959, which involved not only the revolutionary policies of the Leap but took place in the context of (and was directly and heavily influenced by) the struggle against Soviet revisionism. It also marked the Cultural Revolution, in which the proletarian revolutionaries had both a certain freedom to take bold initiative due to the battering that the U.S. was receiving from the national liberation struggles, most especially in Vietnam, and which in turn played no small part in contributing to that battering and to the reawakening of revolutionary struggle within the imperialist countries. Further, the Cultural Revolution rallied the masses in particular to support the struggle of the Indochinese people and stand as a reliable rear base area, and to support other struggles as well (including the Black rebellions in the U.S. in the late '60s). On the other hand, in the final struggle in socialist China in 1976, a temporarily unfavorable balance of forces internationally, including the stepped-up threat of Soviet attack in the context of the two imperialist blocs heading towards war, lent strength to the Rightist and conservative forces in China.

At each of these points all the most basic questions went up for grabs; different positions arose and different forces polarized over support for international revolution, policies on national defense, economic construction, and the struggle in the superstructure. The proletariat had to overthrow the bourgeoisie within the party (or rather the sections of it which jumped out in open opposition to further advance, especially those occupying key leading positions in the state) in order to rise to the challenges and carry out the initiatives and transformations — both international and domestic — demanded by the historic moment. The bourgeoisie, too, had to throw itself into these struggles, not only to protect its material and social base but to seize what it perceived as do-or-die opportunities to reverse the direction of society. And this was true not just of socialist China, but is a universal phenomenon of proletarian dictatorship.

Here the principle enunciated by Mao — that the heart of the bourgeoisie in socialist society resides at the top reaches of the communist party — assumes critical importance. "With the socialist revolution they themselves come under fire," Mao stated, and went on:

> At the time of the cooperative transformation of agriculture there were people in the Party who opposed it, and when it comes to criticizing bourgeois right, they resent it. You are making the socialist revolution, and yet don't know where the bourgeoisie is. It is right in the Communist Party — those in power taking the capitalist road. The capitalist-roaders are still on the capitalist road. (cited in *Immortal*, 298)

While Mao here is specifically pointing to the key junctures of the Chinese Revolution, especially its transition from the bourgeois-democratic to socialist stage, his point has universal significance; the socialist revolution *must* continue to move forward, and at any given time there will be those in the party who will think it's gone far enough and will jump out to oppose further advance.

The Party in Socialist Society

Mao's focus on the party is crucial to correctly understanding (and waging) the class struggle in socialist society. The party is the most critical part of the socialist superstructure; yet it has a dual position and character. On the one hand, until the achievement of communism the proletariat must have a leading core. This has everything to do with the international domination (or in any case remaining strength internationally) of capital, the capitalist birthmarks in socialist society (including the remaining and persistent bourgeois ideological and political influences on the masses, the continuing contradiction between mental and manual labor, etc.) and the fact that *spontaneously* at this point society develops toward capitalism rather than communism. In this regard it is truly the case that the question of whether or not proletarian rule and the cause of socialism are maintained and advanced is concentrated in the question of the correct line and leadership of the party, and the proletarian vanguard must be further built and strengthened as a key part of advancing the worldwide struggle.

On the other hand, the very factors that make the party necessary — along with the fact that it is the leading force in the exercise of political power — mean that if its members, *especially* its leading officials, deviate from Marxism, depart from the socialist road and divorce themselves from the masses, then their position of authority is transformed from guiding the masses in revolution toward communism into one of oppressing the masses and forcing them back toward capitalism — all in the name of "socialism" and "communism."

In sum, with the seizure of power by the proletariat and the socialization of ownership of the means of production, the party becomes both the leading political center of the socialist state and the main directing force of the economy; and the contradiction between the party as the leading group and the working class and masses under its leadership is a concentrated expression of the contradictions characterizing socialist society as a transition from the old society to fully communist classless society. This contradiction can only be resolved through the proletariat continually making revolution to overthrow the bourgeoisie, and progressively digging up ever more of the soil of new bourgeoisies, especially the bourgeoisie among the top ranks of the communist party itself, until the final elimination of *all* bourgeois relations.

These all-out battles between the bourgeoisie and proletariat not only determine whether the proletariat strengthens a specific country as a base area for revolution (or whether bourgeois rule is restored), but also form the main way in which the proletariat is practically tempered to transform all society. They are marked by all-encompassing upheaval, by the masses thrashing things out on a grand scale, and by the entry in a concentrated way of every class onto the political stage. While ongoing socialist education and constant struggle to revolutionize the base and superstructure are tremendously important in advancing towards communism and transforming the proletariat itself (as well as laying a necessary basis for those periods in which more far-reaching leaps can be undertaken), the concentrated, all-out revolutions under the dictatorship of the proletariat in particular give the masses an extraordinary and necessary tempering.

Not only that, such struggles are absolutely crucial to keeping the party red and further revolutionizing it. They are a key way that the masses supervise the party, and through which the party is revitalized and the links between the party and masses are strengthened. Unreformable bourgeois forces are driven out, waverers are given a "political shock" and further remolded in their outlook, and fresh forces from among the masses who come forward and are tempered in these complex struggles are absorbed into the party, strengthening its revolutionary line and role, and raising up new generations of revolutionaries — if, that is, the proletariat is victorious.

These struggles are in reality crucial components of *strengthening* the proletarian dictatorship — that is, the increasing control by the proletariat over every sphere of political and social life — on the basis of a correct line and correct leadership by the party. The kind of political understanding on which that control has to be based can only be forged through the most deep-going struggle, the broadest debate of every important question, really unprecedented mass democracy; but that democracy is not an end in itself (for then it would eventually feed anarchism and ultimately bourgeois hegemony would reassert itself), but a means for strengthening the overall conscious control of every sphere of society by the proletariat. Democracy among the masses and dictatorship over the bourgeoisie, democracy and centralism among the masses and within the party, struggle and unity, criticism and transformation — all these unities of opposites are part of the process through which society is transformed under proletarian dictatorship, as part of the overall process of conquering the whole world.

For all these reasons then, the key link and decisive task of the proletariat in the period of transition to communism is *revolution* — the class struggle against the bourgeoisie and other reactionary forces within the socialist countries and internationally against imperialism, reaction and all exploiting classes. Thus while the state has its origin in the rise of classes and class struggle, it will be the class struggle — and through it the eventual *abolition* of classes — that abolishes the state. In the future communist society, humanity will, as Engels said, "put the whole machinery of state where it will then belong: into the museum of antiquities, by the side of the spinning-wheel and the bronze axe." (*Origin*, 210)

The path to this great goal has been blazed by the struggle and blood of the proletariat and other oppressed classes, and is especially marked by the great mileposts erected at the crucial turns along the way: the Paris Commune, the October Revolution, and the Great Proletarian Cultural Revolution. The study of those experiences and their lessons, as Bob Avakian said, "gives us an understanding and illustrates the need to combine a sweeping historical view with the rigorous and critical dissecting of especially crucial and concentrated historical experiences, and to draw out as fully as possible the lessons and to struggle to forge the lessons as sharply as possible as weapons for now and for the future. And here I'm talking specifically about the immediate future, with the full focus on the conjuncture that is now shaping up. And this, after all, is the importance of summing up history." (*Conquer the World?...*, 9)

5
THE PARTY

"For all the horror and misery they entail," Lenin wrote during World War 1, "wars bring at least the following more or less important benefit — they ruthlessly reveal, unmask and destroy much that is corrupt, outworn and dead in human institutions. The European war of 1914-15 is doubtlessly beginning to do some good by revealing to the advanced class of the civilised countries what a foul and festering abcess has developed within its parties, and what an unbearably putrid stench comes from some source." ("The Collapse of the Second International," *LCW*, Vol. 21, 208)

The targets of Lenin's polemic — the parties of the Second International — had indeed acted in a foul way. The World War was nothing but a massive bloodletting conducted by the imperialist powers. The Second International had for several years predicted just such a slaughter, promised to oppose it, and even vowed to use it to hasten a revolutionary overthrow of the bourgeoisie in every country; but when the war actually broke out, virtually every party went along with the war proclamations of its own government, marshalling the workers it led to kill and be killed by the workers of other nations.

If it did nothing else, the capitulation of these parties highlighted by contrast the action of the Bolsheviks. Led by Lenin, the Bolsheviks took a principled stand at the war's outbreak against *their own* bourgeoisie, and consistently worked to foster the resistance and understanding of the masses, and to "turn the imperialist war into a civil war." And the contrast became even sharper when, after three years of war, the political structure in Europe began to fissure and break, with revolutionary situations developing in a number of countries; then it was the Russian proletariat — led by the Bolsheviks — that alone was able to carry things all the way through to the seizure of power and consolidation of a socialist state.

The complex combination of factors that went into the revolution's success can't be reduced to a single cause. In certain ways the objective situation in Russia was sharper than in other countries[1] and the proletariat had the schooling of the defeated 1905 Revolution. But these differences alone could not a revolution make; had there been no Bolshevik Party, or had that party collapsed in the way that the other parties of the Second International had, there could have been no proletarian revolution in Russia.

The ability of the Bolsheviks to rise to the challenge, when others collapsed or fell short, was something that had been fought for and forged. Under Lenin's leadership, the party's ideological and political line was tempered and developed through a succession of challenges and struggles, in society at large as well as within the revolutionary movement and the party. These included: the experience of the 1905 Revolution; the struggle against the ideological assaults on Marxism in the wake of that revolution's defeat; the fight for an internationalist stand in World War 1; and Lenin's development of the Marxist analysis of imperialism. Within all that, however, the struggle led by Lenin around the basic principles concerning the role and character of the revolutionary party assumes special importance. This struggle — concentrated in Lenin's classic 1902 polemic, *What Is To Be Done?* —

---

[1] This should not, however, be seen as some sort of absolute. For instance, the very things that are often — and generally correctly — cited as part of the more favorable conditions (e.g., the comparative backwardness of Russia, the experience of the 1905 Revolution) also contained negative aspects: the small size of the Russian proletariat relative to the huge peasantry (an effect of backwardness) caused considerable problems, and defeated revolutions inevitably leave a great deal of demoralization (as well as tempering) in their wake.

took in the political, ideological and organizational tasks of the party, and its overall relationship to the masses; in a nutshell, it focused up the question of what it means to *lead*. Its resolution was the foundation on which the Bolshevik Party was built.

The tendency to downplay the party's importance, or in other ways to distort its nature and role, has seriously corroded the revolutionary movement, historically and down to the present, and Lenin's developments on this question have been opposed from a number of angles. This itself should underscore the real and fundamental importance of grasping the Leninist theory of the party. In fact it is hard to *over*estimate its importance; as Bob Avakian has written:

> The party cannot "create" the revolutionary situation, nor can it stand aside cultivating itself until the revolutionary situation develops and then "intervene" to assume (grab) leadership. But, on the other hand, it is through the leadership of the party that, in conformity with the laws of society and the development of the objective situation and the class struggle, the masses are concretely trained and prepared ideologically, politically and organizationally for the revolutionary situation. And it is through the leadership of the party that they are and must be led in making revolution when the situation does ripen. Who else can prepare and then lead the masses in seizing the opportunity — and who else, for that matter, can throw away that opportunity? ("Thoughts on Points for Discussion," a report by Bob Avakian to the Second Plenary Session of the Second Central Committee of the RCP, USA, 1978)

The necessity for a party to lead the revolution, and after that the transition to communism, is rooted in the material contradictions of class society. The division of labor in bourgeois society, the powerful pulls and tugs of everyday life that foster a bourgeois outlook among sections of the masses (e.g., competition between workers over jobs, the structure of relative privilege built up among sections of the proletariat within the imperialist countries, even the unending pressure to "look out for yourself" in the dog-eat-dog scramble to survive), and the bourgeois domination of the superstructure — all this gives rise to conditions where the proletariat will not, in its great mass or majority, become class-conscious or be won to the need for revolution all at once; there is necessarily a gap between the more advanced minority of the proletariat and the rest of the class. To bridge that gap (in class society), to raise the rest of the proletariat to the position of the class-

conscious section, requires a vanguard party. The organizatio
the advanced into a distinct political party does carry with it the
potential problem of the party being set *against* the masses and
becoming either a reformist political machine or, after the revolution, a new ruling clique; still, there is no other means *but* such a
party for bridging that gap between leadership and led, raising the
consciousness of the masses through twists and turns, and
mobilizing them to not only overthrow the bourgeoisie but carry
forward the transformation of society to communism, when
classes — and parties — will be eliminated and transcended.

Political Role of the Vanguard

Preparing for Revolution

"The seizure of power by armed force, the settlement of the
issue by war, is the central task and the highest form of revolution. This Marxist-Leninist principle of revolution holds good universally. . . ." ("Problems of War and Strategy," *MSW*, Vol. 2, 219)

If Mao's point seems basic, it is no less profound and far-
reaching; it implies that all work of the proletarian party (when
out of power) must center on the preparation for and carrying out
— whenever conditions are ripe — of revolutionary war to seize
political power. But only rarely does a situation in which the party
can immediately lead the proletariat to directly "settle the issue"
present itself. Revolutionary situations — speaking especially,
though not exclusively, of the advanced imperialist countries
(more on the differences in the oppressed nations and colonies
shortly) — are extraordinary. Lenin insisted that cataclysmic
changes in the objective situation, independent of the will of any
parties or classes, are necessary — changes which make it impossible for the ruling class to rule in their accustomed way and
which jolt the masses to such a degree that millions are
". . . drawn both by all the circumstances of the crisis *and by the
'upper classes' themselves* into independent historical action."
("The Collapse of the Second International," *LCW*, Vol. 21, 214).
These are necessary prerequisites for any revolutionary attempt,
and such crises obviously don't happen every day.

And even such changes cannot on their own produce a revolu-

tion. "[R]evolution," Lenin continued, "arises only out of a situation in which the above-mentioned objective changes are accompanied by a subjective change, namely, the ability of the revolutionary *class* to take revolutionary mass action *strong* enough to
break (or dislocate) the old government, which never, not even in
a period of crisis, 'falls,' if it is not toppled over." (*LCW*, Vol. 21,
214) Here the importance of the party asserts itself — while the
party cannot create a revolutionary situation, it can and must play
a role in "...revealing to the masses the existence of a revolutionary situation, explaining its scope and depth, arousing the proletariat's revolutionary consciousness and revolutionary determination, helping it to go over to revolutionary action, and form-
ing, for that purpose, organisations suited to the revolutionary
situation." (*LCW*, Vol. 21, 216-217)

The ability to recognize and contribute to a revolutionary
situation, and to seize the opportunity to topple the old regime,
must be *developed*; the proletariat — especially its advanced section at any given point — must be trained and prepared prior to
the full outbreak of crisis. A study of the complex and chaotic
character of revolutionary situations and revolutions themselves
brings this point home; they are anything *but* a neatly drawn battlefield in which the proletariat and bourgeoisie line up like teams
before the "big game," all decked out in jerseys clearly marked to
explain that one side is defending oppression and exploitation
while the other is fighting to end it. Revolutions in the real world
are marked by incredible social upheaval and the emergence of
new and totally unforecast phenomena, and by the flooding into
political life of all sorts of class forces under all sorts of banners, as
well as different political trends within the broad ranks of the
working class itself. In another essay from the same period of
World War 1, Lenin explained that the socialist revolution:

> ...*cannot be* anything other than an outburst of mass struggle on
> the part of all and sundry oppressed and discontented elements.
> Inevitably, sections of the petty bourgeoisie and of the backward
> workers will participate in it — without such participation, *mass*
> struggle is *impossible*, without it *no* revolution is possible — and just
> as inevitably will they bring into the movement their prejudices,
> their reactionary fantasies, their weaknesses and errors. But *objec-*
> *tively* they will attack *capital*, and the class-conscious vanguard of
> the revolution, the advanced proletariat, expressing this objective
> truth of a variegated and discordant, motley and outwardly frag-

mented, mass struggle, will be able to unite and direct it, capture power, seize the banks, expropriate the trusts which all hate (though for different reasons!), and introduce other dictatorial measures which in their totality will amount to the overthrow of the bourgeoisie and the victory of socialism, which, however, will by no means immediately "purge" itself of petty-bourgeois slag. ("The Discussion of Self-Determination Summed Up," *LCW*, Vol. 22, 356)

This then is the character of the situation for which the class-conscious proletariat is *preparing*, and it sharply focuses up a question: how *does* the party prepare the proletariat, how does it imbue in the working class the ability to seize the time when the time for revolution is ripe?[2]

The Spontaneous Struggle and the Revolutionary Movement

The raw material for the political preparation and revolutionary training of the proletariat exists in the basic contradictions of imperialism, and the events and eruptions those contradictions continually give rise to. The wars of aggression launched by the imperialists (and the resistance they encounter), the backward and oppressive social relations which the system rests on (and the out-

---

[2] There are, at the same time, some important particularities to the struggle in the oppressed nations of Asia, Africa and Latin America. In these countries the opportunity to commence the armed struggle is generally nearer than in imperialist countries. This flows from a number of factors: the more backward character of the productive forces (including transportation and communication) which make possible, even before nationwide victory, the survival of people's armies and even zones where the proletariat can temporarily hold power; the more desperate condition of the masses, which make many more people immediately hungry for revolutionary change; the shakier character of the ruling cliques, etc. Given all that, it's still the case that in the oppressed nations too, severe crisis is generally necessary for a final nationwide offensive, and the masses must still be *politically* prepared to wage that struggle; Mao at one point characterized the anti-Japanese war in China as a "period of preparation," and if in this case the preparation took an overtly military form from very early on, and the actual military outcome of this period was crucial, it is nonetheless true that *political* mobilization of the masses was key. This section of the chapter focuses more closely on the tasks of the revolutionary party in the advanced countries; generally, though, the Leninist view of the party and its political, ideological and organizational tasks is universally applicable in most key respects. There are also important ways in which the development of capitalist relations in some sections of the third world — albeit in a lopsided and distorted form — have made many of the political principles more directly applicable. For more on the general point of the tasks of parties in oppressed nations, the reader should turn to *Basic Principles*, 39-43.

breaks of struggle against them), and the severe misery and deprivation, including the mutilation of the spirit, that is visited on the majority of the world's people, all going on in the face of the apparent ability of humanity once freed from the backward imperialist relations to rapidly eliminate that misery — all these continually propel the masses to raise their heads, to question and to rise up in struggle and revolt. Coupled with this is the necessity of the imperialists themselves, as Lenin stressed, to drag the masses into political life, especially in times of crises, in order, for example, to win them to the incredible sacrifices necessitated by world war, to take a concentrated expression of this. All this, then, provides the basis for the emergence and tempering of a class-conscious section of the proletariat, one that is both politically conscious and able to lead in a practical sense when everything goes up for grabs.

But how is the proletarian party to view this "raw material"? This was the nub of the debate addressed in *What Is To Be Done?* — a debate which continues to be fought out today on much the same ground as in Lenin's time. The Economists maintained that the consciousness developed by the masses in the course of their spontaneous struggles — and the Economists particularly emphasized the economic struggle (hence their label) — would itself be sufficient. Lenin insisted on the opposite; the party's tasks, he wrote, must be ". . . to *combat* spontaneity, to *divert* the working-class movement from this spontaneous, trade-unionist striving to come under the wing of the bourgeoisie, and to bring it under the wing of revolutionary Social-Democracy [i.e., communism — LW]." (*WITBD?*, 49)

Why? Because, while the spontaneous struggle, left to itself, can strike important blows against the system, it will ultimately only reproduce the bourgeois political (and economic) framework against which it is rebelling in the first place. Take revolts or uprisings in the third world; while these struggles are continually generated by the basic relations of imperialism, even the most revolutionary of them will remain at bottom nationalist, and ultimately will not break the bonds of imperialism and exploitative relations generally unless and until they are led by a proletarian vanguard party.

In the oppressed nations spontaneity, particularly in the form of revolutionary nationalism, nevertheless plays an important role in the struggle against imperialism, even though that spontaneity must be ultimately (in fact from the very beginning) combatted and diverted; in the imperialist countries it is even more immediately necessary to break the proletariat and oppressed masses out of the channels spontaneously cut by the development of the movement. As Bob Avakian has pointed out:

> . . . [I]f you just go along and link up with the masses [within the imperialist countries — *LW*] where they are at and concentrate on the trade union struggle, then when the war comes along [speaking especially of world war — *LW*], even if you try to make the transition from the trade union to the international arena and attempt to promote proletarian internationalism and revolutionary defeatism, the workers will answer you in bourgeois trade unionist terms — "listen, of course we have to fight these guys for better conditions and so on, but after all this is our country and we are not even going to be able to talk about improving it if we don't go out and win this war. (*Coming From Behind to Make Revolution*, RCP Publications, Chicago, 1980, pp. 15-16)

And even the understanding that spontaneously arises out of struggles in arenas besides the economic struggle — against imperialist aggression by "one's own" bourgeoisie in the third world, or the threat of nuclear war, for instance — while often opposing and even deeply indicting the imperialist power for what it does, at the same time often tends to frame this struggle in a demand that the "true promise" or nature of "the nation" be preserved. This stand will also, when all is said and done, set people up to defend their own bourgeoisie when the existence of "the nation" is threatened (as it must be by revolution, or by war with a rival imperialist power or bloc).

The material basis for bourgeois ideology is large. Not only is there the bourgeois superstructure, with all that entails, but there are also the underlying economic relations of daily life which spontaneously mask their true character — the appearance of wages, for example, as an exchange between equals, or the tendency of commodity exchange to mask relations between people as relations between things. Beyond that, though, are the economic and political relations *between nations* and the importance that assumes with the transition to imperialism. The fact that the economic concessions granted the masses in imperialist countries occur in large part on the basis of the increased ability of the imperialists to plunder the third world creates a tremendous and poisonous basis for economism and chauvinism to reinforce one another, and makes it even more urgent to combat a spontaneity which can easily degenerate into struggling to defend a way of life built up on the backs of the majority of the world's people.

With all that, it is still the contradictions of the imperialist system and the struggles they give rise to — and as an important aspect of that the spontaneous revolt of the masses — that communists and the communist party forge the revolutionary movement out of. To return to and pursue the earlier analogy of spontaneity to raw material, iron ore must be broken down and subjected to forging and tempering before it changes — qualitatively — into steel; so too with spontaneity: the outbreaks of protest and rebellion among the masses, and the drive to take up now this, now that ideology promising some sort of change or liberation, must be broken down, "divided into two" and synthesized into something qualitatively different, something on a qualitatively higher plane — a real *revolutionary* movement.

Role of Political Exposures

In this, the key link is *political exposure* — agitation, but also propaganda[3] focusing on the most important and widely discussed political events of the day, exposure which draws out the real class relations and significance of these events. This kind of exposure amounts to a sort of *political* warfare with the bourgeoisie on the most crucial social dividing lines of the day; connected to that, and more principally, exposure creates public opinion for revolution. Consistently carried out, such exposure presents an all-sided picture of a death-bound system and fosters the conviction that the whole system is worthless. In effect, it helps create and strengthen a revolutionary proletarian "pole" in

---

[3] Lenin explained in *What Is To Be Done?* that agitation takes one glaring event in society (say, something on the order of the Israeli massacre of Palestinians in Lebanon) and drives home a single idea (the nature of imperialist "order" in the third world, for instance) in order to arouse "discontent and indignation among the masses against this crying injustice." (82) The propagandist would unfold a more all-sided analysis of the same event, exposing the role of Israel and its links to U.S. imperialism, the significance of the entire Lebanon crisis in light of the world situation, the role of the Soviet Union, etc. Agitation presents a single idea to many people, while propaganda presents many ideas — and more of an entire world view — to a few.

society through the twists and turns of the entire preparatory period. As part of that, exposure is especially key in developing an internationalist trend in the proletariat; for how else but through the exposures of a thousand concrete instances of imperialist oppression, as they happen, can the masses (particularly within the imperialist countries) acquire a bone-deep internationalist outlook?

Exposures also propel the masses into political action (which in turn creates more public opinion for revolution, and secondarily gathers and tempers forces for revolution). Lenin, while noting that calls to action by the party at times play an important role, stressed the primacy of exposure; posing the question why the Russian worker of his day displayed "little revolutionary activity," Lenin answered:

> We must blame ourselves, our lagging behind the mass movement for being unable as yet to organize sufficiently wide, striking and rapid exposures of all these despicable outrages. When we do that. . .the most backward worker will understand, *or will feel* that the students and members of religious sects, the muzhiks and the authors are being abused and outraged by the very same dark forces that are oppressing and crushing him at every step of his life, and, feeling that, he himself will be filled with an irresistible desire to respond to these things, and then he will organize catcalls against the censors one day, another day he will demonstrate outside the house of a governor who has brutally suppressed a peasant uprising, another day he will teach a lesson to the gendarmes in surplices who are doing the work of the Holy Inquisition, etc. (*WITBD?*, 87-88)

Exposure must focus in the *political* arena. For one thing, the bourgeoisie *rules* politically, and the proletariat must *politically* overthrow it; for another, the interests of all classes in society are *concentrated* in the political arena. Thus for the proletariat to be prepared for its tasks, which include both the mounting of a political revolution and the accumulation of allies for that uprising, it must above all be trained politically. Beyond that, the more fundamental task of the proletariat — the all-around transformation of all society and elimination of classes — demands that it be able to consciously act and lead in *every* sphere, and most especially the political one.

This emphasis has historically been opposed by economism, which basically argues that the workers will first move around the "gut" economic issues, and only later — and on that basis — take up political struggle (which itself is reduced to the struggle for reforms). Economism proposes that exposure principally focus on the economic exploitation of the proletariat, and more, that the revolutionary movement be built by uniting with that struggle for bread and butter, and winning leadership through tactical skill.

But the economic struggle in itself in no way arms the masses with an all-sided and deep understanding of bourgeois society; how could it? While the daily conditions and struggles (especially the really *sharp* struggles) of the masses do provide a source of exposure of imperialism, essentially the battles over wages and working conditions are battles over the terms of sale of labor power, and can be contained within the bourgeois framework of commodity owners haggling over price. The fundamental critical view of capitalist society necessary for the radical rupture simply cannot be wrung from the battles that go on in this sphere because, as Lenin put it, *"that framework is too narrow."* Recall the type of thinking cited earlier by Bob Avakian, or think about how workers willing or even eager to fight around economic questions can be pinned to the political banner of the bourgeoisie on the basis of "protecting jobs" from minority nationalities, or from workers in other countries. This again points to the fact that in imperialist countries a one-sided focus on the economic arena will inevitably degenerate into chauvinism; for without exposing the foundation of the imperialist economies in the oppression and exploitation of the third world, revolutionaries will (whatever their intentions) tend to channel the activity and thinking of the workers into a blind defense of what amount to crumbs and bribes.[4]

Beyond that, though, economism denies the needs of those workers who at any given time hunger to know about and act on political issues on a revolutionary basis. These workers, especially in imperialist countries, will generally be a minority, at least up to those times when society is "sprung into the air" and a revolution becomes a real prospect; but it is the training and marshalling and

---

[4] Economic struggle does often function as an avenue for more backward sections of the proletariat to enter political life and struggle; this is especially marked in a situation of revolutionary political upheaval. But here too, though its importance and potential change, the economic struggle can hardly be made the leading edge; to do so would actually douse that larger movement.

forging into a class-conscious political force of this minority that is key to leading the millions in a revolutionary direction when the times do ripen. To turn away from those workers already awakening to political life, to cede political hegemony to the bourgeoisie on the many political questions which at any time stir even the backward to raise their heads and look around, all in favor of some lowest common denominator that everyone supposedly can rally around (never mind the basis!) — this is tantamount to abandoning the role of *vanguard*, and immersing the party and the advanced section of the proletariat *beneath* the general level of consciousness. It is a recipe for building a *non*revolutionary movement, at best.

In stressing the basic importance of political exposure, Lenin wrote that:

> The masses *cannot* be trained in political consciousness and revolutionary activity in any other way except by means of such exposures. . . . Working-class consciousness cannot be genuinely political consciousness unless the workers are trained to respond to *all* cases, *without exception,* of tyranny, oppression, violence and abuse, no matter *what class* is affected. Moreover, to respond from a . . . [communist], and not from any other point of view. The consciousness of the masses of the workers cannot be genuine class consciousness, unless the workers learn to observe from concrete, and above all from topical (current), political facts and events, *every* other social class and *all* the manifestations of the intellectual, ethical and political life of these classes; unless they learn to apply in practice the materialist analysis and the materialist estimate of *all* aspects of the life and activity of *all* classes, strata and groups of the population. (*WITBD?*, 85-86)

The key medium for this exposure is a regularly appearing party newspaper, distributed nationally and penetrating into every crevice and cranny of society with an overall picture and analysis of imperialism, what that system does around the world and the direction of the struggle to wipe it out. Only such a newspaper can give the party the reach and the depth necessary to create revolutionary public opinion; though not the *only* weapon, it is the *main* weapon of the party in the period preparatory to a revolutionary situation.

Aside from its principal task in creating revolutionary public opinion broadly throughout society, the newspaper serves also as a *collective organizer* of the party and the revolutionary movement, consistently providing political orientation for activists. And it serves as a lifeline back and forth between the party and masses, allowing the party both to keep its hands on the pulse of events and to accelerate that pulse as well. Lenin emphasized the *flexibility* provided by the newspaper, and stressed that:

> . . . [T]he revolution itself must not by any means be regarded as a single act . . . but as a series of more or less powerful outbreaks rapidly alternating with periods of more or less intense calm. For that reason, the principal content of the activity of our Party organization, the focus of this activity, should be work that is possible and necessary in the period of the most powerful outbreaks as well as in the period of complete calm, namely, work of political agitation, linked up over the whole of Russia, illuminating all aspects of life and conducted among the broadest possible strata of the masses. But this work is *unthinkable* in contemporary Russia without an all-Russian newspaper, issued very frequently. The organization which will form around this newspaper, an organization of its *collaborators* (in the broad sense of the word, i.e., all those working for it), will be ready *for everything*, from upholding the honour, the prestige and continuity of the Party in periods of acute revolutionary "depression," to preparing for, fixing the time for and carrying out the *nation-wide armed insurrection*. (*WITBD?*, 217-218)

Create Public Opinion, Seize Power

The RCP, USA, through the struggle to sum up its own experience and, more importantly, the experience of the international communist movement, especially in regard to economism, and through restudying Lenin (as well as important lessons of the Cultural Revolution summed up by Mao) has formulated its central task as *"create public opinion, seize power."* This formulation synthesizes fundamental points on the importance of political exposure and the need to forge the links to the future *revolutionary* situation in nonrevolutionary times, and stands in opposition to the basic orientation of the communist movement since the death of Lenin, which could be summed up fairly accurately as "merge with the basic struggles of the masses and gain leadership of them."[5] In explaining this central task, and especially its link to

---

[5] Reflecting this heritage, the RCP had previously formulated this task as one of building "the struggle, class consciousness and revolutionary unity of the working class and develop(ing) its leadership of a broad united front against the U.S. im-

the actual seizure of power, Bob Avakian has written that:

> The central task does have two aspects — create public opinion and seize power — but they are not separated from each other by a brick wall. We are not creating public opinion to create public opinion, we are creating it toward the goal of seizing power — toward the eventual armed uprising of the masses and toward the leading role of the party to carry it through and establish the dictatorship of the proletariat. Concretely this means that how much the influence of the party's line is spread and how much progress is made in training the advanced as communists, as revolutionary leaders in the fullest sense — in other words, how wide and how deep the conspiracy around the newspaper is developed — is of crucial importance not only in preparing for and building toward such an uprising but in influencing and perhaps even determining both its actual character and its chances of winning real victory. . . .
>
> It is not possible to "win a battle of public opinion" with the bourgeoisie before it is overthrown — nor is that necessary or the point of the central task. The fact is that sooner or later . . . things will reach the point, through the development of the objective situation and the actions of revolutionaries, of various kinds, where there will be the actual attempt by significant sections of the masses to rise up in arms against the system. And it is also quite possible that even if we did not lead things in that direction, such an attempt would occur anyway. But the ability of the class-conscious proletariat to march to the head of that, with the party playing the overall leading role, and the possibility of carrying it through to a fundamental change in the economic and political relations as a whole — that depends both on the work we do between now and then (whenever "then" actually is) and, dialectically related to that, how well not only the party but beyond it the class-conscious proletariat it has trained — and continues to train in the heat of the revolutionary situation and struggle — how well they do in actually winning leadership and coordinating the uprising under their overall leadership. ("Why Our Plan is 'Create Public Opinion . . . Seize Power'," *RW*, No. 92, Feb. 13, 1981)

The Party as Ideological and Theoretical Leader

Bound up with the economist conception of the party is a downplaying of its necessary theoretical tasks and ideological leadership. In a certain sense, this flows from the assumption that

perialists, in the context of the world-wide united front against imperialism aimed at the rulers of the two superpowers."

the party's task is to trail in the wake of the spontaneous struggle of the masses; of what use is Marxist theory in doing that? The idea that the party must develop a thorough and comprehensive understanding of the objective situation (including the contradictions beneath the surface, and their directions of development and interpenetration); that it must critically delve into and sum up the experience of the proletariat worldwide and historically in order to orient itself to its current tasks; that it must take up those sweeping and perhaps only partially — or even incorrectly — resolved problems posed by such monumental historical events as the restoration of capitalism in previously socialist countries — all this simply has no place in the economist universe. Nor is there a place for the necessary theoretical work which the party must undertake, on the basis of the sort of study indicated above, in order to really lead in all the diverse spheres of society in which outbreaks erupt (spheres which must also be transformed as part of the transition to communism).

What economists at bottom either fail to grasp, or outright oppose, is that Marxism, while the ideology of the proletariat, is also a science. It is true that only the emergence of socialized production and the first historic struggles of the proletariat laid the material basis for Marxism, and it is true as well that the communist transformation of all society hinges on the conscious activity of a proletariat grounded in an understanding of its own role in society; but it is also true that that science was developed *outside* the working class by Marx and Engels and that the proletariat cannot absorb this outlook through simply working or struggling, but only by studying this science *as a science.* The class hatred and revolutionary sentiments of the proletariat are necessary, but not sufficient, for the proletarian revolution; this hatred and these sentiments are still not *class consciousness,* still not yet a scientifically grounded (even if basic) understanding of the historic role and task of the proletariat vis-à-vis all of society and the future.

The party then must not only *politically* lead the proletariat, but must also lead in forging the *theory* necessary to do that, and in ideologically training the proletariat in the comprehensive and scientific world outlook and method of Marxism-Leninism, Mao Tsetung Thought.

Mass Line

But the party cannot lead without also *learning* from the masses. This relates back to the twofold nature of spontaneity (as both the "raw material" of the revolutionary movement, as well as something that must be diverted and combatted) and to the fact that, as Lenin put it, communism springs from the pores of life itself. The masses themselves constantly erupt in opposition to the backward social relations of bourgeois society. They bring forward new forms of struggle and new insights into society and the world, and they strain to transform humanity, society and nature, all in the most unpredictable ways and through oftentimes unexpected avenues. All this the party must learn from if it is to lead and divert it; the party must synthesize things to a higher level, yes, but that higher level is not fashioned from mid-air.

This contradiction between learning from and leading the masses is resolved through the application of the mass line, a principle originally developed by Mao. As formulated in the *New Constitution* of the RCP, USA, this entails taking

> . . . the ideas of the masses and the experience of the class struggle (and the struggle for production and scientific experiment), in the U.S. and internationally, and by applying the science of revolution to them concentrate the essential lessons, distinguishing what is correct from what is incorrect, and then return these concentrated ideas to the masses, propagate them widely and deeply among the masses and unite with the masses to apply them to transform the world with class struggle as the key link. This, too, is a continual process which proceeds in an upward spiral, in accordance with the development of the objective situation and the class struggle overall. (*New Programme and New Constitution*, 114)

The party, to sum up, leads through ideological and political line — that is, through applying Marxism to the challenges facing the proletariat, formulating correct political line on that basis, and winning the masses to that line and understanding. But while the vanguard must focus above all on political and ideological leadership, and while the economist orientation of grabbing up organizational positions should be exposed and opposed, this does not at all mean that the proletarian party then yields to spontaneity in matters of organization. As Stalin said,

> The Party is not only the *advanced* detachment of the working class. If it desires really to direct the struggle of the class it must at the

same time be the *organised* detachment of its class. The Party's tasks under the conditions of capitalism are immense and extremely varied.... But the party can fulfill these tasks only if it is itself the embodiment of discipline and organisation, if it is itself the *organised* detachment of the proletariat. (*The Foundations of Leninism*, FLP, 1970, p. 106)

Lenin's struggle against economism also focused up differences over organization. The Economists favored a rather loose organization; Lenin fought for a vanguard, organizationally as well as politically, with a backbone of professional revolutionaries. This core, Lenin said, had to be systematically trained to carry out the key theoretical, political and organizational tasks (depending on their specialty), to lead the party and the masses as a whole, and to combat the political police and ensure the party's ability to not only function but seize the offensive in conditions of illegality and even severe repression. Arguing against the Economists, Lenin wrote that:

> The "economic struggle against the employers and the government" [an economist catchphrase — *LW*] does not in the least require — and therefore such a struggle can never give rise to — an all-Russian centralized organization that will combine, in one general onslaught, all and every manifestation of political opposition, protest and indignation, an organization that will consist of professional revolutionaries and be led by the real political leaders of the whole people. This is but natural. The character of any organization is naturally and inevitably determined by the content of its activity. (*WITBD?*, 122)

This question became especially sharp during World War 1. The Second International had made absolutely no organizational preparations to function illegally in conditions of wartime! While this was obviously linked to and flowed from bigger ideological and political problems, nevertheless this served as a particularly glaring concentration of those weaknesses, and *reinforced* them; had such a party even wanted to carry through a revolutionary line, at best their efforts would have been severely hamstrung, if not made at least temporarily impossible, by their economist organizational line.

For these reasons in particular, then, the organizational principles of the party should be studied in their own right.

Organizational Principles

The vanguard party is organized on the principles of *democratic centralism*. Democratic centralism is intended to combine the fullest discussion of and struggle over the party's line with the firmest and most disciplined implementation of that line. The principles of democratic centralism include the subordination of the individual to the party as a whole, of the minority to the majority, of lower party levels to higher ones, and — finally — of the entire party to the Party Congress (or to the Central Committee chosen by this Congress, when it is not in session).

A centralized party — organizationally "tight" while flexible and supple — is absolutely necessary if the proletariat is to carry through its task. When you think about the discipline and conscious unity necessary to win even a mere struggle for improvements under the existing system, some idea of the dimensions of what's called for in carrying out the fundamental task of the seizure of power itself and the construction of a new social order begins to emerge.

But democratic centralism embodies and reflects more than just the political necessity facing the proletariat; it also reflects the Marxist theory of knowledge, and the correct relation between knowing and doing. And if this is downplayed or incorrectly understood or applied, then the political and ideological character will inevitably deteriorate too, and the party eventually will be turned into its opposite. The party's very ability to formulate (and implement) a correct line pivots on its democratic centralist form of organization.

The party must concentrate and correctly synthesize the experience gained by the membership overall in agitation, in other aspects of practical work among the masses and in theoretical struggle (including the struggle to correctly sum up practice). Its organizational structure must serve that process. This is key in enabling the party as a whole to forge a political line reflecting reality as all-sidedly and deeply as possible — and it's for this purpose (and not the bourgeois notion of "allowing everyone their say" as an end in itself) that inner-party democracy and struggle over line is fostered. Democracy — proletarian democracy — in this case is a means for developing the most correct possible concentration of the broadest experience and struggle, and hence a correct political line with which to guide the revolutionary struggle.

Such democracy is dialectically linked to the party's centralism. Once line is determined, the party must unite as tightly as possible in carrying it out — and this is for two reasons. First because, again, the class war is deadly serious and once a particular initiative is decided upon, steel-like unity is necessary to see it through. More fundamentally, centralism is necessary to continue and push to a higher level the spiral of knowledge.

What is meant here? For one thing, unless a line is carried out in a unified way, there is no way to really determine its correctness (or incorrectness) and deepen (or change) it on a scientific basis. If a particular line or policy is agreed upon but party branches in certain localities refuse to carry it through, and if the policy should fail, it becomes more difficult to determine on what basis it failed — whether the call itself was wrong, or whether it failed due to sabotage of the directives. Of course, even more to the point, the purpose of knowing is doing, that is, the proletarian party strives to understand the world precisely in order to change it, and this chain of knowing and doing must not be severed. In other words, the centralized leadership of the party is necessary to really changing the world, to making the party's line a material force (and on that basis further deepening and developing the line, returning it to practice on a higher level, and so on in an endless and upward spiral).

Through this process, democracy and centralism are not walled off from each other — there is democracy in centralism, and centralism in democracy, and political line is the key link in their interpenetration and mutual transformation. For example, struggle over line throughout the party — an aspect of democracy — cannot be anarchic but must itself be led, if it is to actually contribute to developing and deepening line and changing the world; there has to be central guidance to even figure out what questions to take up, what the terms of the struggle are, where knowledge must be advanced and deepened to correctly or basically resolve questions, etc. Conversely, the party doesn't — or shouldn't — rigidly carry out its line without constantly summing up (and struggling over) experience gained from applying that line to practice and deepening that line.

Without centralism, what meaning does inner-party democracy have? How can the initiative, input and contributions of party members and units to deepening, criticizing and even correcting the lines and policies of the party be unleashed? What ends are served by struggle over the party's line, if the point of such struggle is *not* the implementation of that line and thereby the transformation of reality? And what would be the basis for any genuine supervision of leadership by the membership, if the political line is not understood as something to be implemented in a centralized way, as powerfully as possible? At the same time, without democracy — in the sense of the fullest possible struggle and input from the party members as a whole through party channels — the line actually formulated will tend to be shallow and one-dimensional, and its implementation brittle, bureaucratic and mechanical.

This takes on a concentrated expression in the relation between higher and lower levels of the party, and the principle of top-down leadership. While the basic units of the party are critical to the overall formulation (and implementation) of line, no single unit can develop the overall line of the party on its own, or correctly conduct its work in isolation from that line; each individual unit can — as a rule and overall — grasp less of the overall picture of objective reality, the work of the party and the class struggle worldwide than the centralized leadership of the party. Collective, concentrated knowledge is generally more correct than partial knowledge, and to break the chain of knowledge/chain of command would amount to substituting empiricism for science.

The central bodies of the party, on the other hand, are most able to develop a correct line *not only* because their members are elected on the basis of their ability to apply Marxism, and not only because the division of labor within the party demands that they devote more time to studying major theoretical and political questions, but also because only the party's highest bodies are in a position to synthesize the knowledge of the entire party. The line struggled out there concentrates the struggle at every level on the highest possible plane. Here then is the ideological basis for the subordination of lower to higher levels.

At the same time, none of this "guarantees" that the leadership will always be correct; that too would represent a mechanical view in which truth could be ensured merely by organizational structure. Obviously, it can't. And for that reason, party members, when in opposition to the party as a whole and its leadership, are not only allowed to reserve their opinions and appeal to higher bodies (including the Central Committee itself), but, if convinced of the rightness of their position, the urgency of the question and that an opportunist line has been consolidated, also have the duty to "go against the tide" (as Mao put it) and rebel. Going against the tide of an opportunist line and respecting the discipline of the party, however, are themselves dialectically linked; as a book put out by the Communist Party of China under the leadership of Mao explained, "Both are aimed at preserving the correctness of the Party's line." (*A Basic Understanding of the Communist Party of China*, Norman Bethune Institute, Toronto, 1976, p. 55)

The basic and underlying principle involved here is the responsibility of every member to pay attention to major questions, to struggle as vigorously as possible for what they understand to be correct, and to carry out that struggle with the object of deeper party unity around the correct line and a more thorough transformation of the world. Struggle and contradiction are the lifeblood of the party; Mao wrote that:

> Opposition and struggle between ideas of different kinds constantly occur within the Party; this is a reflection within the Party of contradictions between classes and between the new and the old in society. If there were no contradictions in the Party and no ideological struggles to resolve them, the Party's life would come to an end. ("On Contradiction," *MSR*, 93)

No party is "pure," nor is that an ideal to work toward. Parties arise and exist in class society, and inevitably the thinking of different classes is reflected in them. But only if struggle is conducted vigorously and unity sought on the basis of transforming the world, and if the chain of knowledge and chain of command of the party are built up on democratic centralist principles, is it possible for the party to maintain its proletarian character and more fundamentally lead the masses in carrying out proletarian revolution. Lenin powerfully expressed the importance of organization to the proletariat in his conclusion to the work "One Step Forward, Two Steps Back":

> In its struggle for power the proletariat has no other weapon but organisation. Disunited by the rule of anarchic competition in the

bourgeois world, ground down by forced labour for capital, constantly thrust back to the "lower depths" of utter destitution, savagery, and degeneration, the proletariat can, and inevitably will, become an invincible force only through its ideological unification on the principles of Marxism being reinforced by the material unity of organisation, which welds millions of toilers into an army of the working class. Neither the senile rule of the Russian autocracy nor the senescent rule of international capital will be able to withstand this army. (*LCW*, Vol. 7, 412)

*****

The contradictions between the party and the masses, and the struggle over line within the party, push forward the development of the party throughout its existence. But the ways in which these contradictions express themselves — and their content and importance — change radically when the proletariat seizes state power in a particular country, and the party becomes the leading political and economic force in society as a whole.

Even under capitalism, the gap between leadership and led can become the basis for elitism. But as Bob Avakian pointed out:

. . . [I]n the main, this is more than offset by the fact that to be a party member, or more broadly a part of the advanced forces stepping forward to lead the struggle for the overthrow of capitalism, means to be hunted, hounded, persecuted — harassed, jailed, etc., even murdered — and moreover to take a stance that is not "socially accepted" and does not generally mean greater prestige, etc. (*Communists Are Rebels, Revolutionary Communist Youth* pamphlet, 1980, p. 11)

And while the line struggle within the party under capitalism is critically important, and can at times assume antagonistic character (with opportunist attacks, splits, etc.), this is rarely the principal form of class struggle in society and line struggle is generally conducted as part of waging the all-around struggle against the bourgeoisie.

With the establishment of socialism, this changes. As gone into in depth in the previous chapter, the material and social basis develops in socialist society for sections of the party to be transformed into bourgeois cliques and beyond that into headquarters for attempts at capitalist restoration. Such cliques have in fact developed one after another, waged constant struggle and temporarily triumphed in both the Soviet Union and China.

But something else exists as well — not only the basis to defeat such cliques, but the method with which to struggle against them as a key part of the transition from socialism to communism. This was one of the tremendous contributions made by the Cultural Revolution, and by the leadership of Mao Tsetung, and represents an important deepening of the Marxist understanding of the party.

In socialist society the struggle over the leading line in the party becomes a key struggle throughout society. Indeed, it represents part of the tremendous progress of the socialist revolution when the class struggle within the socialist country, involving millions and millions, is openly fought out over the key and decisive questions of the direction of society and over correct vs. incorrect political line; and when the leadership/led contradiction, endlessly mystified in capitalist society, is openly tackled, dissected, struggled over and moved step by step towards resolution.

The struggle to transform and revolutionize the party through each stage of socialist society (and as part of the larger worldwide struggle and its spirals); the struggle to narrow the gap between leadership and led, to involve increasingly greater sections of society on deeper and deeper levels in thrashing out right and wrong and the direction of society; the struggle to *strengthen* the party's leading role in this way — all this is a key part of the struggle to eliminate classes, *and parties*, altogether and to achieve communism. Then not only will antagonistic classes have been transcended and eliminated and the division of labor characteristic of capitalism surpassed, but the ideological and political level of society as a whole will be developed enough to make the "permanent" and institutionalized division between leadership and led expressed in the party no longer necessary.

But — communism will not and cannot do away with the leadership/led and correct/incorrect contradictions. Different schools of thought will still arise around various questions; struggle and not unanimity will push society forward. And in the struggle between correct and incorrect, some form of leadership will have to be developed to "set the agenda" (even if not permanent in the sense that the party, relatively, is). Beyond that, there will still have to be some form of centralism, even if voluntary, in carrying out a certain line in a unified way to test its correctness (or incorrectness).

The profound difference will lie both in the level and breadth of this struggle under communism, and in the absence of the determining role of class interests in it. That peak, as has been stressed, can and will only be scaled through a protracted ascent, amidst wind and thunder. But if distant in one sense, from an historical vantage point this lofty height is quite near. The contradiction between what human society *could* be, on the basis of the unleashing of the productive forces and the further development of human knowledge unfettered by outmoded class divisions, and what it *is* — enmeshed in the chains of capital's backward social relations — makes itself more and more acutely felt. This is especially so as the fundamental contradiction between socialized production and private appropriation again approaches a nodal point, a conjuncture in which all the basic contradictions of imperialism promise to erupt. The responsibility before the revolutionary proletariat and its vanguard to wrench big chunks of the future out of the flames and ruin will then be great, and the opportunity to carry forward a perhaps unprecedented leap toward communist society may well be in the offing; all this drives home even more forcefully the crucial role of the proletarian party.

"Communism," Mao wrote in 1940, in the middle of the last great world conjuncture,

> . . . is at once a complete system of proletarian ideology and a new social system. It is different from any other ideology or social system, and is the most complete, progressive, revolutionary and rational system in human history. The ideological and social system of feudalism has a place only in the museum of history. The ideological and social system of capitalism has also become a museum piece in one part of the world (in the Soviet Union [then still a socialist country — *LW*]), while in other countries it resembles "a dying person who is sinking fast, like the sun setting beyond the western hills," and will soon be relegated to the museum. The communist ideological and social system alone is full of youth and vitality, sweeping the world with the momentum of an avalanche and the force of a thunderbolt. ("On New Democracy," *MSW*, Vol. 2, 360-361)

The chance to make really world-historic contributions to that goal is a rare one, but it is one perhaps to be granted to this generation of revolutionaries. It is in this light that the task of grappling with and applying the science of revolution — and the role of the party as the essential instrument in carrying out that task — can be grasped in its full and profound importance.

Mao Tsetung once compared revolutionary struggle to a "hurricane, a force so swift and violent that no power, however great, will be able to hold it back."

But the outcome of revolutionary storms — whether they spend their fury and subside on a landscape essentially unchanged, or leave behind purified air and fresh earth for a new beginning — depends in large part on the understanding and consciousness of people. Revolution, as opposed to just resistance, demands a scientific world outlook and analysis.

That science, the body of revolutionary theory developed in conjunction with the great revolutionary movements of the last century and a half, is Marxism-Leninism, Mao Tsetung Thought.

Its foundations and basic principles are brought together and explained in this single volume, an essential work for the experienced activist or the beginning student of Marxism.

ISBN 0-89851-036-8
RCP Publications

$7.95